PRAISE FOR *HOPE IN THE WILDERNESS*

The book of Numbers is often described a bit like the American Midwest. Many people from the East and West Coasts think of it as "flyover country," something without much real substance. However, just as the Midwest has its good (and bad) points, so, too, does the history of the people of Israel recorded in Numbers. R. Reed Lessing has produced a study that will show you how the book of Numbers is relevant to Christians and Christian living today. His book helps you see not only the point of the vivid stories of Israel's sins in Numbers but even the relevance of the census chapters, Balaam and his prophecy-for-hire that did not turn out as Balak hoped, and the worship laws recorded in Numbers 28–29. Lessing's devotional style makes this the ideal book for those who want to know the book of Numbers better while applying it to their daily walk of faith.

—**Andrew E. Steinmann,** distinguished professor emeritus of theology and Hebrew, Concordia University Chicago

HOPE IN THE WILDERNESS

Practical Insights from the Book of Numbers

R. REED LESSING

FOR ASHER,

ONE OF THE TWELVE TRIBES OF ISRAEL,

AND ONE OF MY DEAR GRANDSONS.

Published by Concordia Publishing House
3558 S. Jefferson Ave., St. Louis, MO 63118-3968
1-800-325-3040 • cph.org

Copyright © 2025 R. Reed Lessing

All rights reserved. No part of this publication may be reproduced, stored in a retrieval system, or transmitted, in any form or by any means, electronic, mechanical, photocopying, recording, or otherwise, without the prior written permission of Concordia Publishing House.

Unless otherwise indicated, Scripture quotations are the author's translation.

Scripture quotations marked ESV are from the ESV® Bible (The Holy Bible, English Standard Version®), copyright © 2001 by Crossway, a publishing ministry of Good News Publishers. Used by permission. All rights reserved. Italics added to indicate author's emphasis.

Catechism quotations are taken from the Small Catechism © 1986 Concordia Publishing House. All rights reserved.

The quotations from the Large Catechism are from *Concordia: The Lutheran Confessions*, second edition © 2006 Concordia Publishing House. All rights reserved.

The quotation from the Wisdom of Solomon is from *The Apocrypha: The Lutheran Edition with Notes* © 2012 Concordia Publishing House. All rights reserved.

Quotations marked *LSB* are from *Lutheran Service Book* © 2006 Concordia Publishing House. All rights reserved.

Manufactured in the United States of America

1 2 3 4 5 6 7 8 9 10   34 33 32 31 30 29 28 27 26 25

TABLE OF CONTENTS

INTRODUCTION

The Lord give you peace. (Numbers 6:26 ESV)

Who likes numbers? Mathematicians, accountants, statisticians, and investment bankers. The rest of us? Not so much. That's why we prefer biblical books like Jeremiah, Jonah, John, and James. The book of Numbers? Are we really edified by knowing that the tribe of Reuben has 46,500 soldiers? How does that inspire our life of faith?

When was the last time you looked at Numbers? Maybe it was part of a Bible reading program. To get from Leviticus to Deuteronomy, you had to slog your way through Numbers. And now you're ready for a deeper dive?

Origen (ca. AD 185–253), an early church leader, compared Numbers to food. Did he use adjectives like delicious, delightful, and delectable? Not quite. Instead, Origen described Numbers as food that's "tasteless." He's not alone. Be honest. Your heart probably didn't leap for joy when your church announced, "The next Bible study is going to be on Numbers!"

While I was working on this book, a friend asked me what I was up to. With great enthusiasm, I cleared my throat and announced, "I'm writing a book on Numbers!" His response? "Ha! Good luck finding anyone who wants to read that!" But you're here! There's hope!

Numbers may begin and end with eye-glazing lists—much like telephone books of yesteryear. But Moses, the book's author, also traces Israel's journey from Mount Sinai to the cusp of the Promised Land—describing the nation's highs and lows with dramatic flair. To spice things up, he even throws in a talking donkey. And Numbers has tons of variety: stories, instructions for worship, legal disputes, census lists, a travel itinerary, and military battles.

That said, I need to be honest. There are sections in Numbers that are tough sledding. Have you ever been to a high school track meet?

I have, many times. My son Jonathan ran the 4 × 100-meter relay race (the first event in the morning) and pole-vaulted (the last event in the afternoon). Between the racing and the vaulting, I dutifully sat in the stands. It was like watching paint dry. But it was my son Jonathan, so it was worth it.

Numbers is worth it too. I promise. Why? Because the book paints a beautiful and captivating portrait of Jesus. The background for Christ's bread of life discourse in John 6 is Numbers 11—where Israelites complain about manna. And events in Numbers 21 foreshadow Christ's death on the cross (John 3:14–15), providing the backdrop for the Bible's most famous verse, John 3:16.

Then there's Balaam. His oracles contain remarkable references to Jesus. In his first oracle, Balaam alludes to God's promises to Abraham, Isaac, and Jacob (Numbers 23:10; cf. Genesis 13:16; 28:24)—pointing to the greatness and grandeur of Christ's kingdom. Balaam's second oracle is about Israel's king (Numbers 23:21; cf. Genesis 17:6, 16; 35:11), who comes through the tribe of Judah (Numbers 23:24; cf. Genesis 49:9). This is Jesus, our Lord. In his third oracle, Balaam speaks of Christ's exalted status (Numbers 24:7) and connects the messianic lion of Judah (Numbers 24:9; cf. Genesis 12:3; 49:9; Amos 1:2) to Jesus, who triumphed over the grave (Revelation 5:5). Balaam's final oracle speaks of the Messiah as "not near" (Numbers 24:17). When Christ arrives, however, He will be the star from Jacob (cf. Matthew 2:2; Revelation 22:16) and wield a royal scepter (cf. Genesis 49:10). Jesus will then forever defeat all enemies—including devils, demons, darkness, and even death (cf. Genesis 49:9; Revelation 19:11–21).

In addition to these significant messianic predictions, Moses also composed Numbers to show us how to survive during in-between times.

In-between. It's a seminal idea in Numbers, describing Israel's journey to a tee. Moses and crew are bounded by Egypt to the south and Canaan to the north. They're straddling salvation accomplished (at the Red Sea) and salvation to come (crossing the Jordan River into the Promised Land).

Does this sound familiar? You and I also live between our past and our glorious future. In Holy Baptism, God began a good work in us. He will complete it on the day Christ returns (cf. Philippians 1:6).

If you're like me, during life's betwixt and between times, you chomp at the bit. "Something has to change!" In the meantime? You trudge from one day to the next. It's all so bland and boring—just more details and deadlines and disappointments. "I don't have time for this! Keep doing the same thing today I did yesterday? I want big things with big excitement! And what do I get? A screaming toddler at night; a spouse's morning breath the next morning; and a huge headache at work by noon."

There are a million ways to distance myself from life's dailiness. It's so easy to numb out the monotony and dullness of it all. Soon something BIG will come along and whisk me away. But today? Oh, I'll go through the motions. I'll hold on until this tedious season passes. But I refuse to be a happy camper!

What do I miss with this kind of attitude? Everything! I miss being present in the present. I fool myself into thinking that today is the warm-up so it's not *that* important. It's just spring training. The real games—those that count—they're almost within reach. But not today.

What do people think about me when I have this kind of attitude? "He's detached." "He's got his mind on other things." "He's in a big hurry to get somewhere." "Why, just look at that impatient look on his face!"

There's a better way. We find it in the book of Numbers. Moses teaches us what to avoid, what to do, and how to thrive during in-between times. He also points us to the mercy and might of Jesus, who empowers us to stay faithful when we're circling and stuck in the wilderness.

I invite you get your Bible and a pen. Numbers won't be a quick jog around the block or a short trip to the store. It will be a journey—but a journey worth taking. Let's get started!

A MAP OF ISRAEL'S ROUTE FROM SINAI TO CANAAN

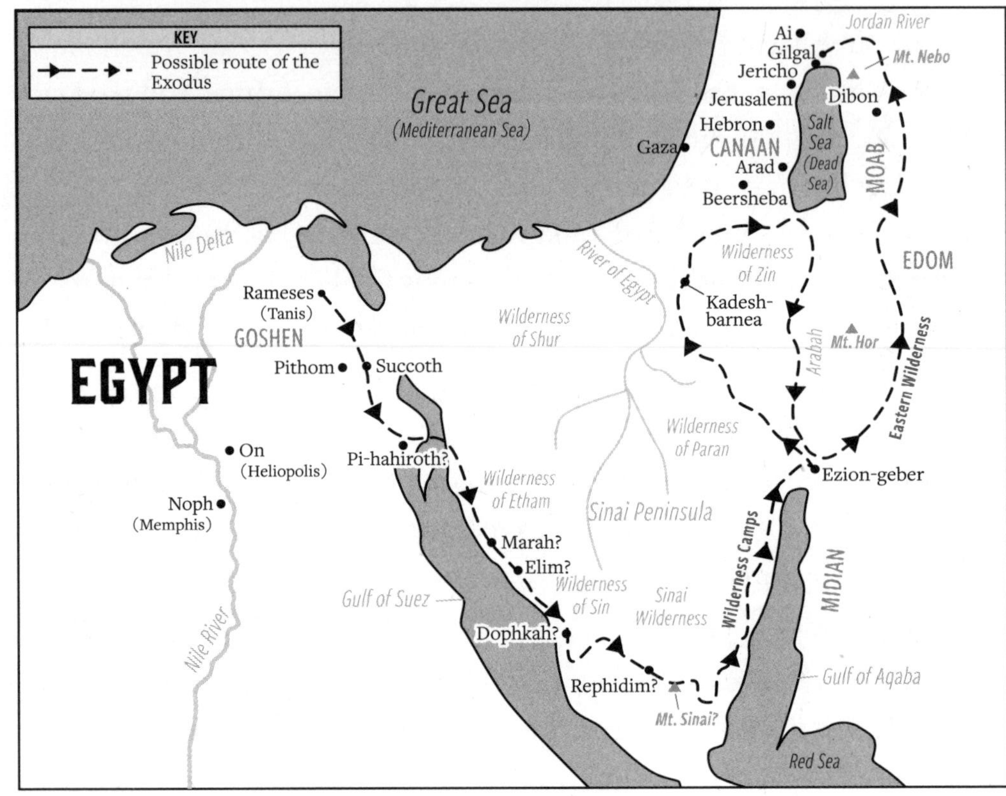

ISRAEL'S ITINERARY

Geographical Location	Duration
Rescue from Egypt (Exodus 3:1–15:21)	Several months
Travel to Sinai (Exodus 15:22–18:27)	One month, fourteen days
Camped at Sinai (Exodus 19:1–Numbers 10:10)	Eleven months and nineteen days
Travel to Kadesh (Numbers 10:11–12:16)	Two to three months
Camped In and Around Kadesh (Numbers 13:1–20:21)	Thirty-seven years
Kadesh to the Plains of Moab (Numbers 20:22–22:1)	Several months
Camped on the Plains of Moab (Numbers 22:2–36:13)	Several months
Total (Numbers 32:13)	Forty years

Note: Kadesh and Kadesh Barnea are synonymous names for the same place located in the desert of Paran, which is in the wilderness of Zin.

CHAPTER 1

NAVIGATING NUMBERS: AN OVERVIEW OF THE BOOK

> He who began a good work in you will bring it to completion at the day of Jesus Christ. (Philippians 1:6 ESV)

One afternoon, three men were walking on an ocean beach when they came across an old lamp. The first man picked it up and began to rub it. Out popped a genie. The genie said, "I'm here to give each of you one wish." The first man didn't hesitate. "I want a million dollars!" POOF! A million dollars appeared before him. The second man exclaimed, "I want a mansion right here on the beach!" POOF! A beautiful mansion appeared, and the genie handed him keys to his new home. The third guy? "Make me irresistible to women!" POOF! The genie turned him into a box of chocolates!

Suppose you had three wishes; what would you wish for? Or maybe you'd take the high road and say, "Thanks, but no thanks. I already have everything I need." What would happen next? The genie would faint and need to be revived with smelling salts!

Our world screams, "You need something bigger, brighter, and better!" Whether it's the latest iPad, big-screen television, or smartwatch, advertisers incessantly tell us what we lack. They're out to addict us to what? They entice us to adopt *when-and-then* thinking.

What does that look like? "When I get a new job, then I'll be happy. When I get a new boss . . . When I get new car . . . When I get a new husband . . . When I get rid of my old husband . . . When I make 10K more a year, lose thirty pounds, move out on my own, get married, move to a different city, join a different church, go on cruise, win the lottery, pay off my mortgage, then I'll be happy. When my wife quits bugging me, when my boss starts paying attention to me, when my mom quits griping at me, when my dad quits yelling at me, then—and only then—will I be happy."

Welcome to the book of Numbers.

Before the Israelites place their feet on Canaan's soil, God commands a census be taken, has Moses organize the twelve tribes, dictates how Levites and priests will serve, and gives directives about vows, blessings, sacrifices, and worship. Everything goes like clockwork throughout Numbers 1–10. People appear to be patient, calm, and accommodating. However, once God's glory cloud lifts and begins leading Israel (Numbers 10:11), the nation shows its true colors. *When-and-then* thinking strikes with a vengeance.

After living as state slaves in Egypt, camping at Mount Sinai for almost a year, then saddling up for the journey to the Promised Land, the Israelites quickly become disgruntled. "When we cross the Jordan River, then we'll be happy. When we defeat Jericho, take Jerusalem, and settle in Joppa, then we'll be happy. But now? In the wilderness? Argh!"

Numbers 11–25 describes Israel's callous ingratitude, perpetual complaining, and blindness to God's ongoing mercies. Longing to go back to Egypt, people reject Moses' leadership, have little faith in divine promises, and even get caught up in worshiping other gods. At the root of it all? *When-and-then* thinking.

The Israelites weren't going to break camp at Sinai and defeat the Canaanites the next day. It was going to take time. What do we call that? Living in-between. Between the exodus and land inheritance; between deliverance and the grand goal: life in the Promised Land.

If God's people were going to make their goal, they needed to become satisfied with manna from the sky, water from the rock, and God's guidance through a pillar of cloud by day and a pillar of fire by night. How did the Israelites fair? They caved in to the when-and-then syndrome—time after time. They never found a genie in a bottle.

IN-BETWEEN

Did you know that trapeze artists become good friends? This doesn't surprise me. If I'm flying through the air, I wouldn't want the person catching me to have any lingering resentments toward me! When the flyer lets go of the trapeze, it's too late to reach back for the bar and too soon to be caught. The flyer's job is to be as still as possible and wait for the catcher to catch her. The flyer is where? In-between.

Moses also tells us about a journey that's in progress. Let's drill down into some of the book's details.

The Israelites celebrate the first Passover on the fourteenth day of the first month in 1446 BC. They leave Egypt the next day (Numbers 33:3; cf. Exodus 12:2, 6), arrive at Mount Sinai roughly a month later (Exodus 19:1), and then take a year to learn about God's laws as well as build the tabernacle (Exodus 40:2, 17). One month later, the nation begins preparing to leave Sinai for the Promised Land—the first day of the second month in 1445 BC (Numbers 1:1). On the twentieth day of the second month, the cloud goes up from over the tabernacle and the Israelites begin their journey from Sinai to Canaan (Numbers 10:11–12).

For the next forty years? Things were better than they were in Egypt, but not as good as they were going to be in Canaan. The Israelites lived between freedom from slavery and entry into the land flowing with milk and honey. They were bounded by the known and the unknown, the familiar and the scary, the past and the future. What's that like?

We know. In Christ, the new creation has broken into this present age (cf. 2 Corinthians 5:17; Hebrews 6:5), yet we still experience setbacks, besetting sins, and crushing rejection. John puts it this way: "We are God's children *now*, and what we will be has *not yet* appeared" (1 John 3:2). Now. Not yet. We straddle the present evil age and the glorious age to come. We long for Jesus to return and transform this world into paradise. In the meantime, in the between time, like Israel, we stumble through the wilderness.

Oh, we happen upon an oasis every now and then. Thank God! But they're the exception, not the rule. The rule? Like Israelites in the book of Numbers, we're between the promise issued and the promise inherited. We know God can, but He hasn't yet—at least not finally and fully.

"I'm at the *midway* point of my project." "Welcome to *Intermediate* Algebra." "I'm *halfway* home." Oh, the thrill of starting! Oh, the ecstasy of finishing! But being in between? Ugh.

Interim seasons don't come for our comfort. God uses them to mold and shape us to become more like Christ. In-between days are God's invitation to learn how to wait and grow in faith. We don't need less of these times. We need more insight into how to mature from them.

No doubt about it!

I'm a lot like the grousing and griping Israelites. During between times, my attitude can become sour. I can protest and pout with the best of them. I get depressed and down in the mouth. This outlook even impacted Moses. He became so despondent in the wilderness that at one point he prayed to die (Numbers 11:10–15). The more the winds howl and the sand blows, the more vulnerable we become to when-and-then sinking thinking. At that point, we're tempted to make bad decisions and hook up with bad actors. We end up in bad places. Why? We want the Promised Land right *now*.

HURRY UP AND WAIT

None of us likes to wait. We scowl at the person who dares, *who dares*, to take eleven items into the ten-item express line. We weave through traffic like we're in the Daytona 500, looking for the fastest lane. We sit at red lights, inching our car ever closer to the one in front of us, saying under our breath, "Come on! Come on!" None of us likes to wait. Not on the doctor. Not on the traffic. Not on the pepperoni pizza.

The teenager? Waiting to make the team. The young couple? Waiting to get pregnant. The man with the depressed look? Waiting for a second chance. The elderly woman with the cane? Waiting for one painless day.

Adam waits for Eve. Noah waits for flood waters to subside. Abraham waits for a son. Jacob waits to marry Rachel. Hannah waits for a child. Jesus spends forty days in the wilderness as He waits to begin His public ministry. The point?

Change is slow. It takes time. Don't believe me? Look out your window and you'll probably see some trees. Trees play the long game. Trees, by their very nature, refuse instant gratification. So does most of creation—that is, with one exception. People.

Delays? Postponements? Not now!

Transitional times are defining—for nations and for individuals. They define our character and chart the course for our future. The decisions we make during these seasons are pivotal—a truth we repeatedly encounter in the book of Numbers.

THE MIDDLE INNINGS

Baseball fans! How much glitz and glamour is there in being a middle relief pitcher? None! Who gets the spotlight, as well as the money? Starting pitchers and closers. Taking the mound in the sixth inning and pitching through the bottom of the eighth doesn't win you a lot of fans.

How often do we find ourselves in the middle innings? Driving from work to home. Mediating between two upset children or two angry adults. Waiting for a new job, a new relationship, or a new school. How do we respond? We moan and groan and pick a bone.

The highlight reel of our lives includes events like finishing college, getting married, having children. It might also feature promotions, breakthroughs, advances, and dream vacations. Our response? "Hip, hip, hooray, and hallelujah! Life is great and oh so grand!"

Then there's the rest of life: losses, heartaches, hospital stays, goodbyes, breakups, funerals, and rock-bottoms. Hopeless knocks on the door. We let him in. And it goes downhill from there. It feels like our hurt will never leave. We give up, give in, and go down with the ship. "Why is this taking so much time?"

All we see is regimen and routine. The ordinary, the mundane, the dull, and the predictable. SSDD. Same stuff, different day. "Give me a mountain to climb, a project to tackle. I'm ready!" But in between, time grinds to a halt. Ticktock. Ticktock. Ticktock.

In-between doesn't have a lot of glitz and glamor. It's raising toddlers. Waiting in line at the gas station. Staring out the window wondering what's next. Wouldn't it be great if we could get in a Formula 1 race car and speed past these days? Cut in line and get to the front? Skip it all and get on with getting on?

No, it wouldn't. Why? We'd miss life. Sunrises and sunsets. Building relationships. Getting on our knees repeatedly and crying out to God for help and forgiveness and love.

The more we let impatience call the shots, the less we enjoy the now. In our longing for the extraordinary, we miss the ordinary. These moments and these days. This season. If we want to live life to the glory of God, we must embrace the present reality. Yes, it can be agonizing. And frustrating. Waiting is never a walk in the park.

What if we never learn how to embrace our in-between seasons? What if we succumb to when-and-then thinking? What if (God forbid!) we become like Israelites in the book of Numbers? Much of life will be wasted. Is that putting it too strongly? I don't think so.

SMARTPHONE ADDICTIONS

What occupies us during in-between times? When we're waiting and waiting and waiting? That's easy. It's our smartphone. Do you check your phone regularly for some form of message (Facebook, Instagram, text, email, and so on) even when you don't get a notification? Do you always keep your phone with you or in close proximity? Do you sleep with your phone? Do you feel your phone vibrating or hear it ringing when it isn't? If you answer yes to any of these questions, you may have what psychologists call "nomophobia"—the fear of not having access to a mobile phone or mobile phone services. "I can't believe it! There's no cell-phone service here!"

The reason we check our phones so often is because of dopamine, the hormone of happiness. Every time we get a notification, our dopamine level rises because we believe something new and interesting is happening. Our phone becomes our slot machine—we may win big or lose it all. Is there something better to do with my in-between times than be obsessed with my phone? How about this? Study the book of Numbers.

THE BOOK OF NUMBERS IN 1 CORINTHIANS AND HEBREWS

We're learning that, far from being musty, dusty, irrelevant accounting of Israelite history, Numbers is a book for today, for Christians, for our times, for our lives. That's also what we find in the books of 1 Corinthians and Hebrews.

Paul reminds the cantankerous Corinthians that the journey to the heavenly promised land begins just like Israel's did—through water and God's Word. "All were baptized into Moses in the cloud and in the sea" (1 Corinthians 10:2 ESV). Paul uses the word *all* five times in 1 Corinthians 10:1–4. God was rich in mercy to every Israelite. They all passed through the sea. They all were baptized. They all ate the same spiritual food. They all drank from the Rock. Men and women. Rich and poor. Young and old. God loved them all.

Next, Paul teaches Christians in Corinth that Christ is the Rock that sustained God's people during their in-between times (1 Corinthians 10:4). Just as Israel's Red Sea deliverance points to Christian Baptism and its spiritual food and drink prefigure God's gifts in the Holy Supper, so also the Rock that followed the Israelites foreshadows Jesus.

Despite these Gospel gifts bestowed upon the Israelites, Paul says that "with most of them God was not pleased" (1 Corinthians 10:5 ESV). What a massive understatement! The fact of the matter is that two—just *two*—Israelites from the cohort of adults that left Egypt made it to Canaan: Joshua and Caleb. Why? The others grew tired and succumbed to impatience. "If we can't be in Canaan in less than two weeks, forget it!"

Paul further reminds the Corinthians about Israel's sins. These include worshiping the golden calf (1 Corinthians 10:7; cf. Exodus 32), engaging in sexual immorality (1 Corinthians 10:8; cf. Numbers 25), testing God (1 Corinthians 10:9; e.g., Numbers 21), and grumbling against Moses (1 Corinthians 10:10; e.g., Numbers 11, 12, 16). Paul's point? These Israelites were a tough group! Don't become like them!

The New Testament book of Hebrews provides another Christian application of Numbers. The author warns us about becoming rebellious and unbelieving like the Israelites (Hebrews 3:16–19). Yet that book's chief way of interpreting Numbers is through Psalm 95:7–11. "*Today*, if you hear His voice, do not harden your hearts, as at Meribah, as on the day at Massah in the wilderness, when your fathers put Me to the test and put Me to the proof, though they had seen My work. For forty years I loathed that generation and said, 'They are a people who go astray in their heart, and they have not known My ways.' Therefore I swore in My wrath, 'They shall not enter My rest'" (ESV). Hebrews 3:7–11 quotes these verses almost word for word.

In his application of Psalm 95, the writer of Hebrews emphasizes the word "today." It appears in Hebrews 3:7, 13, 15; 4:7 (two times). By highlighting the present moment, "today," the Hebrews author places us into the narrative of Numbers—just like Paul does in 1 Corinthians 10. You and I are traveling in the wilderness now, *today*!

The author of Hebrews further points out that, like God's people in Numbers, his audience had experienced God's saving gifts but may end up rejecting Him (Hebrews 6:4–6; 10:29; 12:25). Sluggishness (Hebrews 6:12) could lead to something far worse—apostasy (Hebrews 10:26). Take heed, God says to the recipients of Hebrews. Don't be like the Israelites, who failed to spiritually mature (Hebrews 5:11–6:2).

Those who left Egypt as adults, who fizzled so miserably throughout Numbers 11–25, provide further impetus for the clarion call in Hebrews not to neglect God's Word (Hebrews 2:1–4; 3:7–4:13; 5:11–6:8). Neglect may turn into contempt, and contempt may turn into hardened revolt. Those who "turn away from the living God" (Hebrews 3:12) reject the sacrifice for sins provided by Christ and therefore negate His saving power (Hebrews 6:6; 10:29). This leads to life's ultimate tragedies: the loss of salvation (Hebrews 2:2–3), the loss of promised rest (Hebrews 4:1), the loss of the heavenly homeland (Hebrews 11:14–16), and the loss of the lasting city (Hebrews 13:14).

What do 1 Corinthians 10 and the book of Hebrews want to hammer into our hearts? *Israel's story in Numbers is our story as well.* Through Holy Baptism, we've come out of Egypt and are on the way to our heavenly promised land. That's our past and our future. What about today? Grave dangers and enticing temptations await us while we're in between.

OUTLINING NUMBERS

Understanding how a biblical author frames ideas is essential. Faithful interpretation and application hinge on seeing how a book is organized and what is accented. Outlining Numbers, therefore, is like looking at a map before beginning our trip—which is always a good idea!

At first glance, Numbers appears to be a map put together by an incompetent committee of cartographers! They hastily threw the book together then went on their merry way. Switching metaphors, Numbers might remind us of a cluttered garage. The book jumps from lists to laws to lessons learned—then back again. Numbers often feels haphazard and incoherent. In fact, one scholar studied thirty-three commentaries on Numbers and discovered eighteen significantly different outlines. All is lost!

Not so! There are two approaches to the book; both are helpful. The first way is to look at Numbers geographically. The initial third of the book describes events in the Sinai wilderness (Numbers 1:1–10:10). *Orientation* is the theme. The second part describes Israel's wilderness travels (Numbers 10:11–21:35). These chapters chronicle the nation's *disorientation*. The last third of the book occurs on the Plains of Moab, on the east bank of the Jordan River, opposite Jericho (Numbers 22:1–36:13). These chapters focus on *new orientation*.

Though it's insightful to consider Numbers from the vantage point of geography, this approach doesn't help us understand the book spiritually.

After all, Moses' intent isn't to teach us about different locations. His main reason for writing Numbers is to showcase Israel's spiritual highs and lows, along with God's steadfast, immovable love. Looking at the book spiritually puts the spotlight on the two generations in Numbers. Understood this way, the two censuses in chapters 1 and 26 rise like twin towers above the book's thirty-four other chapters.

I find this approach to be the most fruitful way to understand Numbers. The main gist isn't geography. It's *generations*. Two of them, to be exact. Those who left Egypt as adults and their children. The first group failed. The second succeeded.

The book of Numbers, therefore, is very straightforward. The end of the old. The beginning of the new. That's not bad, is it? Two generations and two censuses. Part A and part B.

God directs the first census in the second month of the second year after the exodus (Numbers 1:1). He commands Moses and Aaron, along with tribal leaders, to count the first generation of post-Egypt Israelite men—twenty years and older (Numbers 1:1–4). The second census occurs in the fortieth year after the exodus. It's goal is to count the second generation of post-Egypt Israelite men, also twenty years and up (Numbers 26:1–4). Numbers 1 and 26, then, are pivotal—and they're virtually alike. The order of the tribes varies in these chapters, but only through reversing the names of "Manasseh" and "Ephraim." That's not a lot of slippage!

It follows that, like victory banners, Numbers 1–10 and Numbers 26–36 display Israel's steadfast trust in God's promises. The first third of the book highlights the first generation's obedience (e.g., Numbers 1:54; 2:33–34; 4:49; 8:20, 22; 9:5). The last third highlights their children's faith (Numbers 26:4–63; 31:7, 31; 36:10).

Yet, like Death Valley, the book's middle section in Numbers 11–25 describes the cohort of adults who came out of Egypt—their doubt and defiance—along with God's ongoing attempts to deliver this wayward generation. These are the stories we're most familiar with: grumbling about manna and Moses, twelve men sent to spy on Canaan, Korah's rebellion, the bronze serpent, and Balaam with his talking donkey. In spite of Israel's constant carping and compromising in this part of the book, God's river of mercy continues to flow.

Numbers thus accents two groups of people—the exodus generation's fears and the new generation's faith. The first fails to enter Canaan because of unbelief. The second generation is faithful. In the book of Joshua, they enter the Promised Land.

There are numerous connections between the first part of the book (Numbers 1–25) and its second part (Numbers 26–36). The links invite us to compare and contrast the two cohorts of Israelites. Look at a few examples:

Legal issues involving women (Numbers 5; 27)

Passover celebrations (Numbers 9; 28:16–25)

Victory over Sihon and Og (Numbers 21:21–35) and assigning their land to the tribes of Reuben, Gad, and half of Manasseh (Numbers 32)

Tribal lists of spies (Numbers 13) and leaders (Numbers 34)

Wilderness travel (Numbers 10–25) and the journey's itinerary (Numbers 33)

Provisions for Levites (Numbers 18:21–32; 35)

What do these parallels suggest? Moses wants us to read Numbers with an eye on what went wrong with the adults as well as what went right with their children. How big is the contrast? You tell me.

Everyone over twenty years old when Israel left Egypt died in the wilderness—with the exception of Joshua and Caleb. How many recorded deaths are there of the second generation? Zero. Zip. Zilch. Nada. None. Numbers 26–36 records military victories, solved problems, and several directives for life in the Promised Land. The difference between the two groups is the difference between cats and dogs, night and day, peanut butter and jelly—pick your own contrasts. They all work!

Will those who are in-between—straddling Egypt and Canaan—make it to the Promised Land? The answer for the first cohort is a resounding *no*. The answer for their children is an affirming *yes*. Moses wants every reader of Numbers to follow the second generation's faith-filled example and learn how to trust God during life's in-between times.

Numbers' lessons, however, are not merely moral. They're also Christological. Christ travels with both generations. He's not only their Rock (1 Corinthians 10:4), but in the fullness of time, Jesus shows Himself to be the perfect, obedient Israelite. In the wilderness, our Savior met every temptation of Satan and conquered him through God's Word (Matthew 4:1–11; Luke 4:1–13). That same Word empowers us in our journey, making us more like the Israelites of the second generation.

GENERATIONS

What generation do you belong to? The Greatest Generation—those born before 1928? The Silent Generation—those who came of age in the postwar era? The Baby Boom generation—people (including me) who were part of the spike in fertility that began in 1946, right after World War II? Or maybe you identify as a Gen Xer, those born from 1965 through 1980. Or you may be like my three children—a Millennial born after 1980. Perhaps you're a proud member of Gen Z (1995–2009), Generation Alpha (2010–2024), or the latest group of Americans, called Generation Beta, beginning in 2025. I know. This can quickly get confusing! Not in the book of Numbers. Moses provides an in-depth look at just two generations—adults who left Egypt and the next generation, their children.

God calls these and every generation to pass on the legacy of faith to their children. Here's a sampling of some verses.

> "The Lord, the God of your fathers, the God of Abraham, the God of Isaac, and the God of Jacob, has sent me to you." This is My name

> forever, and thus I am to be remembered throughout all *generations*. (Exodus 3:15 ESV)
>
> This day shall be for you a memorial day, and you shall keep it as a feast to the LORD; throughout your *generations*. (Exodus 12:14 ESV)
>
> All native Israelites shall dwell in booths, that your *generations* may know that I made the people of Israel dwell in booths when I brought them out of the land of Egypt. (Leviticus 23:42–43 ESV)

The Israelites who left Egypt—who were the initial recipients of these commands—were impatient, idolatrous, faithless, and prone to complain, a lot! What about us? What kind of legacy are we leaving to the next generation? All it takes is one bad decision for the train to come off the track.

For King Jeroboam (931–910 BC), this decision happened at the height of his career. He started out with great promise. Catching the eye of his boss, Jeroboam got promotion after promotion—right up the ladder! At one point, he was made superintendent of Israel's public works. God even promised Jeroboam He would prosper him as He had prospered David (1 Kings 11:38). Jeroboam had a bright future. Then his judgment faltered. He set up two golden calves and told his people, "It is too much for you to go up to Jerusalem. Here are your gods" (1 Kings 12:28). Through this one faithless act, he led Israel into the sin of idolatry.

Jeroboam could have had an enduring legacy—one like David. Instead, when future evil kings of Israel arose, their legacy was compared to Jeroboam's. Nineteen times the Bible says, "He didn't depart from the sins of Jeroboam son of Nebat, who made Israel sin" (e.g., 2 Kings 10:31). Like a broken record, Jeroboam's sad and sorry legacy was repeated over and over.

What about us? Day by day, we write our life's legacy; we make choices that impact generations to come. The most important gift we can leave won't be etched on the pages of a will. It won't be given to our children when we die. Our greatest legacy is imparted over a lifetime—steadfast love, faith, and devotion to Jesus Christ. This is a life shaped by the Spirit that exudes humility and honesty.

Statistics show this handoff of faith has hit some tough times. The percentage of Christians holding a biblical worldview (i.e., those who believe and build their lives on core scriptural truths) has drastically declined over the last four generations of Americans. Here are the sobering statistics. The Pew Research Center found that the number of people who identify as Christian is dropping precipitously: from 85 percent in 1990 to 65 percent in 2019.[1] A Barna study found that 22 percent of millennials who once identified as Christians no longer do.[2] A further 30 percent still identify as Christians but aren't connected to a faith community anymore.

No family is perfect. And there's no family too broken to rediscover the value of passing on a Christian legacy. If you find that hard to believe, consider Manasseh—Judah's worst king (2 Kings 21:1–18). His grandson, Josiah, was one of Judah's best kings (2 Kings 22–23). That's what I call a comeback!

It's never too late to build bridges, make amends, and talk about Jesus with our family. Regardless of the past, God can still use us—moms and dads, grandmas and grandpas—to encourage our loved ones to develop biblical thinking and godly living. Here are a few more generational verses to direct you:

> We will not hide them from their children, but tell to the coming *generation* the glorious deeds of the LORD. (Psalm 78:4 ESV)
>
> Tell your children of it, and let your children tell their children, and their children to another *generation*. (Joel 1:3 ESV)

1 "In U.S., Decline of Christianity Continues at Rapid Pace," Pew Research Center, October 17, 2019, https://www.pewresearch.org/religion/2019/10/17/in-u-s-decline-of-christianity-continues-at-rapid-pace/ (accessed December 23, 2024).

2 "Almost Half of Practicing Christian Millennials Say Evangelism Is Wrong," The Barna Group, February 5, 2019, https://www.barna.com/research/millennials-oppose-evangelism/ (accessed December 23, 2024).

To Him be glory in the church and in Christ Jesus throughout all *generations*. (Ephesians 3:21 ESV)

"IN THE WILDERNESS"

The Hebrew title for Numbers is *bemidbar*, or "In the Wilderness." "Wilderness," in this case, denotes a place that can't provide enough food and water to sustain people. That would be southern Arizona, western Nebraska, or pretty much the entire state of Nevada. The Hebrew word for "wilderness" appears 271 times in the Old Testament. Forty-eight of those times are in the book of Numbers—where all the action takes place in locales bounded by Mount Sinai and Canaan.

Paul knows about in-between places. He writes, "He who began a good work in you will bring it to completion at the day of Jesus Christ" (Philippians 1:6 ESV). The good work has begun—we've been baptized and born again. But look around. What do we witness? Wars, famines, pandemics, sickness, cancer, breakups, death, and sometimes complete despair. What do you hear?

"No one will *ever* love me."

"*This* can't be redeemed."

"*Everyone* is against me."

"Future? *What* future?"

Yes, God has begun a good work. No, it's not finished. What's that sound like? The book of Numbers. Let's begin at the beginning—Numbers 1.

CHAPTER 2

I HAVE CALLED YOU BY NAME: NUMBERS 1

The sheep hear his voice, and he calls his own sheep by name. (John 10:3 ESV)

If we had been on the British Coast in 1845, we might have seen two ships boarded by 138 of England's finest sailors. Their task? Chart the Northwest Passage around the Canadian Arctic to the Pacific Ocean. Sir John Franklin, the expedition's captain, hoped the journey would be the turning point in Arctic exploration. History shows that it was. Not because of its success but because of its utter failure. The explorers never returned. Every crew member died. Those who followed Franklin's path learned an all-important lesson: If you're going to survive the journey, you must plan ahead.

Though the voyage was projected to last three years, Franklin only carried a twelve-day supply of coal for his auxiliary steam engines. What he lacked in fuel, however, he made up for in entertainment. Each ship carried more than 1,200 books, china place settings, and expensive wine goblets—along with sterling silver flatware. You've got to wonder if the crew was planning for an Arctic expedition or a Caribbean cruise.

In the first third of Numbers (chapters 1 through 10), we can't accuse the Israelites of failing to plan. The list of details (and more details!) for their journey from Mount Sinai to Canaan begins in chapter 1. Let's start with a deliberate look at the book's first verse.

"THE LORD . . ."

Meet Yahweh—translated "Lord" in English Bibles—the God of Abraham, Isaac, and Jacob. His name appears a whopping 6,828 times in the Old Testament. He even gives us His nickname, *Ya*—as in "Hallelujah," or "praise Ya." An insightful definition of Yahweh comes in Numbers

15:41. "I am the Lord your God, who brought you out of the land of Egypt to be your God: I am the Lord your God." Here's an outline of this verse:

I am the Lord your God,

who brought you out of the land of Egypt to be your God,

I am the Lord your God.

The Gospel is in the middle. Israelites were state slaves in Egypt. There was no way out. No way, that is, until a voice spoke from within a burning bush. It shocked the sandals right off Moses' feet, literally! Moses is the Lord's first-round draft pick. His assignment? Get Israel out of Egypt.

As slaves in Egypt, Israelites had no legal status, no worth, no value, no hope, and no future. Their sons were murdered, tools of torture brought mayhem, and their daily quota of mud, bricks, and straw meant a life of endless monotony.

It was like getting braces *on* your teeth and never getting them *off*. It was like being sixteen and never getting your driver's license. It was like working and never getting paid. But then there were frogs and flies and fire, and a mighty hand and an outstretched arm, and God rescued Israel through the Red Sea that became dry ground.

This is the Lord your God! The Gospel God! He lavishes His people with love, liberates them with power, and launches them into the world with His redemption story. Numbers 1:1 goes on to say that the Lord (Yahweh) is anything but silent.

"THE LORD SPOKE . . ."

Question: Who speaks more? Men or women? I bet you know the answer! Here's some research to back it up. Studies show that most women speak on average twenty thousand words per day. That's approximately thirteen thousand more than the average man. Why is that? Women possess higher levels of the FOXP2 gene. The FOXP2 gene provides instructions for making the language protein called forkhead box

P2. Researchers find 30 percent more forkhead box P2 protein in the brains of women. Who knew?

Here's another question. Whose words carry the most power? I bet you know that answer too. It's Yahweh! His Word has ultimate power. My! By His Word, He created the universe in six days. By His Word, He sent forth a worldwide flood, toppled the tower of Babel, inspired the prophets, and climactically burst forth in the flesh, in Jesus Christ, our Lord. God's Word is the most powerful force in the universe. "He spoke, and it came to be; He commanded, and it stood firm" (Psalm 33:9 ESV).

In addition to God's words, Numbers records a handful of other people's words. Some we implicitly trust, like those of Moses. But what about others? Hobab, Moses' brother-in-law, appears believable. Balaam's donkey speaks the truth. What about Balaam himself? He's mostly dependable, but as we'll see, he also has some questionable character traits. In other sections of Numbers, outsiders shouldn't be trusted, like Midianites in chapter 25. What about Israelites? Are we to believe them simply because they're Israelites? Not at all! Miriam and Aaron are envious of Moses (Numbers 12). Korah and his rebels certainly aren't credible (Numbers 16). And even mighty Moses' words aren't always dependable. He makes the mistake of his life, saying, "Shall *we* bring water for you out of this rock?" (Numbers 20:10 ESV). There is, however, one voice that we can bank on every single time. It's the voice of the Lord our God.

While this should be evident, sometimes we hear well-meaning Christians use phrases like this: "The Lord spoke to my heart and said . . ." "I feel like God is telling me to . . ." Driving these statements is the false notion that the Bible offers religion but God offers a personal relationship, beyond the Bible, where He speaks directly to our hearts—apart from His revealed Word in Holy Scripture. "Since the Lord spoke to Elijah in a still, small voice, He'll do the same for me."

Do you understand where this leads? There's nothing concrete. There's nothing to hold on to. There's nothing of substance. I may think

God told me to tell you to sell all your possessions and give the proceeds to me. Who says God isn't speaking a divine oracle through me? Probably you!

Thank God He's told us where He speaks. Not in our hearts or feelings or intuitions or hunches or dreams. God speaks through His Spirit-inspired Bible. *The will of God is only revealed in the Word of God.* Paul says as much. "Do not go beyond what is written" (1 Corinthians 4:6).

God speaks to Moses (and sometimes includes Aaron) sixty times in Numbers. All told, the Lord speaks over 150 times in the book. Here's an illuminating fact. "When Moses went into the tent of meeting to speak with the LORD, he heard the voice speaking to him from above *the mercy seat* that was on the ark of the testimony, from between the two cherubim; and it spoke to him" (Numbers 7:89 ESV; cf. Exodus 25:22).

Did you catch that? God speaks from *the mercy seat*. What's a good definition of God's mercy? Superlatives don't cut it. Neither do superlatives of superlatives. Will a thesaurus help? Nope. We need a thesaurus supplement. Divine mercy stretches the limits of our language.

God understands this. That's why He finally sent Mercy to lie in a manger, to preach to the multitudes, and to heal the sick, the lame, and the broken. Mercy loves fools and stubborn rebels like you and me. Mercy finally hangs on a God-forsaken cross between two malefactors. Three days later, Mercy swallows up death forever. Mercy has a name. *Jesus*.

"THE LORD SPOKE TO MOSES . . ."

When people hurt us—when they blame us and shame us and game us—we can do what Miss Havisham did. Remember her in Charles Dickens's novel *Great Expectations*? Jilted by her fiancé just prior to their wedding, how did she respond? She closed all the blinds in her house, stopped every clock, let the wedding cake on the table gather cobwebs, and continued to wear her wedding dress until it hung on her body in yellow decay. Humiliated and heartbroken, from that day on, Miss Havisham was alone in her mansion, until she adopted a daughter to further her revenge on men. Miss Havisham was defined by her broken heart for most of her life.

Moses understands unsettling setbacks. Throughout the book of Numbers, he's rejected, abandoned, critiqued, and condemned—all by his own people! Yet Moses manages to survive. He refuses to get lost in despair. He clings to God's Word.

The expression "the Lord spoke to Moses" appears forty-nine times in Numbers. While God reveals Himself to other Israelites through dreams (e.g., Genesis 41:1) and visions (e.g., Isaiah 1:1), He speaks to Moses "mouth to mouth" (Numbers 12:8 ESV; cf. Deuteronomy 34:10). And what's the most life-transforming Word God speaks to Moses? The Gospel.

Note, for instance, that immediately after Israel's complete collapse in Numbers 14, God's next words are Gospel words. "The Lord spoke to Moses, saying, 'Speak to the people of Israel and say to them, *When* you come into the land you are to inhabit, which I am *giving you*.'" (Numbers 15:1–2 ESV). "When." Not "if." "Giving you." Not "that you must earn." This is exactly what Moses needed to hear—God's guarantee of a gracious new beginning. Countless more Gospel words in Numbers await us! They're all previews and predictions of God's final Word—the Word made flesh, Jesus Christ, our Lord.

"THE LORD SPOKE TO MOSES IN THE WILDERNESS OF SINAI . . ."

Experts say that to stay alive in the wilderness we need to know how to build a shelter, forage for edible plants, find water, and build a fire. And don't underestimate the necessity of a fire. The most likely cause of death in the wild isn't starvation or even dehydration. It's hypothermia. Could you get a fire going from scratch in five minutes? Not many people could. I sure couldn't!

In the Old Testament, the wilderness is a place of desolation and death. It's "formless"—to use a word from Genesis 1:2 that Moses employs in Deuteronomy 32:10 when he describes Israel's journey in

Numbers. What does "formless" imply? No boundaries, no structure, no shape, no plan—nothing we can get our hands on. No wonder biblical authors use "wilderness" symbolically to describe feelings of being lost, confused, and hopeless. Sarah exiles Hagar and Ishmael to the wilderness (Genesis 16:7). Elijah falls faint there (1 Kings 19:4). And John maintains that the church lives and moves and has her being in the wilderness (Revelation 12:14).

During wilderness wanderings, we try to make sense of our formless and shapeless situations. I call them the big D's—debt, depression, divorce, demons, darkness, devils, and the last enemy: death. These adversaries mess with our minds, pillage our peace, and steal the joy of our salvation.

Yet it's in the wilderness, in places of obscurity and the unknown, that God shaped Jacob, Moses, John the Baptist, and Jesus. The wilderness is where God births new dreams and desires. It's where He creates character and resilience. It's where lives are sharpened, deepened, and strengthened. And take heart! God provides for His people in desolate and dry places. "I have led you forty years in the wilderness. Your clothes have not worn out on you, and your sandals have not worn off your feet" (Deuteronomy 29:5 ESV).

"THE LORD SPOKE TO MOSES IN THE WILDERNESS OF SINAI, IN THE TENT OF MEETING"

The God of Abraham, Isaac, and Jacob isn't far off; He doesn't live on the dark side of the moon. God is in the midst of His people; He lives with them in a tent of meeting—His tabernacle. Whatever the wilderness threw at the Israelites, one thing was for sure. They weren't alone. The Lord God of heaven and earth was with them.

In one of their most sober moments, the Israelites understood that God's presence was their greatest gift. It takes place in Exodus 33. The chapter begins with these words: "The Lord said to Moses, 'Depart; go up from here, you and the people'" (Exodus 33:1 ESV). While God pledges safe passage to Canaan—out of mercy, lest He destroy Israel—He tells Moses that His presence will no longer accompany His people. The Israelites take this as "a disastrous word" (Exodus 33:4 ESV). God's decision not to go along with His people to the Promised Land isn't a minor change to the plan or a slight delay. *It's the end of everything.*

In a moment of stark realization, the Israelites come to their senses. Without God's presence, everything will be in vain. Safety and abundance aren't enough in Canaan. Nothing is complete without divine companionship. "Whom have I in heaven but You? And there is nothing on earth that I desire besides You" (Psalm 73:25 ESV).

God leaves the door open to change His decision. "If for a single moment I should go up among you . . ." (Exodus 33:5 ESV). Judgment isn't set in stone. A glimmer of light appears! By the end of Exodus 34, Moses has convinced God to abide among His people in the tabernacle—a mini Mount Sinai, a portable sanctuary, a place for God's presence with His people.

The tabernacle was 145 feet long, 72 feet wide, and 7 feet high (Exodus 27:18). There was an outer court, as well as an inner section divided in two—a Holy Place and the Most Holy Place, the inner sanctum where only the high priest entered once a year on the Day of Atonement. Moses goes into great detail when he writes about the tabernacle's blueprint in Exodus 25–31. God's dwelling place shares at least five features with ancient Near Eastern kings' royal palaces:

Israelites brought their offerings to the Lord (Exodus 25:1–9), just as subjects would bear tribute to their king (e.g., 2 Kings 17:3).

Israelites stood before the Lord (Deuteronomy 10:8), just as servants would stand before one in authority (e.g., 1 Kings 1:28; 3:16; Esther 8:4).

Israelites adorned the tabernacle to make it fit for a king (Exodus 25:10–26:37; 30:1–10).

Priests wore vestments (Exodus 28) to minister before the King (e.g., 1 Kings 10:5).

The tabernacle had a throne room (Psalm 99:1; Isaiah 6:1–2).

In the New Testament, God's kingly presence doesn't reside on a mountain, or in a tent, tabernacle, or temple. John 1:14 states that the Word (Jesus) became flesh and tabernacled among us, full of grace and truth.

At times, we get lonely—sometimes desperately so—but we're never alone. Christ's name is "Immanuel," God with us (Isaiah 7:14; Matthew 1:23 ESV). We can live with this promise. We can die with this promise. And we can face today—in the wilderness—with God's promise that He will never leave us or abandon us.

"THE LORD SPOKE TO MOSES IN THE WILDERNESS OF SINAI, IN THE TENT OF MEETING . . . AFTER THEY HAD COME OUT OF THE LAND OF EGYPT"

The story of Israel's departure from the land of the Nile begins when a new Egyptian king comes to power and sees Israelites as a threat to his rule. The pharaoh not only enslaves God's people, but he also begins a systemic program to kill Hebrew baby boys. After God calls Moses and Aaron, the two elder statesmen confront Egypt's genocidal policies. The result? I'll summarize it in six words. More bricks. No straw. More whips.

You know how things finally turn out. The pharaoh huffs and puffs. God blows everything down. Ten plagues completely ruin the land. Then God defeats Egypt's brightest and best. "Pharaoh's chariots and army He has hurled into the sea. The finest of Pharaoh's officers are drowned in the Red Sea" (Exodus 15:4–5).

With a mighty hand and outstretched army, God defeated Egypt and rescued His people from misery and hopelessness. The exodus became the defining mark of God's power and provision for His people. That's how Numbers 1:1 ends, highlighting the Gospel. And for Paul? It's a template for what God has done in Christ Jesus. In Romans 6–8, Paul applies Israel's history—summarized in the first verse of Numbers—to the baptized.

ROMANS 6–8: A RECAP OF ISRAEL'S HISTORY

In Romans 6, Paul announces that God liberates people enslaved to sin through the waters of Holy Baptism. In Romans 7, the apostle argues that there was nothing wrong with the Ten Commandments. The problem was with Israel, not with God. Israel was—to use one of Paul's terms—"of the flesh," a warning Moses makes throughout Deuteronomy 32. Hebrew prophets also testify to Israel's hard heart and described it in their preaching. This meant, just like Adam and Eve (who were thrust out of Eden), Israelites were eventually removed from their land—first in 721 BC then in 587 BC. Israel ended up repeating Genesis 3. Is that the end of the story?

Not even close! Sin, a dark power wielded by Satan, needed to be condemned. God carried out the sentence. Through Christ, He condemned sin in the flesh (Romans 8:3). God placed all sin on Jesus, who dealt with it once and for all. Dying under the weight of humanity's rebellion, Christ drained sin of its power. "There is now no condemnation for those who are in Christ Jesus" (Romans 8:1). The rest of Romans 8 announces that the Holy Spirit comes to tabernacle in our hearts, giving us new life.

Do you see what Paul is doing? He's following Israel's story of passing through the Red Sea (Romans 6) and arriving at Sinai (Romans 7). The apostle then understands God's dwelling in the tabernacle and promise of Canaan as the Holy Spirit with us, leading us into the new creation.

Viewed this way, these words are pivotal. "You did not receive the spirit of *slavery* to fall back into fear, but you have received the Spirit of adoption as sons, by whom we cry, 'Abba! Father!'" (Romans 8:15 ESV). Paul's argument? Don't even think about going back to being slaves, stuck in darkness and unbelief! Remember? This was killing you. You're baptized exodus people. Working with Israel's history, Paul goes on to maintain that the Spirit (not a pillar of fire and cloud) leads the baptized. "All who are led by the Spirit of God are sons of God" (Romans 8:14 ESV). *God's dealing with Israel, then, is how He deals with us—writ large in Christ Jesus.*

ISRAEL'S FIRST CENSUS

On June 6, 1944, Allied forces landed on Omaha Beach. We call that day D-Day, though the official code name was "Operation Neptune." Since we're studying Numbers, you might like to know about the numbers connected to D-Day. The Allies employed 1,213 warships, 4,126 transport vessels, 736 supplemental crafts, and 864 merchant vessels. Germans tried to hold the beachhead with eight artillery bunkers, thirty-five pillboxes, four artillery pieces, six mortar pits, eighteen anti-tank guns, forty-five rocket launcher sites, eighty-five machine gun sites, and six tank turrets. Allied forces consisted of 43,250 infantrymen, while the Germans only mustered 7,800 soldiers. Before the day was over, 4,200 soldiers on both sides had been killed.

At the burning bush on Mount Sinai, God commissioned Moses to lead Israel in its own D-Day assault against Canaanites. While Israelite forces would be a key element to taking the Promised Land, trusting God was at the heart of the nation's strategy. Moses combines this divine and human approach. "Know therefore today that He who goes over before you as a consuming fire is the Lord your God. He will destroy them and subdue them before you. So you shall drive them out and make them perish quickly, as the Lord has promised you" (Deuteronomy 9:3 ESV). *God takes the initiative. Israel follows.*

Before Moses could lead the charge across the Jordan River, he had to organize his army. After all, these would-be soldiers were—until recently—a rag-tag group of slaves. No one had graduated from a military school. In fact, no one had graduated from any school! There were no experts in riding horses, driving chariots, or wielding swords, spears, bows, and arrows. But they must have had an accountant or two, as well as a few folks with management degrees. These Israelites could certainly count and get organized!

Numbers 1 tells us about it. For the most part, the chapter consists of a list with names and numbers. Run for cover! Better yet, run for the New Testament! What spiritual truths could there possibly be in Numbers 1? This isn't an inviting way for a book to begin. Didn't Moses get the memo? Yes, he did—probably from the IRS!

Peter Frampton and Mark Robilliard wrote a book called *The Joy of Accounting*, published in 2020. Perhaps you're an accountant and you find great joy in your work. Or perhaps you're like most people, who know just enough about digits, equations, and computing to stay out of jail. That's why our eyes might glaze over as we read a whole lot of names.

NAMES

Who likes to hear unknown names rattled off, one after another? Not me. I know the drill. As a university professor who is mandated to attend four commencement exercises every year (three in May, one in December), I often get antsy and impatient during these ceremonies. "I've got important things to do. People to see. Projects to complete!"

Should the university administration ever ask me, I'd suggest they streamline things. How? Have all the graduates stand. Invite those gathered to clap, hoot, holler, whistle, and shout—but only for thirty seconds. Follow this with the university president announcing, "I now declare that everyone standing has earned their degree. You're all dismissed." In two minutes, we'd be done. Finished, complete, and on to other things!

What would we miss? A lot. We'd miss the graduates' names. And names matter. They matter to us, and they matter to God. "Ben, Courtney, Teresa, Abdifatah, Vignesh, Amanda . . ." "Barb, Noah, Caitlyn, James . . ." When families and friends hear the name of their loved one, they shout and scream and cheer—sometimes they shed a tear.

Names matter. Names also matter to God. God values names—your name, my name, every name. He even calls us by name.

While Numbers 1 provides a lot of names, it doesn't list the names of all 603,550 men—those twenty years and older able to go to war. Why? A normal page in a book has about 250 to 300 words. If Moses listed every name, that would mean adding another 2,100 pages! All 603,550 names were recorded somewhere else, indicating that the total number of Israelites was close to three million.

Where are our names recorded? In God's heart. Want an example? Early on Easter morning, Mary goes to Christ's tomb, sees the stone rolled away, then runs to tell Peter and John (John 20:1–2). She returns to the tomb and weeps (John 20:11)—so devastated that when Jesus stands next to her, Mary thinks He's the gardener (John 20:13–15). Everything changes when He calls her name, "Mary." She recognizes Him and exclaims, "Rabboni!" (John 20:16 ESV).

Jesus calls you by name too. It's not what others have called you—like Stupid Idiot, Big Mouth, Loser, Old, Short, Of-No-Account. And Jesus will not use any of the names you call yourself—Rejected, Friendless, Lonely, Forgotten, Abandoned, Over-the-Hill. Jesus calls you by new names—Beloved, Cleansed, Forgiven, Priceless, Gifted, and Heaven-Bound. And get this. Your name is written with crucifixion ink in the Lamb's Book of Life—never to be erased.

How do I approach university commencements after taking a close look at Numbers 1? With joy! With delight! Celebrating academic achievements and clapping for each name!

NUMBERS IN NUMBERS

I take the numbers in Numbers 1 and 26 literally. They demonstrate that God sticks to His promises. What promises? Consider just a few—the ones He gave Abraham.

> I will make you into a great nation. (Genesis 12:2)
>
> "Look toward heaven, and number the stars, if you are able to number them." Then He said to him, "So shall your offspring be." (Genesis 15:5 ESV)

> You shall be the father of a multitude of nations. (Genesis 17:4 ESV)
>
> I will surely bless you, and I will surely multiply your offspring as the stars of heaven and as the sand that is on the seashore. (Genesis 22:17 ESV)

A census of sorts appears at the beginning of Exodus (Exodus 1:2–5). The total? Seventy. While in Egypt, "the Israelites were fruitful and greatly increased . . . so that the land was filled with them" (Exodus 1:7). Was it ever! Pharaoh became scared that the rapidly multiplying Hebrews would overrun his country (Exodus 1:9–12).

A literal understanding of Numbers 1 and 26 also harmonizes with an earlier census taken during the first year in the wilderness (Exodus 30:12–16; 38:26), as well as with other texts that address the number of adult men who left Egypt (Exodus 12:37; Numbers 11:21). The numbers don't lie!

PREPARING FOR BATTLE

Israelites aren't going on vacation in Canaan. They are going to war. To prepare, they need to conduct a military census, muster soldiers, and organize the rest of the people. Israel's leaders not only need to know the size of their fighting forces (Numbers 1) but also how to arrange the masses (Numbers 2:1–34; 3:13–49) as well as how to break camp and march (Numbers 2:3–31). There's only one way to do this: count the noses—tribe by tribe (Numbers 1:5–15).

> From *Leah*: Reuben, Simeon, Judah, Issachar, and Zebulun
>
> From *Rachel*: Ephraim and Manasseh (Joseph's sons) and Benjamin
>
> From *Bilhah* and *Zilpah*: Dan, Asher, Gad, and Naphtali

What about the Levites? The Levites aren't listed because they don't go to war and neither do they inherit land; thus, they drop off the list of twelve. The solution? God divides the tribe of Joseph in two—Manasseh and Ephraim. This even dozen is so important that within Numbers, tribal lists recur in 2:3–31; 7:12–83; 10:14–28; 13:4–15; 26:5–51.

A CALL TO ARMS

God also calls us to arms. What? Really? "The whole world lies in the power of the evil one" (1 John 5:19 ESV). I know what some of you might be thinking: "Lessing, aren't we too grown up for devils and demons, ghosts and goblins, along with ladders and lakes of fire? Aren't we all too sophisticated to believe in the dark side and Darth Vader?"

During World War II, the Germans were led in North Africa by General Erwin Rommel, otherwise known as "The Desert Fox." Rommel was invincible until British Field Commander Bernard Montgomery began to study his tactics and strategies. Soon Montgomery was able to predict and plan for Rommel's next move. Within a few months, Allied forces drove the Germans out of North Africa.

We minimize the devil's reality to our own demise. Conversely, when we learn more about his tactics and strategies, we increasingly gain the upper hand.

Where did Satan come from? Isaiah tells us. "You [Satan] said in your heart, 'I will ascend to heaven; above the stars of God I will set my throne on high; I will sit on the mount of assembly in the far reaches of the north; I will ascend above the heights of the clouds; I will make myself like the Most High" (Isaiah 14:13–14 ESV). Though Isaiah is mocking the Assyrian king Sargon II, who died in battle in 705 BC, the prophet's description also matches what Satan did when he revolted against the God of heaven and earth. What's the devil like? Jesus' words are spot on. "He was a murderer from the beginning, and has nothing to do with the truth, because there is no truth in him. When he lies, he speaks out of his own character, for he is a liar and the father of lies" (John 8:44).

The Hague Conference of 1907, the Geneva Protocol of 1925, and the Geneva Convention of 1929 all produced agreements so that nations would fight wars in a more humane way. Nerve gas, biological germs, and bullets that expand on impact were all prohibited because they produce more suffering than the conferees believed necessary.

What about Satan? He has no rules, no regulations, and no restraints. Our enemy uses weapons that inflict maximum pain. Nothing is too mean, too cruel, or too vicious. Some of his favorites? Gossip, ugly lies, damaging words, emotional abandonment.

And the devil has allies—more fallen angels called demons. The Bible speaks about them over a hundred times, calling them evil and unclean spirits, rulers, authorities, powers, dominions, thrones, and leaders. This may sound like science fiction—but it's all very real. How does the devil operate? First, he comes as tempter. "Now the serpent was more crafty than any other beast of the field that the Lord God had made. He said to the woman, 'Did God actually say, "You shall not eat of any tree in the garden"?'" (Genesis 3:1 ESV). Indulgence—that's the satanic temptation. Whatever we feel like doing, Satan gives us these marching orders. "Ready. Set. Go!"

After that, Satan comes as a deceiver. "But the serpent said to the woman, 'You will not surely die. For God knows that when you eat of it your eyes will be opened, and *you will be like God*, knowing good and evil'" (Genesis 3:4–5 ESV). "You will be like God." Sound familiar? Recall Isaiah 14:14, where the devil says, "I will make myself like the Most High" (ESV).

The 1939 film *The Wizard of Oz* created several illusions. For instance, the tornado was really just a big sock. The farmhouse in the tornado was only three feet high. And the threatening army of monkeys? They were six inches tall and hung by piano wire. Underneath the monkey costumes were small, battery-driven electric windshield wiper motors that made their wings go up and down.

It's hard to distinguish illusions from the real thing. Just ask Eve. "When the woman saw that the tree was good for food, and that it was a delight to the eyes, and that the tree was to be desired to make one wise, she took of its fruit" (Genesis 3:6 ESV).

Here's Satan's strategy: Tempt. Deceive. Accuse. "Then the eyes of both were opened, and they knew that they were naked. And they sewed fig leaves together and made themselves loincloths" (Genesis 3:7 ESV). Satan says to our first parents, "You're now washed up with God. You just committed the unforgivable sin. It's all over!" This game plan reminds me of the cheer squad chants in my high school. Rush 'em. Mush 'em. Crush 'em. Flush 'em.

During the fall of Cambodia in 1980, the Khmer Rouge found an effective way of keeping prisoners in line. They took a long needle, threaded it with string, and passed it through the palms of their captives' hands. The prisoners completely conformed.

So do we. It's painful to give up that habit, that excuse, that pet sin. "Why, I'll die if I lose that!" So, we follow the temptations, deceptions, and accusations—hook, line, and sinker, until we're sunk.

A five-year-old boy answered the phone. The call was from a credit card salesman.

> Salesman: "Is your mom home?"
>
> Little boy (in a whisper): "Yes, but she can't come to the phone right now."
>
> Salesman: "Is your dad home?"
>
> Little boy (in a whisper): "Yes, but he can't come to the phone right now."
>
> Salesman (curious): "Is there any adult there that I can talk to?"
>
> Little boy (in a whisper): "Yes, there's a policeman, but he can't come to the phone right now."
>
> Salesman: "Is there anyone else?"
>
> Little boy (in a whisper): "Yes, there's a fireman, but he can't come to the phone right now."
>
> Salesman: "With all those people there, why can't one of them come to the phone?"

Little boy (in a whisper): "Because they're looking for me!"

God comes looking for us. When we fall *again* for Satan's same bag of tricks, God drops everything to seek and save us. "They heard the sound of the LORD God walking in the garden in the cool of the day, and the man and his wife hid themselves from the presence of the LORD God among the trees of the garden" (Genesis 3:8 ESV). Our God moves heaven and earth to find us. He did it climactically through His Son, Jesus, who paid it all. Jesus paid the price for all sin, for all people, for all time. And He did it with His own blood. "If the Son sets you free, you will be free indeed" (John 8:36 ESV).

In Numbers 1, Israel prepares for battle—deliberately, methodically, and faithfully. What about us? How do we get ready to fight our enemy? With the truth—God's truth in His Word. Under the Second Petition of the Lord's Prayer in his Large Catechism, Martin Luther writes, "Dear Father, we pray, give us first Your Word, so that the Gospel may be preached properly throughout the world. Second, may the Gospel be received in faith and work and live in us, so that through the Word and the Holy Spirit's power, Your kingdom may triumph among us. And we pray that the devil's kingdom may be put down, so he may have no right or power over us, until at last his power may be utterly destroyed. So sin, death, and hell shall be exterminated" (paragraph 54).

Amen. Let it be so!

CHAPTER 3

GOD WITH US: NUMBERS 2–3

> You, O LORD, are in our midst, and we are called by Your name; do not leave us. (Jeremiah 14:9 ESV)

Mushers—people who drive dog sleds—train their dogs to endure races in the cold, arctic wilderness. Even so, during long races, like the Alaskan Iditarod, some dogs get hurt. Others become exhausted. Still other dogs lose interest in running for eighteen hours every day in the ice and snow. (I can't say that I blame them!) Injured, tired, and bored dogs are called "dropped dogs." Dropped dogs are placed in bags to stay warm. Then they're loaded onto an airplane and sent home. Dropped dogs will never pull a sled again. They worked hard toward a goal, only to fall short.

Have you ever felt like that? You excelled in college and were ready to land a great job. Nothing has opened up for three years. Now your education looks like a huge waste of time and money. You planned with great precision for a summer wedding with hundreds of family members and friends. But your outdoor wedding was rained out. Only thirty-six people showed up. You worked and saved for the vacation of a lifetime. The travel company called and canceled, but now you can't get your money back. You sweat bullets to get your business up and running. Now it's hanging on by a thin thread. You punched the clock for forty years. In retirement, all you want is to spend time with your grandchildren, but your son got a job transfer, and they moved a thousand miles away.

We can all relate with dropped dogs. The past is past, and the future is uncertain. "God, where are You?" "God, why is this happening?" "God, please take away all this pain!" These are cries of people in transition. Yesterday is history, and a new day hasn't yet dawned.

What's God's response? He's with us—for Israel in the tabernacle and for us in Christ Jesus. Let's see what that means.

THE CAMP'S ARRANGEMENT

While most of Numbers 1 provides a census of Israel's fighting men, it also stipulates for Levites to form a protective inner ring around the tabernacle to guard it from unauthorized entry (Numbers 1:52–53). Moses further mandates in Numbers 2 that Israel's tribes camp around the tabernacle—joining the Levites—to guard God's presence from outside forces. Moses then explains the camp's arrangement. It's simple—a square with God in the middle and Israel's tribes, beginning with the Levites, camped around it.

Why are there so many cautionary measures connected to the tabernacle? The prophet tells us. "Great in your midst is the Holy One of Israel" (Isaiah 12:6 ESV). The great, holy, transcendent, righteous, perfect, eternal, awesome Yahweh has descended to live with His people. This is a two-edged sword. God's presence can bring great healing. God's presence in the tabernacle can bring great harm.

Divine holiness is a life and death matter! People who unlawfully enter God's holy space will be killed (Numbers 1:51). They will be dealt with as though they were Egyptians—God will unleash a plague upon them (Numbers 8:19; 16:46).

THE IMAGE OF GOD

The Most Holy Place was the most important part of the tabernacle. Was there an image of God there? While the Lord commanded the Israelites to place the ark of the covenant in His inner sanctuary, He expressly prohibited them from making any image of Him. If a non-Israelite ever looked into the tabernacle's holiest place, he would have been shocked. There was no statue of God, no sculpture, no painting, no molten image. All the gods and goddesses in the ancient Near East, Israel's cultural milieu, were depicted in carvings, poles, and images. Not

ARRANGEMENT OF THE CAMP

Numbers 2; 3

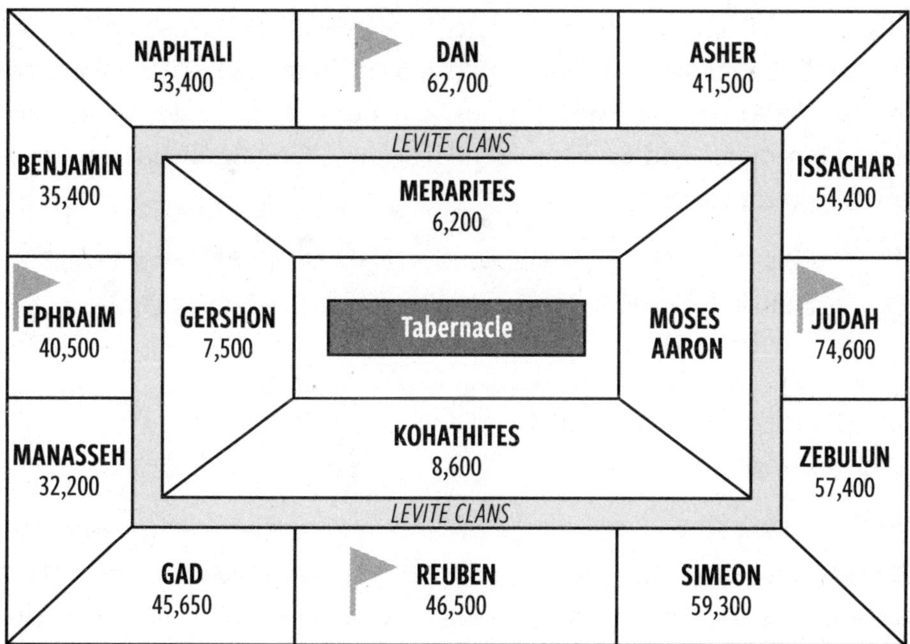

the God of Abraham, Isaac, and Jacob. Depictions of angels, animals, and flowers were in the tabernacle, but there wasn't an image of God—not yet.

In July of 1994, scientists watched as Jupiter, a gas giant, was struck by a comet. They marveled when a huge plume of vapor rose into Jupiter's atmosphere. Scientists soon theorized about the planetwide effects of the massive collision.

It took a while, but eventually, someone asked the obvious question. "What if that had been us?" If the heavens ever converged with earth, that would change everything—no doubt! Brace yourself, because the collision already happened!

God descended upon earth. Ground zero of this eternity-changing event was where? An animal feeding trough in the little town of Bethlehem. That's what John 1:14 says. Most English versions of the

Bible render the first part of this verse as follows: "The Word became flesh and *dwelt* among us." The word "dwelt," however, misses the close connection between God's presence in Israel's tabernacle and God's presence in Jesus. It's better to render John's Greek as "tabernacled." Here's my amplified translation of the first line in John 1:14: "The Word, the Second Person of the Trinity, Jesus, our Lord, became flesh and tabernacled among us and we have seen His *glory*." God finally has an image of Himself on earth!

> The god of this world has blinded the minds of the unbelievers, to keep them from seeing the light of the gospel of the glory of Christ, who is the *image* of God. (2 Corinthians 4:4 ESV)

> He [Christ] is the *image* of the invisible God, the firstborn of all creation. (Colossians 1:15 ESV)

How does Christ, the image of God, reflect divine glory? After all, the Israelites saw God's glory too. Moses describes the dedication of the tabernacle with these words: "The cloud covered the tent of meeting, and the *glory* of the LORD filled the tabernacle" (Exodus 40:34 ESV). God's glory comes through a cloud—an awe-inspiring cloud of power and beauty that radiated majesty and might.

We might suppose that Christ's glory was similar. Several thoughts could come to mind. Jesus walking on water. Jesus feeding five thousand. Jesus raising Lazarus, healing the sick, cleansing lepers, and making broken people whole. Christ's glory must mean that He walked an inch above the ground, right? Christ's glory must denote that He was always emitting a glowing, heavenly light. Right? Wrong. Dead wrong.

Christ's supreme and ultimate glory was His unjust suffering and agonizing death. This is what Jesus says on His way to the cross:

> The hour has come for the Son of Man to be *glorified*. (John 12:23 ESV)

> Now is the Son of Man *glorified*. (John 13:31 ESV)

> Father, the hour has come; *glorify* Your Son. (John 17:1 ESV)

We see Christ's supreme glory in Gethsemane, at Gabbatha, and on Golgotha. Roman executors used whips of leather strips with lead balls on each end to beat Him. They shoved a crown of thorns on His head, caking His hair with blood. Their clenched fists struck His face and their nails pierced His hands and feet. Christ's greatest glory is to love us, forgive us, and come to us right where we are—when we feel lost and forlorn, like a dropped dog.

Jesus comes to heal the divorced and the desperate; to comfort the bitterly broken; to cleanse the soiled and the shamed. The stock market doesn't rattle Him. Politics don't frighten Him. Diseases don't surprise Him. And death will never defeat Him. *Death will never defeat Jesus*. This is the holy God who tabernacles with us. At the cross, we see His glory. In His Word, we behold His grace and truth.

YAHWEH SHAMMAH

Ezekiel furthers the idea that our holy God comes to dwell among His people. In the last verse in his book, the prophet writes, "The name of the city from that time on shall be, 'The LORD Is There'" (48:35). The Hebrew is *Yahweh Shammah*. The new city's name isn't "The LORD *Was* There." "The LORD *Used* to Be There." "The LORD *Might* Be There." No. "The LORD *Is* There." *Yahweh Shammah*. God is present with His people. God is graciously present with us.

When we're lonely, God invites us to believe *Yahweh Shammah*. In their 1966 song titled "Eleanor Rigby," the Beatles asked this: Where do all the lonely people come from? They certainly come from America. Today almost 30 percent of American households consist of one adult living alone. Living alone can be depressing. Some days its absolutely crushing. And the medical world reminds us that it's dangerous for both our mental and physical health.

Abraham was all alone on Mount Moriah, about to sacrifice Isaac on an altar. Then God showed up (Genesis 22:11). Jacob was all alone at the Jabbok River, wrestling all night before meeting his estranged brother, Esau, the next day. Then God showed up (Genesis 32:30). Gideon was all alone against the mighty, menacing Midianites. Then God showed up (Judges 6:12).

When we're stressed, "The Lord Is There." What are you stressed out about? Artificial intelligence? Climate change? Political dysfunction? Money? Sometimes we get sick with worry—literally. High anxiety creates back pain, neck pain, and stomach pain.

Worry often works like this. I must pass a test tomorrow. If I don't pass this test, I'll go on academic probation. If I go on academic probation, I'll get thrown out of school. If I get thrown out of school, I'll never find a job. If I never find a job, I'll never be able to buy a house. If I never buy a house, I'll never get married. If I never get married, my life will be one, huge, empty nothing. Don't you see? If I don't pass the test tomorrow, it will be the end of the world!

Do you remember a series of movies called *Back to the Future*? Marty McFly and Emmett "Doc" Brown had a DeLorean that took them into the past and into the future. How exciting! Hollywood at its finest!

I've got bad news. Those movies? They aren't real. We can't live in the past or in the future. We still try, though, don't we? We're convinced worry will change the past. We're convinced worry will change the future. No. Sorry. Worry only destroys today. The solution? "Cast all your anxieties on Him, because He cares for you" (1 Peter 5:7). Countless times—too many to remember—I've fallen asleep at night with this verse on my lips and in my heart.

What about our broken hearts? *Yahweh Shammah*, "The Lord Is There"! Jesus isn't an impersonal force. He's not some far-off, distant power. He's close to the brokenhearted and binds up those crushed in spirit (cf. Psalm 34:18).

I'm often with people whose names are in the Bible—Hannah, Aaron, James, Sarah, and the like. I tell them, "My name is in the Bible too!" They shake their heads and say in unison, "No way, José!" Then I cite Isaiah 42:3: "A bruised reed He will not break" (ESV). The response?

Many moans and great groans!

Seriously, though, I love that verse because I've been bruised a lot. My guess is that you have too. Jesus won't break you. Jesus won't crush you. When we cry out, "God, where are You?" Jesus says, "I'm on the cross—bleeding, suffering, and dying for you." Jesus says, "I feel your loneliness. I feel your worries. I feel your brokenness. But the day is coming when I will wipe away every tear from your eyes. There will be no more death, no more crying, and no more pain. For the old order of things will pass away."

How can we be so sure? Jesus promised, "Because I live, you will live also" (John 14:19). The empty tomb shouts from the rooftops that the day is coming when we'll live in Ezekiel's new city. Then we will forever delight in the splendor and beauty of the eternal God.

What a name! "The LORD Is There." We can believe this now, in our hardest places. We can believe this in our most confusing places. We can believe this in places when it doesn't look like God will ever show up. God is there—in our most painful place, with all of His mercy and might in Jesus, our Lord. *Yahweh Shammah*!

THE MARCHING ORDER

<table>
<tr><td>Dan</td><td>Ephraim</td><td rowspan="3">Kohathites carrying tabernacle furniture</td><td>Reuben</td><td rowspan="3">Gershonites and Meraites carrying the tabernacle</td><td>Judah</td></tr>
<tr><td>Asher</td><td>Manasseh</td><td>Simeon</td><td>Issachar</td></tr>
<tr><td>Naphtali</td><td>Benjamin</td><td>Gad</td><td>Zebulun</td></tr>
</table>

We've all probably been to parades and football games and marveled at a marching band that executes with military precision. What would you think of a high school marching ensemble that had over 800 members? You'd probably think you're in Texas, and you'd be right! They do everything big in the Lone Star State—especially the Allen Eagle Escadrille marching band at Allen High School, with its 800 musicians on the march. Multiply 800 by 3,750, and you'd have the size of Israel's outfit—over 3 million marchers!

In Numbers 2, Moses uses words like "regiments," "companies," and "ensigns"—they point to the military nature of Israel's marching columns. Armies rise or fall based upon their organizational strategies and discipline. There's good reason, therefore, that the tribe of Dan is on the left and last in Israel's marching order. God wants to protect His army from surprise attacks from the rear, so He has His best soldiers, the Danites, positioned there. In fact, the nation's vanguard and rearguard tribes have the biggest armies (Numbers 2:16, 31). Unlike Israel's other tribes, Levities walk in the same formation as they camp. Whether marching or stationary, they are to guard and protect God's presence among His people (Numbers 2:17).

What place is Judah in Israel's marching order? In front (Numbers 2:3) because they're the biggest among the twelve tribes. Additionally, Genesis 49:8–12 compares the tribe of Judah to a cub, a lion, and a lioness. Judah's warriors are ready to rumble in the jungle with great power and might! When Jacob blesses Judah, he also includes this promise of victory: "Your hand shall be on the neck of your enemies" (Genesis 49:8). This aligns with God's promise that Eve's Seed would crush the head of the serpent; that is, the Messiah will subdue and conquer the devil himself (Genesis 3:15; cf. 1 John 3:8). Jacob further promises, "The scepter shall not depart from Judah, nor the ruler's staff from between his feet, until tribute comes to him; and to him shall be the obedience of the peoples" (Genesis 49:10).

A dazzling picture of a warrior King emerges from the book of Genesis. He will rule and reign over the entire world by defeating and destroying the serpent. All the tribes of Israel will bow before Judah's greatest descendant, and all the nations will worship Him as King and Lord.

In the fullness of time, Christ came into the world to fulfill these prophecies. Jesus is the King of kings (1 Timothy 6:15; Revelation 19:16) as well as the Lion of the tribe of Judah (Revelation 5:5). Like Judah of old, our Savior takes the lead. As the Pioneer of our faith, Christ paves the way, makes a way, and is the Way. "From victory unto victory His army shall He lead till every foe is vanquished, and Christ is Lord indeed" (*LSB* 660:1).

A LIFE-AND-DEATH JOB

I suspect that most of us don't have a life-and-death job. Me? I'm a university professor and a part-time pastor. While students sometimes give me the impression that they're dying from boredom, I doubt that my droning on is catastrophic. None of my classrooms have signs that say, "Danger: Safety Helmets Required to Enter."

Let's say you're a history teacher and you forget when Abraham Lincoln was assassinated by John Wilkes Booth. (By the way, it was shortly after 10:00 p.m. on April 14, 1865.) No one is going to die. Someone points out your error, and you respond, "No harm, no foul."

On the other hand, if you're a nurse or medical doctor or a parachute packer, you mess up, and that could be that! Air Force pilots have a saying: "There are old pilots and there are bold pilots, but there are no old, bold pilots." If you cut corners and make too many dicey moves, you probably won't enjoy Florida sunshine in your seventies.

Which category are Israelite priests and Levites in? They're in the do-or-die category. In fact, two died—Nadab and Abihu (Leviticus 10:2). Their first day on the job was their last day on the job. Note well. By reiterating the short-lived careers of Nadab and Abihu, Numbers 3:4 bolsters the warnings in Numbers 1:51, 53. Both warn people that if they get too close, God's wrath may kill them.

The Israelites couldn't just barge into an earthly king's throne room (cf. 1 Kings 1:15–23; Esther 4:11). This etiquette applies to the heavenly King's presence all the more. Properly serving Him was a life-or-death matter. And if a Levite failed to guard the tabernacle? It was a capital offense (Numbers 1:51; 3:10, 38; 18:22). The Lord's holy place must never be defiled. Little wonder, then, that Moses summarizes the

Levites' job description with this warning: "That they [fellow Israelites] may live and not die when they come near to the most holy things" (Numbers 4:19).

God's people were welcome to stand "before the Lord" (e.g., Leviticus 1:3; 3:1, 7), but they couldn't get too close. Levites were there to make sure boundaries were respected and maintained. That's because divine presence delivers both forgiveness that brings life as well as blazing holiness that condemns and kills. Thus, Numbers 3–4 highlights the Levites and their role in worship as well as in handling the holy things of God.

LEARNING TO LOVE THE LEVITES

Health-care professionals that oversee surgical rooms don't let any Tom, Dick, or Harriot simply waltz in whenever they feel like it. Contagions and pathogens might sicken or even kill people. In an analogous way, Levites were to serve at the tabernacle and guard it to prohibit impurity from defiling God's throne room—where the King of heaven resided on earth.

We need a bit of background information.

After constructing the tabernacle in Exodus 35–40, Moses describes God's descent: "Then the cloud covered the tent of meeting, and the glory of the Lord filled the tabernacle" (Exodus 40:34 ESV). God dwells with His people. Hurray! But no one can enter His presence. You don't say! "Moses was not able to enter the tent of meeting because the cloud settled upon it, and the glory of the Lord filled the tabernacle" (Exodus 40:35 ESV). The book of Exodus ends with a dilemma. God now resides on earth, but people can't get near Him—not even Moses. What can be done? The solution comes with God's choice of the Levites.

Levi was the third son of Jacob and Leah (Genesis 29:34). He had three sons: Gershon, Kohath, and Merari (Genesis 46:11). Aaron and Moses descended from Kohath (Exodus 6:16–20). Prior to the books of Leviticus and Numbers, Moses only refers to the Levites several times. Their devotion to God is noted in Exodus 32:26–28, and they are briefly mentioned in Exodus 38:21.

The book of Numbers greatly expands upon God's plans for the Levites. They're to serve as a bridge between His holy presence and His sinful people. Therefore, God distinguishes between Israelite laity and Levites, Levites and priests, and priests and the high priest. Try putting this book down and repeating the prior sentence from memory. As soon as you can do that, you're on your way to learning to love the Levites. Now try this: *All priests are Levites, but not all Levites are priests*. This, too, will be helpful to keep in mind.

Levites were excluded from military service because they were only to concern themselves with the tabernacle (Numbers 1:47–53; cf. Numbers 2:33). Since God didn't plan for Levites to go to war, their census is different from the other tribes. There are two for the Levites (Numbers 3:14–39; 4:1–49). The first census is for all Levites, one month and up. The second is for those between ages 30 and 50 who will work in and with the tabernacle.

Moses divides the Levites into two groups: priestly (Aaron's descendants) and nonpriestly (those not in Aaron's family). While all the Levites are to work in the tabernacle's sacred spaces (Numbers 1:47–53), only Aaron's sons—a subset of the tribe—were to function as priests (Numbers 3:5–10; 4:16). God authorizes priests to enter the tabernacle, handle sacrifices, serve at the altar, and teach God's Word. Levitical priests also lead the tribe of Levi (Numbers 3:32; 4:28, 33).

On the other hand, non-Aaronic Levites guarded the outside of the tabernacle and were responsible for erecting, dismantling, and carrying it. No one else could perform these tasks. Though these Levites could serve in the sanctuary, they weren't allowed to offer sacrifices or preside over sacred rites (e.g., Numbers 3:38; 8:26; 18:1–32). An example might help.

As a Levite, Korah rejected God's distinctions, arguing that "the entire congregation, all of them, are holy" (Numbers 16:3). Korah and his followers, especially Dathan and Abiram, maintained that priests had no divine right to their special status. Though Korah and his kindred carried the most holy things (Numbers 4:1–20), they wanted more. God, however, had given priests to Israel (Exodus 28–29) who were ordained by divine mandate (Leviticus 8–9). To usurp this order was to reject the way God had chosen to deliver forgiveness and blessing to His people.

God deemed Aaron and his sons ritually holy through their ordination (Leviticus 8–9). A different rite conferred an elevated state of purity upon the nonpriestly Levites (Numbers 8:5–22) whom God set apart to serve in the tabernacle environs as well as handle its furnishings for transport (Numbers 3:21–37; 4:1–33). The Levites' dedication is similar to that of the Levitical priests' ordination, though the latter group is anointed with blood and oil as well as dressed in holy garments.

Who is the most important Levite? Aaron, Israel's first high priest. Numbers 3:1 begins with the expression "These are the generations." While the phrase only comes here in Numbers, it appears eleven times in the book of Genesis—extending from Genesis 2:4 through Genesis 37:2. What are we to make of Moses' usage of "These are the generations" in Numbers 3:1? He's following God's orders—elevating his older brother, Aaron, to the same level of the patriarchs, Abraham, Isaac, and Jacob. "This is the account of the family of Aaron and Moses" (Numbers 3:1). However, the next three verses only list Aaron's sons. These are VIPs—Very Important Priests!

Here's a summary: God provided two ways to protect His holiness while distributing divine gifts. First, He set aside the tribe of Levi to camp around the tabernacle—thus guarding its ritual purity. He also tasked these Levites with packing, transporting, and setting up the tabernacle and its accoutrements. Second, God elevated one family within Levi's tribe—Aaron's family—to serve as priests who offered sacrifices at the altar and presented gifts to the Lord. Only Aaron and his sons were high priests.

SUBSTITUTION

About 23 percent of Americans are free from personal debt. What about our national debt? As I write this sentence today, it stands at forty trillion dollars and is increasing by one trillion every one hundred days. We pay four hundred billion dollars a year to service this debt. Here's an idea, though. What if every American man, woman, girl, and boy chipped in one hundred thousand dollars? We could bring America's debt down to zero. Good luck running on that political platform!

I invite you to go to West 44th Street in Lower Manhattan, New York, and spend a few minutes looking at the US National Debt Clock. The sign is 25 feet wide, weighs 1,500 pounds, and uses 306 light bulbs. It announces constantly, mercilessly, and endlessly the US debt and each family's share.

Did you know God has a debt clock? It keeps track of everyone's insults, ugly words, raised fists, cold shoulders, and failed promises. How much do we owe? The debt is astronomical. How are we going to pay? Only God knows.

Sometimes we confuse the Gospel with God saying, "Your sin isn't that big of a deal. I'll wave My hand, and that will be that!" But God doesn't work that way. He's holy and just, so He must punish sin. But God is also loving and merciful, so He provides a substitute. God explains it. "Behold, I have taken the Levites from among the people of Israel instead of every firstborn who opens the womb among the people of Israel. The Levites shall be Mine, for all the firstborn are Mine. On the day that I struck down all the firstborn in the land of Egypt, I consecrated for My own all the firstborn in Israel, both of man and of beast" (Numbers 3:12–13 ESV).

When God struck down Egypt's firstborn sons and animals in the tenth plague (Exodus 12:29–38), He also demanded that the Israelites give their firstborn sons and animals to Him (Exodus 13:11–16). Now in Numbers 3, He substitutes the Levites for Israel's firstborn.

Israel's other tribes counted men twenty years and older. However, Levites counted males one month and older—these were the substitutes. In the first counting, there were 22,273 (Numbers 3:43). "Take the Levites instead of all the firstborn among the people of Israel, and the cattle of the Levites instead of their cattle" (Numbers 3:45 ESV).

Every time parents of a firstborn son saw a Levite, they probably thought something like this: "If it wasn't for the Levites, we wouldn't have our son living with us. He would have been given over to tabernacle service. That's because when God rescued us from Egypt, He saved us on a night when all of Egypt's firstborn died. Israel's firstborn didn't. While God then demanded our firstborns, in His mercy, He provided substitutes—for our first son and our firstborn animals."

Israelites repeatedly learned about God's gift of a substitute—and not only through Levites and their animals substituting for Israel's firstborn sons and beasts. God further drove this point home through sacrificial ceremonies where people placed their sins on an animal by the laying on of hands. Then the animal was slaughtered—not because it had sinned but because people had. The animal died as a substitute.

God drilled substitution into His people because one day one man would stand as a substitute for the sin of everyone of all times and places. Ironically, God uses a high priest, Caiaphas, to state the idea: "It is better for you that one man should die for the people, not that the whole nation should perish" (John 11:50). Would you like a theological title for this? Substitutionary Atonement.

Our spiritual debt is big enough to bankrupt us forever. But Jesus forgives it. Jesus wipes the slate clean. Jesus did it by going to the cross—the horror and the nightmare of the cross. At Calvary, Jesus exhausted God's righteous and holy anger, taking it all for us.

Alive on the third day, Jesus doesn't say, "I paid for some of your debt." "I paid for most of your debt." "I paid for the vast majority of your debt." No. Jesus says, "I paid for *all* your debt; past, present, and future." Jesus paid using crimson currency. Here's my prayer: "Jesus, make this legal right my deep, personal delight."

WHAT A FRIEND WE HAVE IN JESUS

The Great Depression in the 1930s almost destroyed Mary Cushman. Her husband's weekly paycheck was just sixteen dollars. Among other ways to save money, Mary dressed her five children with hand-me-downs from the Salvation Army. One day, she lost hope. Mary took her youngest child into her bedroom, plugged up the windows with rags, and turned on the gas heater. She didn't light the heater; instead, she lay down in her bed with her five-year-old daughter and waited to die.

The kitchen radio was still on. Mary heard a song with the words "What a friend we have in Jesus." Then, suddenly, she realized she had faith in Jesus—mustard seed faith, but mustard seed faith is all it takes! Mary jumped up, turned off the gas, opened the door and raised the windows. "What a friend we have in Jesus, all our sins and griefs to bear" (*LSB* 770:1).

Jesus bears all our sins and all our griefs. He's our perfect Substitute. Why carry any burden ever again?

CHAPTER 4

BOUNDARIES: NUMBERS 4–5

Through Him we have also obtained access by faith into this grace in which we stand. (Romans 5:2 ESV)

What's your favorite biblical image of God? Is it the caring Shepherd (Psalm 23)? The living Redeemer (Job 19:25)? The loving Friend (John 15:15)? The humble Servant (Philippians 2:7)? Chances are, "The Holy One of Israel" doesn't make your top ten.

In church, we sing "holy, holy, holy"—in hymns and in the Holy Communion liturgy. What does it mean that God is holy? It's common to associate divine holiness with ideas like righteous, pious, perfect, and morally upright. But in the Bible, holy primarily denotes what is separate.

In Isaiah's call, the prophet sees angels cover their faces and their feet as they cry out to God, "Holy, holy, holy" (Isaiah 6:3). When Hebrew words are repeated three times, it's called a super-superlative. Holy, holy, holy, then, denotes that God is absolutely removed, completely separate, altogether different. Stating the same idea poetically, entire nations are like a drop in the bucket before Him, like dust on a scale (Isaiah 40:12). He sits above the earth, and from there, we look like grasshoppers (Isaiah 40:22). Yahweh is in a league of His own, yet He longs to live among His people. That's the tension throughout Numbers 4–5. The Holy One living among the unholy ones.

OUR HOLY GOD

Nuclear radiation accomplishes great things. Nuclear radiation has the capacity to destroy all things! What should we do in the case of a nuclear emergency? Get inside, stay inside, stay tuned, move away from windows, and put as many walls between you and the outside as possible.

God's holiness is like that. It has great power for good. It also has great power to do great harm. God's attributes include purity, life, health, wholeness, order, and peace. In contrast, we display the attributes of disease, decay, disorder, and death. The separation between God and people makes any incorrect contact between them volatile and dangerous. Unregulated contact with God's holiness results in death, regardless of motive. For example, God kills Uzzah when he steadies the ark (a holy object), in spite of his good intention (2 Samuel 6:6–11).

How would you feel if, on a rainy day, a friend came to your home, didn't take off her shoes, and tracked mud all over your brand-new white carpet? It would be the height of disrespect. Just so, entering God's holy presence without proper preparation shows contempt for Him. "The reason I don't respect your property is because I don't respect you."

THE HOLY GOD COMES TO EARTH

The book of Exodus begins with God seeing Israel's plight and coming down to Moses in the burning bush—a place God calls "holy ground" (Exodus 3:5). Subsequently, God descends on Mount Sinai (Exodus 19:9, 16; 24:15–16, 18). Then, at the end of the book, He comes down to fill the tabernacle with divine glory (Exodus 40:34–35). The book of Exodus, therefore, is the story of how our holy God enters our sinful world. The goal is for Him to take up residency on earth without destroying people.

The focal point of Exodus is the encounter at Mount Sinai. Moses accentuates the separation by describing God at the summit of the mountain and the Israelites camped below (Exodus 19:1–3). God's solution to this separation is to command Moses to build a tabernacle as well as set aside men to serve as priests. The tabernacle (or sanctuary) brings heaven to earth, and the consecration of priests with their liturgical service allows God to live among His people. Problem solved!

Two spaces lay at the heart of the tabernacle. The first room was the Holy Place. When priests entered it, they saw the golden seven-branched menorah. It looked like a tree. Priests would also see a beautiful tapestry made up of angels. Angels? Along with a tree? *The Most Holy Place is the new Garden of Eden.*

With this arrangement in place, the book of Numbers mandates that Israelites guard the tabernacle (Numbers 1:53) and keep their camp pure (Numbers 5). Only those with proper protection—that is, in a state of ritual holiness—could come near (Numbers 4:15; 18:3, 7). Why is that? Because when God condescends to dwell among His people, it's like putting a fire in the middle of a munitions factory. The Lord is the infinite, eternal, all-powerful, all-knowing, and holy God—yet, in His great mercy, He yearns to be present with His people. The comingling, though, must happen carefully. Divine regulations must be followed meticulously. When they are, God overcomes the separation and delivers Gospel gifts. He gives us access.

ACCESS

I began playing baseball in fourth grade. My dad was the coach. I continued fielding ground balls, catching high fly balls, and striking out (a lot!) through high school and college. You can imagine that there are a number of Major League stadiums that I love access to: Wrigley Field, the Friendly Confines, home of the Chicago Cubs since 1914; Busch Stadium, home of the eleven-time World Series champion St. Louis Cardinals; Fenway Park, home of the Boston Red Sox, my favorite team as a child. When I gain access to these places—after putting down a pretty penny—my heart overflows!

What about access to our thrice holy God? Doesn't sin keep us out? Aren't there massive barriers between the Holy One and unholy people? Didn't the angels shut the door and lock the gates? Aren't we rejected, lost, forever hopeless? No. Through the blood of Jesus, we have access.

In the Old Testament, only one person had access into the Most Holy Place. That was the high priest—but only once a year on the Day of Atonement (Leviticus 16). Now, in the New Testament era, the wonder of it all is that Christ has become our great High Priest. By His death, resurrection, and ascension to the Father's right hand, Jesus gives access to Fort Knox Gospel wealth—free of charge. How could God be so gracious?

Rome's strategy was singular. Beat Jesus within an inch of death and stop. Soldiers then march Christ to Calvary. His back is lacerated by lashes, and He stumbles carrying the crossbeam on His back. When Jesus came to Calvary, they nailed Him to wood. There He hung—crushed by the sin of the world. For Him? It was total rejection. For us? It means ultimate access.

Hebrews 10:19 states, "Therefore, brothers, we have *confidence* to enter the Most Holy Place by the blood of Jesus." We're not cowards in a crowd. We're not scared or discouraged. We have confidence. Confidence to live. Confidence to speak. Confidence when we suffer. Confidence when we pray. Confidence when we die.

Why stay stuck, thinking that you don't have access to the Holy One of Israel? Because you do. Unlimited access, by the blood of Jesus. It's God's good and perfect gift, for you!

SELECTED FOR SERVICE

You probably know how an organizational chart works. Leaders are on top; the lowly are on the bottom; middle managers are, well, in the middle. In Israel, the priests are at the top of the nation's org chart (Numbers 3:6, 9, 32; 4:16, 28, 33). God authorizes them to perform duties connected to the tabernacle functions. Next in line are the nonpriestly Levites whom God tasks with packing up and moving the tabernacle (Numbers 3:7–8; 4:1–33). At the bottom of the chart are Israel's tribes. They could only participate in the tabernacle's worship (Leviticus 1–5; 23).

And yet!

God didn't designate Levites to be His go-betweens because they were better, more faithful, or more worthy of this great honor. Someone needs to deliver divine absolution and oversee the tabernacle's liturgical service. This means that Levites aren't the end. They're a means to an end—to connect people to the Lord. He set apart priests and Levites for one reason: to serve the rest of the Israelites (Numbers 3:7, 38). God doesn't concentrate power in a few so the rest are forced to blindly follow. No. *Selection is for service.*

That's what Peter says about pastors: "Not domineering over those in your charge, but being examples to the flock" (1 Peter 5:3 ESV). Peter would know. Jesus, the King of kings and Lord of lords, once stooped down to wash his feet.

The most common mode of travel in first-century Judea was walking. Many of the roads were dirt. Since most everyone wore sandals, after several hours of walking, a person's feet got dirty. Thus, the practice of foot-washing was an ordinary, everyday occurrence. When you visited someone's home, the host would send his servant to bring a basin of water and wash your feet. This was as common as a host taking our coat when we arrive at her home. If a servant or slave wasn't available to wash feet, the duty would fall to the lowest ranking one in the crowd. This person, in Peter's case, was Jesus (John 13:4–17).

Get it? The way up is down—down to wash feet, with a towel in one hand and a water basin in the other. There's no place for pride when God calls us to serve. Peter knows this. So does Paul.

> For I am the least of the apostles, unworthy to be called an apostle. (1 Corinthians 15:9 ESV)
>
> I am the very least of all the saints. (Ephesians 3:8 ESV)
>
> Christ Jesus came into the world to save sinners, of whom I am the foremost. (1 Timothy 1:15 ESV)

After washing His disciples' feet, Jesus puts it this way: "If you know these things, blessed are you if you do them" (John 13:17 ESV). God calls leaders to lead through serving.

TWO MEN AND A TRUCK

I used to see a vehicle with the words "Two Men and a Truck" on the side and think, "How quaint. Two men own that truck, and they're in the moving business. What an endearing mom-and-pop company." Boy, did I get that wrong!

The company is headquartered in Lansing, Michigan, and has 350 franchises throughout the United States, Canada, and Ireland. Yes, at one time, it was a mom-and-pop company—or more accurately, a brother-and-brother team, Brig and Jon Sorber. In 1985, their mother, Mary Sheets, bought their 1966 Ford pickup truck for four hundred dollars and took over the business. What happened after that? Let's just say that today, Mary is a very rich lady!

In Numbers 4, we read about the fourth census in the book. The first three are as follows: (1) for the Israelite army, men, twenty years old and above (Numbers 1:2–46); (2) for service in the tabernacle, Levites a month old and above (Numbers 3:14–39); and (3) for redeeming Israel, Israel's firstborn males (Numbers 3:40–43). The focal point of the fourth census is on non-Aaronic Levites who will be responsible for moving the tabernacle (Numbers 4:1–49).

To move Israel's tabernacle, though, the nation needed more than two men and a truck! Levites used six wagons and twelve oxen (Numbers 7:3). Others weren't so lucky. They had to carry tabernacle parts on their shoulders (Numbers 7:9). Numbers 4:1–33 discusses how the three Levitical nonpriestly groups would move the tabernacle furnishings and its accoutrements.

The Gershonites (Numbers 4:21–26) were to camp behind the tabernacle on the west side. Their job was to carry the tabernacle's outer coverings, its pegs, hangings, screens, and ropes. Kohathites (Numbers 4:27–32) were to camp on the south side. They were to transport the most holy things such as the ark, along with its table, lampstand, altars, and vessels (Numbers 4:4). Though this was a privileged duty, probably because Aaron and Moses were descendants of Kohath (Exodus 6:16–20; 1 Chronicles 6:2–3), the Kohathites could only pack and unpack sacred objects. They couldn't look at them (Numbers 4:20) and certainly couldn't touch them—a duty reserved for priests (cf. 1 Samuel 6:19–20; 2 Samuel 6:6–7). Merarites (Numbers 4:33–37) were to camp on the tabernacle's north side. Moses commissioned them to carry frames, bars, pillars, bases, and so forth.

Since transporting the tabernacle and its equipment was both dangerous (due to the proximity of divine holiness) and heavy, men had to retire at fifty years old (Numbers 8:24–25).

GOD'S MOVING COMPANY

Who likes to move? Surely not I, Lord! First, you have to buy 3,586 boxes and stuff them with all of your earthly belongings. Then, if you go the discount route, you load it all into a rental truck. Next, you drive to your destination—fasting and praying that nothing gets broken, bent, or busted. Finally, you repeat the process in reverse. After you unpack, you'll spend three weeks looking for the can opener.

Once, while moving the cheap way, I lost a bookshelf when it fell off the back of a pickup truck. It rolled down a hill and had enough momentum to go over a cliff. During another move, I had to saw a bookshelf in half and throw it off the balcony because it wouldn't fit down the stairs. I guess you might say that I don't have the best luck with bookshelves!

We all have moving stories. Some make us laugh because they're so unbelievable. Some make us cry because they were so stressful. Here are a few ideas to keep in mind the next time you move:

After the move, get used to the phrase, "Honey, where's the ____?"

At some point in the process, you'll cry out, "Everything must go! Sell it! Donate it! Burn it all!"

> You'll find things you thought were lost forever. I once found some old baseball cards I thought I had sold when my oldest daughter, Abi, was born. Hello, Mickey Mantle!

When God's pillar of fire and cloud moved, Israel moved as well. Imagine tearing down the tabernacle, packing its pieces, loading them, and then carrying everything to a new place. The best estimate is that Levites did this twenty-nine times on their way from Sinai to Canaan. One word comes to mind—*logistics*. For instance, only priests could wrap the objects—beginning with those connected to the Most Holy Place (Numbers 4:5–6) then moving outward (Numbers 4:7–14). The result? Six large packages that Kohathites carried away (Numbers 4:15).

Fabrics used to wrap the objects were blue, scarlet, and purple—colors connected with royalty (2 Samuel 1:24; Esther 1:6; Ezekiel 23:6). And, just as a king was carried by his servants (Song of Solomon 3:7), so these holy items are carried for King Yahweh by hand and not by cart (Numbers 7:7–9).

The following statistics may give you an idea as to how much was moved; fabric measurements are in square feet, and metals are in pounds.

Tabernacle curtains: 2,520

Tent: 2,970

Tent covering: 2,970

Tent outer covering: 2,970

Tent entrance covering: unknown

Courtyard curtains: 3,375

TOTAL: 14,805 square feet (plus the tent entrance covering)

Gold: 2,193

Silver: 7,544

Bronze: 5,310

TOTAL: 15,047 pounds

Bear in mind that the Levites also had to haul their personal possessions. And if a Levite was married and had children? They had lots of stuff they just couldn't live without!

HOLY, CLEAN, AND UNCLEAN

The first four chapters in Numbers discuss Israel's military, Levites, and priests—their countings and their callings. In Numbers 5, Moses transitions to addresses the rest of the nation, their purity, and their holiness. He warns that Israel's camp could become contaminated through the following:

Bodily contagions (Numbers 5:1–4)

Wrongdoing (Numbers 5:5–10)

Sexual infidelity (Numbers 5:11–30)

In Numbers 5, we encounter the Old Testament's three ritual states: holy, clean, and unclean. They aren't just moral categories. They're also access categories. Impurity barred people from being part of certain ceremonies and places.

Here's an analogy to help you understand how it worked in Israel. I have the sniffles and walk into a hospital, wanting to hold a newborn grandchild. What do the nurses say? "Get lost!" Not because I'm a sinner, but because I have a common cold.

In several cases, Israelites could be barred from the camp or the tabernacle's court—not only because of a moral lapse but also because of the boundaries God established through Moses. Need an example? Consider Numbers 9:6: "There were certain men who were unclean through touching a dead body" (ESV). In this case, they were barred from celebrating the Passover.

Jesus turns the categories—holy, clean, and unclean—on their head. When Christ touched unclean people (such as lepers), He didn't become unclean. Instead, the unclean became pure. Remember the account about a woman who had been unclean for twelve years because of her menstrual bleeding (Mark 5:25–34)? She reaches out, touches Jesus, and, instead of rebuking her, He commends her faith. Jesus absorbs our uncleanness and in return heals us and makes us whole.

Biblical holiness is concrete. It's not a feeling, concept, or abstract idea. Instead, holiness is a day, a priest, a tent, a sacrifice. God's presence makes something or someone holy. It was inevitable, therefore, that, because God is fully present in Jesus, Christ is called "the Holy One of God" (Mark 1:24; John 6:69 ESV).

The Gospel's irony is that our most holy Savior became the most unholy sacrifice. It happened when He took our sin into His body. He then declared us righteous, forgiven, and forever loved (cf. 2 Corinthians 5:21; 1 Peter 2:24). Our reply? "Holy, holy, holy is the Lord of hosts; the whole earth is full of His glory!" (Isaiah 6:3 ESV).

GOD'S BOUNDARIES

I like to stroll through the Minneapolis Institute of Art. What would happen if, one Saturday afternoon, I nonchalantly walked up to some of the museum's most precious paintings and sculptures and began to touch them? I'd quickly be handcuffed and carted off to spend a few nights in the Hennepin County Jail! The beauty is there, but so are unyielding boundaries.

That's a good summary of Numbers up to this point. God's beauty and holiness are present for Israel, but God also mandates strict boundaries that include, with the tabernacle's Most Holy Place, the tabernacle proper, and Israel's camp. Everything and everyone outside the camp was considered unclean.

Moses not only commands boundaries for places. He also gives instructions regarding people. Israel's high priest was the holiest person in the community—in fact, "Holy to the LORD" appears on the front of his turban (Exodus 28:36–37 ESV). Next come Levitical priests, then the nonpriestly Levites, followed by Israel. Numbers 28–29, for its part, delineates sacred time—days, weeks, months, and years. Thus, spaces, people, and times provide order amid a chaotic world and boundaries instead of disorder and disarray.

Remarkably, none of these boundaries separated people according to their income, social status, ethnicity, or race. None of Moses' instructions teach that non-Levitical Israelites are second-class citizens. As a result—looking forward into Numbers 6—any Israelite could take a Nazirite vow and be set apart to God for a season.

A Nazirite's top priorities were to refrain from alcohol, cutting their hair, and contact with the dead (Numbers 6:1–21). Samson is the only Nazirite in the Old Testament mentioned by name (Judges 13:5, 7, 24; 16:17), although Samuel appears to have been one (1 Samuel 1:11, 22). The use of the proper noun "Nazirites" in Amos 2:11 is the only place in the Hebrew Scriptures where God describes their selection as a sign of His goodness to Israel.

Boundaries—whether for Levites or Nazirites—are part and parcel of biblical faith. In fact, the Bible begins with them. God separates light from darkness (Genesis 1:4), waters below from waters above (Genesis 1:6), day from night (Genesis 1:14), and men from women (Genesis 1:27). He goes on to distinguish between the Sabbath and the other six days of the week (Genesis 2:3) as well as what Adam and Eve can and can't do with the tree of the knowledge of good and evil (Genesis 2:17). We all know how that went! Our first parents lost the farm when they failed to recognize God's boundaries. Ever since then, people have ignored, neglected, or rejected divine barriers and borders established for our own welfare.

How does God respond? Does He hunker down, take His marbles, and go home? No. God created the world, owns the world, and loves the world. That's why He commissions His people to be a kingdom of priests and a holy nation (Exodus 19:6). God never wanted holiness to remain confined to the tabernacle nor that its transformative power be restricted to Levitical priests. Instead, God wanted all Israelites to receive holiness and to become holy themselves—then take His holy presence into the world.

HOLINESS FOR ALL

The biblical story develops historically and geographically. Historically it moves from one nation, Israel, to every nation. Geographically it moves from one place, the tabernacle, to every place—to the ends of the earth.

This is a grand vision of holiness, where God's presence spreads throughout the world. It's a vision where the priestly vocation of ordained Levitical priests in the tabernacle and the priestly vocation of Israel's laity in the world work in consort to fulfill God's vision of a transformed world where everything becomes holy (cf. Zechariah 14:20–22).

God works with Israel on a small scale to bring His holiness to the world—that's large-scale. The entire creation will one day reflect God's original plan (Isaiah 11:9; Habakkuk 2:14; Psalm 72:19). Contrary to what we might think, the Bible doesn't end with people going up to heaven. It ends with heaven coming down to earth—this earth, where God will dwell with His reconstructed and revivified creation in a new Most Holy Place (Revelation 21:15–21). John writes, "I saw no temple in the city, for its temple is the Lord God the Almighty and the Lamb" (Revelation 21:22). God's divine holiness will permeate His renewed creation. One small tabernacle tent will expand to include all things. Now that's thinking big!

And we deeply desire that everyone receive this gift.

TO THE ENDS OF THE EARTH

Yogi Berra once said, "If you don't know where you're going, you might end up somewhere else." That's called being lost. There are a lot of lost people in the world who don't know they're lost. How do I know?

Study after study shows that three out of every four Americans don't believe in biblical truth. And without biblical truth, there's no moral code. And without a moral code, there's no guilt. And without guilt, there's no need for a Savior because, by definition, a Savior is someone who saves you from guilt. The challenge is huge.

At least three methods are employed to communicate the Good News of Christ to the lost.

The first is "The Intellectual Inquisition." Proponents of this evangelism strategy insist the more talk the better. In fact, it gets really good when an already vague discussion shifts from Bahá'í to Buddhism to Baptists; from the pros and cons of prayer in public schools to the rapid growth of the Church of Jesus Christ of Latter-day Saints. But there's never a direct discussion of forgiveness of sins through Christ's death and resurrection.

Next is "The Mute Movement." It says the less talk the better. The believer who settles for this method could be tagged a "Clairol Christian"—only God knows for sure! Somewhere down the line this person began to swallow one of Satan's tastiest tidbits: "All God expects of you is a good, silent life. Others will ask you about Christ if they're interested." But even Jesus, who lived a sinless life, had to talk.

How about "The Essential Peter"? It says the more courage the better. Peter shows us his courage on Pentecost when he preaches in Jerusalem, where Jesus had been crucified just fifty-three days earlier. Peter had great courage.

Peter tells us, "But in your hearts set apart Christ as *Lord*" (1 Peter 3:15). Lord, or *Kyrios* in Greek, was what people called Nero, the Roman emperor. Peter is contesting that title. Nero isn't Lord. Jesus is Lord. Peter says honor the emperor (see 1 Peter 2:13–15), but don't call him *Kyrios* or Lord. Honor your job, your country, and your financial obligations, but don't make them Lord. Honor sports, hobbies, vacations, and your health, but don't make them Lord. Only Jesus bled and died for you. Only Jesus conquered death for you. Only Jesus will come back for you. He alone is Lord.

The essential Peter also includes a defense carefully prepared. The apostle writes, "Always being prepared to make a defense to anyone who asks you for a reason for the *hope* that is in you" (1 Peter 3:15 ESV). "Hope" is one of Peter's favorite words (cf. 1 Peter 1:3, 13, 21; 3:5).

It's a sin is to sing "Jesus loves me, this I know; *that's all I really want to know*." Peter wants us to grow in the knowledge of God's Word (cf. 1 Peter 2:3). Then we'll be able to defend our hope.

Peter ends his teaching about witnessing for Jesus with this warning: "Yet do it with gentleness and respect" (1 Peter 3:15 ESV). Peter has something to say about humility.

> Be compassionate and *humble*. (1 Peter 3:8)
>
> Clothe yourselves with *humility*. (1 Peter 5:5)
>
> *Humble* yourselves under God's mighty hand. (1 Peter 5:6)

After His resurrection, Jesus opens the disciples' minds so they understand the Old Testament and its mission. Then He says, "This is what is written" (Luke 24:46). Jesus doesn't go on to quote a specific Old Testament verse. Instead, He's saying something along these lines: "God's rescue plan begins in the Old Testament. It's fulfilled in My suffering and rising from the dead on the third day. And it continues through you to all the nations. This is Israel's story. Now it's yours. Go now and preach the Gospel to the ends of the earth."

PERSONAL BOUNDARIES

Some of my boundaries are well defined—they're black and white. For example, the government tells me when to pay taxes, when to renew my license plates, as well as how fast I can go on interstate highways. God has also placed boundaries in my life. Paul describes it this way: "He made from one man every nation of mankind to live on all the face of the earth, having determined allotted periods and the *boundaries* of their dwelling place" (Acts 17:26 ESV).

We encounter boundaries all the time. Fences, walls, doors, windows, laws, traffic signs, and speed limits. Most of us have personal boundaries that dictate what we eat, what we do in our spare time, and how far we're willing to bend in a relationship.

Failure to abide by biblical boundaries is costly. Let's think about that. If my boundaries aren't thought out and acted upon, I open myself up to emotional, financial, and perhaps even physical pain. Without a firm no, people or institutions may try to control me and dictate how I should live. There are few things more destructive than being taken advantage of because we lack clear boundaries.

What happened the last time you were at an intersection and the stoplights weren't working? The situation probably turned into every man for himself! Drivers became confused. They didn't know when to turn, when to stop, or when to move ahead. The same is true for the signals we send to other people. They need to be crystal clear.

Why are boundaries difficult to make and enforce? Because no one likes conflict. We don't want others to get mad, angry, upset, or—heaven forbid—reject us and abandon us. So, we smile, shrug our shoulders, and go along for the ride. After all, it's best to be nice. Don't make waves. Take one for the team. But then we're not being ourselves. Then we present a different person than who we really are, just so people won't frown upon us. But God created us to have boundaries. "This far, and no further."

The foundation for healthy, biblical boundaries is to know where I end and you begin, to connect with people but still be our true selves. That's the triune God. He consists of three distinct people—Father, Son, and Holy Spirit. Yet the people in the Godhead aren't fused together to the point that They abandon Their individual identities. The Trinity exhibits diversity in unity. Each person is a self without being self-centered.

Think of healthy boundaries as a fence around your home. There are some people you'll let on the property—even into your living room and kitchen. "Come on in and sit a spell!" Others? You might call 911! Don't allow manipulators, liars, passive-aggressive players, emotionally immature blamers, shamers, or gamers to take up permanent residence in your life.

Stand your ground. Don't go along just to be liked and loved. And don't deny your feelings, thoughts, or yourself. "I'm not going to lose me just to love you." Instead, claim your baptismal birthright. You're a Bible-believing child of the one true King. You're heaven bound, Spirit led, and grace filled. "Let what you say be simply 'Yes' or 'No'" (Matthew 5:37 ESV).

Boundaries. They're good for God. They're good for Israel. And they're good for us.

CHAPTER 5

THE LORD BLESS YOU: NUMBERS 6–7

> Blessed be the God and Father of our Lord Jesus Christ, who has blessed us in Christ with every spiritual blessing in the heavenly places. (Ephesians 1:3 ESV)

We all know what a Save button is. When we press down on it, we reshape our computer's hard drive. Words on the screen enter the core of our machine. As long as the words are just on our screen, however, they can be lost. But once we save our work, it's safe. I hit the Save button every three seconds. One can never be too sure!

How often do I hit the Save button when it comes to God's promises? I wish I could tell you every three seconds. Sometimes it's hours, days, weeks. Ugh! Yet, in His long-suffering mercy, God still offers forgiveness of sin, reconciled relationships, resurrection, and eternal life—all in the name of Jesus. I don't want to lose these gifts. "Oh God, empower me regularly to save these promises on the hard drive of my heart!"

Moses invites us into a gold mine brimming with promises—the Aaronic benediction. We're going to take a close look at his words at the end of Numbers 6. The goal? That this benediction goes deep into our hearts—never to be forgotten, lost, or casually set aside.

NUMBERS 6:24–26: THE BACKGROUND

Here's the background of the Aaronic benediction. Numbers 5 records rubrics to find out if a wife has been unfaithful to her husband, while much of Numbers 6 dictates laws for people who take Nazirite vows. These two chapters present people at the opposite ends of the spiritual spectrum—faithless (Numbers 5:5–31) and faithful (Numbers 6:1–12).

Which of these are Israelites most like? The faithless wife or the obedient vow-taker? If you don't readily have an answer, I suggest you keep reading the book of Numbers. What will you find? Grumbling. Fear. Envy. Strife. Hard hearts. Sinister accusations. And in Numbers 25? Unbridled and unhinged illicit sex. God, who knows that all of this will happen, still commands Aaron to bless His people. Amazing!

Here's more background information on Numbers 6:24–26.

At the beginning of the twentieth century, there weren't any ancient copies of the Hebrew Scriptures. The oldest dated back to about AD 1000. People therefore questioned the Old Testament's accuracy. But in 1946, the Dead Sea Scrolls were discovered, pushing back the date of the oldest existing Hebrew Scriptures by 1,200 years. When these scrolls are compared to the more recent copies of Genesis to Malachi, the newer ones were found to be remarkably accurate.

But in 1979, an even older fragment of a biblical text was discovered in a burial cave in Jerusalem's Hinnom Valley. Two tiny silver scrolls were found. It took several years for Israeli scientists to clean and unroll the parchments. What did they see? The oldest known fragment of the Old Testament, dating back four hundred years before the Dead Sea Scrolls—to about 600 BC. What was inscribed on them? The most famous words in the book of Numbers—the Aaronic benediction.

GOD LOVES TO BLESS

God loves to bless. God longs to bless. God lives to bless! God put Adam and Eve in a garden—not a rock pile, a desert, or a swamp. God's first words to people weren't words of shame and contempt; they were words of blessing (Genesis 1:28). After the worldwide flood, the Lord repeated these blessings to Noah (Genesis 9:1, 7). As a matter of fact, the word *bless* appears over four hundred times in the Old Testament.

God's blessing is the foundation of His covenant with Abram (Genesis 12:2–3), which He reaffirmed to his descendants (e.g., Genesis 26:2–4; 28:13–15). God promised to bless Jacob even before he was born (Genesis 25:23). It's not surprising that divine blessings are central to

Israel's life with God (Leviticus 26:3–13; Deuteronomy 28:1–14).

A closer look reveals that God's promises to Abram in Genesis 12:2–3 employ the term *bless* five times. Why five? Because there are five curses leading up to Genesis 12. God cursed the serpent (Genesis 3:14), the ground (Genesis 3:17), Cain (Genesis 4:11), the ground a second time (Genesis 5:29), and Canaan (Genesis 9:25). *God's blessings triumph over His curses.* God's final word is always blessing. Need another example? Throughout Numbers 22–24, God turns Balaam's curses, prompted by King Balak, into blessings for Israel and for the nations.

Israel will enjoy divine blessings once they're in the Promised Land. Right? When God's people reside in Canaan, that's when the milk and honey will flow; when enemies are defeated, that's when the land long promised to Abraham will finally be theirs. Yes. But God's blessing goes with Israel through the wilderness places of Sinai, Paran, and Zin; through the nation's massive setbacks, bitter disappointments, and the deaths of almost all who left Egypt as adults. Every step of the way—throughout Numbers—God blesses His people. There are no conditions. No fine print. No ifs, ands, or buts.

Divine blessings for Israel were also intended for the nations (Genesis 12:3; 22:18). The movement is to be from God, to Israel, then to the world. "May God be gracious to us and bless us and make His face to shine upon us, that Your way may be known on earth, Your saving power among all *nations*" (Psalm 67:1–2 ESV).

What do God's blessings entail? The list in Leviticus 26 is instructive. Verses 3–10 pledge protection from enemies and an abundance of food. Verses 11–13 pivot to include the spiritual gifts of God's presence and protection. Specific blessings in the book of Numbers include numerous descendants, provision for the journey, and the promise of Canaan. The most precious blessing, however, is God's abiding presence through the tabernacle.

Climactically, in Christ, God blesses us with every spiritual blessing in the heavenly places (Ephesians 1:3). He lavishes them upon us

(Ephesians 1:8). Consider Niagara Falls. Every minute, 200,000 tons of water plunge over these falls. God could've used less water, but He didn't. God could've made the cliffs lower, but He didn't. God's blessings aren't squeezed out from an eyedropper. They aren't carefully rationed like water during a drought. God's blessings are a Niagara of superabundance!

WE NEED GOD'S BLESSING

Paul's sorry story is ours as well. "But I see in my members another law waging war against the law of my mind and making me *captive* to the law of sin that dwells in my members" (Romans 7:23 ESV). "Captive" here denotes exile. That's how the Pentateuch begins—with God exiling Adam and Eve from the Garden of Eden. And this is how the Pentateuch ends—with God setting life and death before Israel, while also warning them of exile (Deuteronomy 30:15–20). Israel ended up repeating Adam and Eve's sin and rebellion.

I reprise Adam and Eve. So do you. We're stuck in a cycle of sin. We're captive to our low-road choices and high-minded pride. "Who will deliver me from this body of death?" (Romans 7:24 ESV). God's solution is to shower upon us His unmerited and unconditional blessings—fulfilled in Christ, our Lord.

A CLOSER LOOK

The Aaronic benediction in Numbers 6:24–25 comes out of the blue—literally. Aaron didn't ask for it. Moses didn't request it. Miriam didn't sing a song with the lyrics: "God, we've been really great and totally first-rate. How 'bout opening up heaven's pearly gate?" Instead, the blessing comes out of God's generous heart, without any merit or worthiness on Israel's part.

Here's my wooden translation of the Aaronic benediction. Note that the English words connected with hyphens signal one word in Hebrew.

> Bless-you the-Lord and-keep-you. (Three words in Hebrew)

> Shine the-LORD His-face to-you and-be-gracious-to-you. (Five words in Hebrew)
>
> Lift the-LORD His-face to-you and-place to-you peace. (Seven words in Hebrew)

The blessing expands and grows. It begins with three words in the first line, has five in the second, and ends with seven in the third line. A small trickle becomes a gushing river whose goal is shalom, peace. It's Numbers' version of Niagara Falls!

Do you see the threefold use of God's name? "The LORD . . . the LORD . . . the LORD." This represents the fullness of God's blessing. He blesses and blesses and blesses again. It takes us forward to the threefold angelic song in Isaiah 6:3: "Holy, holy, holy is the Lord God Almighty." The triple use of a word intensifies its meaning. "A threefold cord is not quickly broken" (Ecclesiastes 4:12 ESV).

Additionally, the "you" in the blessing is singular, not plural. It's "you," not "you all." Hebrew can make this distinction. English can't—at least not properly. "Ya'll" might fly in Texas, but not in an English grammar book. The Hebrew singular "you" denotes a focus that's individual and intimate, particular and personal. God's care is cosmic and universal—to be sure. "God so loved the world" (John 3:16 ESV). Yet, to emphasize the value God places on individuals, He employs singular "you" six times in the Aaronic benediction. It's you, you, you, you, you, and you! The blessing is specific, reserved, and exact. It's you! "I will bless *you*!"

THE LORD KEEP YOU

Like them or not, in a crisis, the IRS knows exactly what to do. The IRS Handbook states, and I quote, "During a state of national emergency, the essential functions of the IRS will be as follows; assessing, collecting and recording taxes." While everyone panics, the IRS knows exactly what to do. Get our money! The Lord likewise knows exactly what to do when He sees evil threatening us.

The evil that seeks to swallow us whole isn't abstract. This evil isn't *out there*. It's not a nebulous force. This evil is concrete. It's located in a fallen angel. Satan is his name. He's the evil one.

Psalm 121 is a resounding celebration of God's power to keep us safe from all evil designed by the evil one. In fact, the verb *keep* comes six times in the psalm's eight verses.

> He who *keeps* you will not slumber. (Psalm 121:3 ESV)
>
> He who *keeps* Israel will neither slumber nor sleep. (Psalm 121:4 ESV)
>
> The LORD is your *keeper*. (Psalm 121:5 ESV)
>
> The LORD will *keep* you from all evil; He will *keep* your life. (Psalm 121:7 ESV)
>
> The LORD will *keep* your going out and your coming in from this time forth and forevermore. (Psalm 121:8 ESV)

Peter summarizes God's keeping power when he writes that we're kept "through faith for a salvation ready to be revealed in the last time" (1 Peter 1:5 ESV). Once God gets hold of us through Holy Baptism, He guards and keeps us in Christ Jesus all our days. "I give them eternal life, and they will never perish, and no one will snatch them out of My hand" (John 10:28 ESV). God will never let you go—ever!

GOD'S SHINING FACE

Yes, it's great to drive off the lot in a new car. It's wonderful when our favorite team wins the championship. It's awesome to vacation in London, Paris, Rome, and Venice. But the best blessing—bar none—comes when God's face shines upon us.

Have you ever seen children open Christmas presents? Have you ever watched a groom and bride walk down the aisle on their wedding day? Have you ever witnessed a thrilling, come-from-behind victory—when your team scored just enough points with the clock ticking down to zero? In every case, people's faces shine with utter elation.

That's our God. Can you envision His kind and loving face beaming over you? Is this too good to be true? Not on your life! Because of Christ Jesus, your heavenly Father's face lights up every time He thinks of you—which is all the time! The Aaronic benediction is God's majestic smile, from ear to ear, and from His heart full of love. Psalm 80 includes this prayer to God—not once, but three times: "Let Your face *shine*, that we may be saved" (Psalm 80:3, 7, 19 ESV).

What do you think of when you read the word *shine*? Clarity might come to mind. So might warmth and gladness. And don't forget brightness and joy. The opposite of shining? Darkness. God's shining face dispels darkness. All darkness. Every form of darkness. And that includes the prince of darkness—the devil and Satan himself.

The Hebrew verb translated "shine" in Numbers 6:25 also comes in Numbers 8:2. What Aaron announced ("the LORD make His face *shine* on you" [ESV]) is tethered to the lampstand's light in the tabernacle ("the seven lamps shall *shine* in front of the lampstand"). The lampstand with its seven branches, located in the tabernacle's Holy Place, announced God's presence with His people—even in their darkness.

The tabernacle's lampstand also points us to where we see God's radiating presence in its most profound way. Paul states that God "has shone in our hearts to give the light of the knowledge of the glory of God in the *face* of Jesus Christ" (2 Corinthians 4:6). The face of Jesus beams over His beloved Bride, the church—that's us!

I encourage you to walk in the light of God's love, even in your most profound darkness—when it threatens to destroy you. Stake everything on these words: "The light shines in the darkness, and the darkness has not overcome it" (John 1:5 ESV).

THE LORD BE GRACIOUS TO YOU

The Hebrew word translated “grace” describes people in positions of power (like God) who show kindness to people who have no power (like us). We don’t earn God’s grace through obedience, and we don’t lose it through disobedience. Grace is what God abundantly gives to His dear children.

Suppose you’re driving along and you see your daughter—who’s eight years old—sitting on a downtown street corner. She has a sign that says, “Please Help Me.” What do you do? You slam on the brakes, pull up to the curb, and ask, “Honey, what in the world are you doing?” She looks up and says, “You’ve taken care of me for eight years. I figure that now I’m on my own.” “That’s crazy,” you insist. “I love taking care of you. It’s what I delight in doing!”

There are times when life takes a wicked turn and we feel like sitting on the street corner with a sign that says, “Please Help Me.” We say to no one in particular, “I figure that now I’m on my own.” What does God say? “My dear child! I love being gracious to you. It’s what I delight in doing!”

Grace is everything for nothing. Grace sees us at our lowest moment and gently picks us up. Grace saves us, sanctifies us, and sets us on the path to eternal life. It’s understandable that Peter, who received grace after he denied Christ three times, calls our triune God “the God of all grace” (1 Peter 5:10 ESV).

THE LORD LIFT UP HIS FACE UPON YOU

“That was a slap in the face.” “He’s good at showing a poker face.” “How can she be so two-faced!” “Wow, you just saved face!” And if you live in the land of hockey, like I do—the great state of Minnesota—you get used to face-offs.

The Aaronic benediction mentions God’s face—not once but twice. First, God’s face shines on us. Second, God lifts up His face toward us. David connects God’s face to the gift of goodness. “There are many who say, 'Who will show us some *good*? Lift up the light of Your *face* upon us, O Lord'" (Psalm 4:6 ESV).

What does the catch-all word *good* mean? A department store Santa asks little Susie, "Were you good this year?" and Susie says, "Oh, yes, Santa. I was very good. I only kicked my brother in the shins ninety-seven times." Or Carl comes back from being out, and his wife asks, "Where were you?" Carl says to his wife, "Don't worry, honey. I was good." Or the head of a sales team fails to close a deal, so he tells his boss, "I know *you* would have done much better." On the way out of the meeting, a coworker whispers, "Oh, you're good." Yet true goodness, lasting goodness, eternal goodness only comes from God. In fact, the word *good* derives from what word? *God.*

The Bible defines God's goodness in two ways. One has to do with His character; the other has to do with His actions. Psalm 119:68 captures both when it says, "You *are* good and You *do* what is good."

SHOWING GOODNESS

John Gilbert loved basketball, but he couldn't play the game. When he was five years old, John was diagnosed with Duchenne Muscular Dystrophy—a genetic, progressive, debilitating disease. Every year, John Gilbert lost something. In time, he even lost the ability to talk.

One day, John attended a fundraising auction. When it began, one particular item caught his eye—a basketball signed by the 2015 NBA champion Golden State Warriors. John desperately wanted that ball, so when it came up for a bid, he raised his hand. John's mother quickly pushed it down. They didn't have *that* kind of money.

The bidding on the basketball rose to over ten thousand dollars. Finally, a man made a bid that no one else could match. Taking the basketball in hand, he walked across the room and gently placed it into the thin, small hands of the boy who would never dribble, pass, or shoot a basketball.

John Gilbert, while he was still able, wrote these words: "Have you ever been given a gift that you could have never gotten for yourself? Has anyone ever sacrificed a huge amount for you without getting anything in return?"[3]

All of us can answer that question. "Yes. All of God's goodness flows to me from my Savior's five wounds, empty tomb, and blood-bought redemption." Jesus is good—very, very good. How do we know? His face forever shines upon us.

THE LORD GIVE YOU PEACE

Caesar Augustus (63 BC–AD 14) promoted Roman peace (*pax Romana*) through his court prophets and historians—but also through statutes, including his famous Altar of Peace (*Ara Pacis*). You can see it today in Rome with its detailed marble carvings of agricultural bounty and civic harmony. The subtext is clear. "You live in the best empire with the best government, so don't *ever* consider trying to undermine or rebel against us. If you do, we'll dispatch our ruthless legions. They'll not hesitate to unleash our fury through terror, rape, pillaging, killing, and countless crucifixions." The upshot? The only peace Rome offered was—at its core—completely forced.

Would you like another example of this kind of "peace"? The French Revolution (1789–99) was hailed as history's greatest moment. The upheaval promised freedom from an oppressive monarchy and its antiquated religion. What did the French Revolution end up giving its people? The guillotine.

Then there was Germany. The world's greatest intellectuals hailed from the land of the Rhine. You name it, and the Germans knew it. These intellects led to World War I, World War II, and the Holocaust.

If Roman, French, and German offers of peace look horrifying, consider what our age promotes. "I have my truth. You have your truth.

3 Previously published in John Ortberg, *Everybody's Normal Till You Get to Know Them* (Zondervan, 2003), 198. Used by permission of Gino Grunberg, Gig Harbor, Washington.

There is no absolute truth other than the truth that we must tear down everything from the past." Are there any plans after it's all gone? No. But we're told that it will be a time of peace.

The Hebrew word for "peace" is *shalom*. Shalom is completely different from the world's peace. Shalom denotes restoration, repair, resurrection, and renewal. Shalom includes an abundant life (Proverbs 3:2) as well as security and safety (Psalm 4:8). It's God's final word in the Aaronic benediction.

In the liturgy of Holy Communion (e.g., *LSB*, pp. 160–66), *peace* is the last word after the pastor consecrates the bread and wine, Christ's true body and blood. "The peace of the Lord be with you always." Peace is also the last word in the Agnus Dei: "Lamb of God, You take away the sin of the world; grant us peace." Often communicants are dismissed with the words, "Depart in peace." And, having sung Simeon's song after Communion for decades, I've asked God for His words to be my last words before I die: "Lord, now You let Your servant go in peace."

What a way to live. What a way to die. God's peace comes freely and abundantly through Jesus Christ. In Romans 8:32–34, unlike anywhere else in his thirteen letters, Paul summarizes why Jesus is our source of everlasting peace. He was given up, died, raised, ascended, and now is interceding for us. *Jesus is our Prince of Peace.*

GOD'S NAME ON US

We've all been shopping in a grocery store and overhead people's conversations. Normally they go something like this. "Oh no! Did she say three cans of tomatoes or four?" At other times, though, supermarket speech can be downright ugly. A small child reaches for a bag of candy, and she gets scolded by her mother. "You're such a *bother*!" In the bakery section, a husband berates his wife, "Quit being so *indecisive*." A customer in the checkout aisle rails against the clerk, "Why are you being so *slow*?" Has anyone ever called you "Bother," "Indecisive," or "Slow"? Have you ever called yourself any of these names?

Names can do great harm. Names can bring great healing.

In the Aaronic benediction, God puts His name upon us. "So shall they put My name upon the people of Israel, and I will bless them" (Numbers 6:27 ESV). What is God's name? The Old Testament records over eighty names for God, so let's take a look at all eighty. Just kidding! We are, however, going to focus upon one name. It's God's personal name in the Old Testament. That would be *Yahweh*.

The most thorough definition of Yahweh appears in Exodus 34:6. We might even call this verse Israel's Apostles' Creed. "Yahweh, Yahweh, the compassionate and gracious God, slow to anger, abounding in steadfast covenant love and faithfulness." Yahweh's name points to the most wonderful name on the planet: *Jesus*. His name means "Yahweh Saves." Does He ever! In Jesus' name, we're saved, redeemed, and loved forevermore.

That's not all.

Jesus blesses His disciples at the same time He ascends into heaven. "While He blessed them, he parted from them and was carried up into heaven" (Luke 24:51 ESV). Could it be that Christ used the Aaronic benediction? Luke also writes, "This Jesus, who was taken up from you into heaven, will come in the same way as you saw Him go into heaven" (Acts 1:11 ESV). Get the connection? Jesus will return in the same way He went into heaven—blessing His people. What is Jesus doing between His ascension and second coming? *Blessing His people with His all-powerful name.*

THE TRINITARIAN NATURE OF THE AARONIC BLESSING

In 1523, Martin Luther proposed a number of changes in worship, including the use of the Aaronic benediction at the end of the Divine Service. In the process, the reformer highlighted the trinitarian nature of Numbers 6:24 26—taking his cue from Paul's benediction: "The grace of the Lord Jesus Christ and the love of God and the fellowship of the Holy Spirit be with you all" (2 Corinthians 13:14 ESV).

The apostle's words not only invoke the fullness of God's blessings upon Corinthian believers but also provide one of the clearest biblical expressions of the doctrine of the Trinity in Holy Scripture. The Son is God. The Father is God. And the Holy Spirit is God.

What about the Aaronic benediction? Does it have a trinitarian framework? Its first line magnifies God's creation and its gifts—gifts spelled out in Genesis 1, where God provides everything we need for our body and life. With its reference to God's face, Numbers 6:25 points Christ's face that shone like the sun at His transfiguration (Matthew 17:2). The third line of the Aaronic benediction concerns peace. "To set the mind on the Spirit is life and peace" (Romans 8:6 ESV). Peace is one of the Spirit's fruit (Galatians 5:22).

By ending the Divine Service with the Aaronic benediction, congregations take part in the Gospels' stories, their trinitarian stories. Those in worship hear about the Father's gift of Jesus—whose birth, ministry, passion, death, and resurrection were guided and directed by the Holy Spirit. This is so central that three of the four Gospels include trinitarian endings.

> Go therefore and make disciples of all nations, baptizing them in the name of the Father and of the Son and of the Holy Spirit. (Matthew 28:19 ESV)
>
> I am sending the promise of My Father upon you. (Luke 24:49 ESV)
>
> "As the Father has sent Me, even so I am sending you." And when He had said this, He breathed on them and said to them, "Receive the Holy Spirit." (John 20:21–22 ESV)

BECAUSE OF JESUS

Doesn't God know how the rest of Numbers is going to unfold? Doesn't He realize what's right around the corner? Shouldn't He hold back a bit? See if Israel really deserves to be blessed? Why give it all away? And to such undeserving people!

Divine blessings flow because there would be a day when God would withhold His blessings. Not from Israel, but from His Son, our Savior, Jesus. The Father didn't keep Christ from mocking and spitting. He didn't dispense twelve legions of angels when the whip, thorns, and nails bloodied His body. And God's face? For the first time since eternity, the Father hid His face from His Son. "My God! My God! Why have You abandoned Me?" (Matthew 27:46).

We know why the Father abandoned His Son. "He was pierced for our transgressions; He was crushed for our iniquities; upon Him was the chastisement that brought us *peace*, and with His wounds we are healed" (Isaiah 53:5 ESV). Please reread that verse. What word also appears last in the Aaronic benediction? That's right. Peace, shalom, restoration.

We live in a moral universe. God is holy. We're not. We sin. We die. If we're going to be reconciled with God, someone has to pay for our sin. God knows we can't. God knows only Jesus can. Jesus never committed sin. Never. Not even once. When Christ was pierced and crushed, it was to forgive us, yes. But to bring us peace as well. That's what Paul says: "And through Him [Jesus] to reconcile to Himself all things, whether on earth or in heaven, making *peace* by the blood of His cross" (Colossians 1:20 ESV).

Numbers 6 is an exceedingly precious blessing for us. Numbers 6 is an exceedingly costly blessing for Jesus.

GENEROUS GIVERS

A young couples' Sunday School class was studying the story of Abraham and Sarah, who in their old age were blessed with a son named Isaac. The teacher asked, "What lesson do we learn from this story?" A young mother blurted out, "They waited till they could afford it!" However, if we wait until we can afford to give, we'll probably never give. Yet look at the example set by the Israelites. Out in the middle of nowhere, camped at Mount Sinai, Israelites could hardly afford to give—yet Numbers 7 says they did, exceedingly so.

A point of clarification is in order. Numbers 7:1–9:14 is chronologically in the wrong place. The events happened one month *before* Numbers 1–6. More exactly, Numbers 7:1 refers back to the tabernacle's construction during the *first* month of the second year (Exodus 40:17; Numbers 9:1). Numbers 1:1 begins the book with events on the "first day of the *second* month, in the second year after they had come out of the land of Egypt."

What happened after Exodus 40:33? After the Israelites finished building the tabernacle? Numbers 7:1–9:14 tells us. Then Numbers 9:15 states that the cloud covered the tabernacle, thus coinciding with Exodus 40:34–38. Why the flashback? To highlight Israel's lavish generosity. How else can you respond to the Aaronic benediction? *Gifted people give.*

With eighty-nine verses, Numbers 7 is the second longest chapter in the Bible. Psalm 119 is the longest with its 176 verses. Numbers 7:10–88 describes a lengthy twelve-day ceremony. Israel's twelve tribal leaders bring offerings to dedicate the altar. Their arrangement follows the sequence of tribes in Numbers 2.

I need to warn you. Numbers 7 has a lot of numbers and a lot of details. Why? The Lord loves facts and figures. He counts things. *We can be glad He* does. The very opening of the Bible begins with numbers. Day one, day two, day three, and so on throughout Genesis 1. The last chapters of the Bible number the city limits of the new Jerusalem, the gates of pearl, and the jewel-filled foundations of our heavenly home. Additionally, Jesus says the heavenly Father numbers the very hairs of our heads and the Good Shepherd knows the number of His sheep—the ninety-nine that are safe and the one who is lost. The Savior also knows that five loaves and two fish will feed over five thousand men.

The numbers in Numbers 7 don't deviate. They're exactly the same. A silver plate and basin with oil and flour, a gold dish of incense, a bull, a ram, a lamb, a goat, two oxen, five rams, another goat, and five more lambs. Why not state the list once, indicate that every tribe gave the same offerings, then move on? Short and to the point usually wins the day.

That's not what happens. Israel's biggest tribe, Judah, boasted 74,600 soldiers. The smallest tribe, Manasseh, had only 32,200. *However, every tribe gave the same amount, thus underscoring tribal unity*. Up to this point, the nation had been plagued by jealousies, strife, and bitter feelings. Recall how Joseph's brothers sold him into slavery in Egypt. Then, when Jacob died, the brothers were overcome with fear. Would Joseph settle the score? Or would his descendants? The nation that gives together stays together.

GOD'S ALTAR

Tribal gifts in Numbers 7 were given to dedicate the altar. Altars play a significant part in God's salvation story. God took away Gideon's doubts and despair at an altar (Judges 6:24). God atoned for Isaiah's uncleanness at an altar (Isaiah 6:6–7). The movement in the first half of Isaiah 56:7 begins at God's holy mountain, continues into His house of prayer, and concludes with His altar. When the temple's altar was destroyed by the Babylonians in 587 BC, the first order of business for Judeans, according to Ezra 3:2, was what? To build an altar.

God's ultimate goal is to bring all people to an altar called Golgotha—that's Aramaic for "the Place of the Skull." Golgotha was Jerusalem's rubbish heap. Jesus was sacrificed on the altar of the cross there—in a pile of junk—to take away sin, atone for transgression, and set us free. At Golgotha, Christ carried the sin of the whole world (2 Corinthians 5:19; 1 John 2:2). In the garbage, Jesus bore our garbage—He took it away and now announces that we're spotless and clean through His shed blood.

Furthermore, when we come to the Sacrament of the Altar, God delivers this cleansing power that Christ purchase for us. Packaged into our Savior's true body and blood are the gifts of washing, renewal, absolution, and love.

Would you like a summary of Numbers 6–7? Here it is. "The Lord is God, and He has made His light to shine upon us. Bind the festal sacrifice with cords, up to the horns of the altar" (Psalm 118:27 ESV).

CHAPTER 6

ARISE, O LORD: NUMBERS 8–10

Arise, O LORD, and go to Your resting place, You and the ark of Your might. (Psalm 132:8 ESV)

In a novel called *Cat's Cradle*, an important book comes to light. It's called *What Can a Thoughtful Person Hope For, Given the Experience of the Past Million Years?* People can't wait to read the book. However, when they do, they're shocked. The book consists only of one word: "Nothing." *What Can a Thoughtful Person Hope For, Given the Experience of the Past Million Years?* Nothing! That's what we have without faith in the triune God. No hope. No life. Nothing to live for. Nothing to die for. Absolutely nothing.

That's so not Israel! God's people are headed for Canaan—a land brimming with abundance, blessings, and bounty. Here's how Moses describes Canaan in Deuteronomy 8:7–10. It has

- a. **brooks of water, along with fountains and springs;**
- b. **wheat and barley, vines and fig trees and pomegranates, olive trees and honey;**
- c. **bread without scarcity; and**
- d. **stones that are iron and hills of copper.**

Life in this land is worth preparing for. We pick things up in Numbers 8–10 as the Israelites continue getting ready for their new life in Canaan.

WE'LL LEAVE THE LIGHT ON FOR YOU

You're probably familiar with that line. Tom Bodett made it famous for Motel 6. The hotel franchise hired Bodett in 1986, and on his first day in the recording studio, he ad-libbed the line "We'll leave the light on for you." It was an instant success—becoming one of the top one hundred best advertising slogans in the twentieth century.

We may liken God's tabernacle to a Motel 6. God directs Aaron to have its seven lamps lit at all times (Numbers 8:1–4). Why go to all this trouble? Why leave the lights on? And why make sure bread will always be present (Exodus 25:30) and that incense will always be offered (Exodus 30:7–8)?

I'll answer those questions with a question. When we expect guests, how do we prepare? We turn the porch light on. Cook a meal. And make sure there are no foul smells. (Translated: Clean out the kitty litter box!) These are God's objectives too. He wants Israelites to know that He's home, anticipating their arrival—so He makes sure the lit lamps are lit, the bread is ready, and that incense takes care of any nasty smell. God awaits His guests with great anticipation. He can't wait to see them! *What Can a Thoughtful Person Hope For, Given God's Meticulous Accommodations?* Forgiveness, life, and salvation!

THE PASSOVER

Numbers 9 continues to describe the events that began in Numbers 7:1—a section of the book that looks back to what happened during the *first* month of the second year after God rescued His people from Egypt. (Moses commences the census in Numbers 1 on the first day of the *second* month after Israel's exodus from Egypt.) We hear, therefore, about Israel's second celebration of Passover—the first took place in the land of the Nile (cf. Exodus 12).

What's different in Israel's second Passover celebration? Moses prohibits several men from participating in the feast. Why? They had touched a dead body. Others miss the meal because they are away on a trip. What does God want Moses to do? Tell them to wait till next year? Take a number, sit down, and wait? Not at all. God wants every Israelite to partake of the Passover's gifts. He takes great delight in delivering the Gospel to as many people as possible. Why? Because everyone needs Vitamin F.

VITAMIN F

They don't look like much or taste very good, but they sure are popular. Each year, Americans spend fifty billion dollars on vitamins and vitamin supplements. If you're eating well, you shouldn't have to take pills with Vitamins A, B, and C. However—and this is a *big* however—everyone in the upper Midwest should take a Vitamin D supplement. That's because sunshine is the main source of Vitamin D, and we (at least us good folk in Minnesota) don't get any warm sunshine in the winter, fall, or spring—and just a tad in the summer!

There's another vitamin that we all *must* have: Vitamin F. Without Vitamin F, we die. Without Vitamin F, we die and our relationships die. Without Vitamin F, we become bitter, petty, small, and vengeful. What's Vitamin F? Vitamin F is forgiveness. When Jesus, our Passover Lamb, suffered, died, and rose again, He won for us complete forgiveness of sin.

Sometimes, however, we doubt it. We struggle with it. "Has Jesus really forgiven *that* sin? I don't feel like it's forgiven." What does Jesus do? He provides a way for us to receive Vitamin F—straight into our mouth, and body, and heart. He does it through Holy Communion.

Paul warns us, though. He teaches that we can take the Holy Supper unworthily. Then we bring condemnation upon ourselves. It's easy, however, to obsess over the apostle's words "unworthy," "guilty," and "judgment" (1 Corinthians 11:27–29)—and fall into self-condemnation. "I'm unworthy! I'm guilty! I deserve judgment!" Feeling unworthy doesn't disqualify us from taking Communion. Feeling guilty or deserving of judgment doesn't disqualify us either. Self-examination before we participate in Holy Communion doesn't imply self-condemnation.

By unworthy eating and drinking, Paul has in mind the type of behavior described in 1 Corinthians 11:21–22. "In eating, each one goes ahead with his own meal. One goes hungry, another gets drunk. What! Do you not have houses to eat and drink in?" The Christians in Corinth celebrated Holy Communion during a fellowship meal after their worship service. It might seem strange to us to distribute the Sacrament during a potluck, but that's the way they did it.

By the time some Corinthians got around to receiving Christ's body and blood, they were already drunk from all the wine they had consumed at their potluck meal. Compounding the problem, some feasted while others had nothing to eat. (As an aside—that often happens to me at church potlucks. People inevitably take all the pecan pie!)

Who receives this Sacrament worthily? It's all about Vitamin F—forgiveness. Martin Luther writes in his Small Catechism, "Fasting and bodily preparation are certainly fine outward training. But that person is truly worthy and well prepared who has faith in these words: 'Given and shed for you for the forgiveness of sins'" (The Sacrament of the Altar, "Who receives this sacrament worthily?"). With Vitamin F, we live. What a gift!

In the Holy Supper, Christ forgives quickly. He doesn't hem and haw. He doesn't make us sit and squirm. Jesus doesn't say, "Let Me get back to you on that." No. He forgives quickly. As soon as we receive Christ's last will and testament—His body and blood—we're absolved.

People sometimes do strange things when they write up their will. Economist Jeremy Bentham left a large fortune to the University College in London on the condition that his preserved corpse annually "attend" the board of directors meetings. For many years, Bentham was recorded as "present but not voting."

Mark Gruenwald, of Marvel Comics fame, left instructions for his heirs to blend the ashes of his body with ink and use the mixture for a comic book. Four thousand copies of Gruenwald's "ink-and-ashes" edition were sold in 1997.

And then there was a Portuguese man—Luis da Camara—who had no family so he randomly picked names out of a Lisbon phone book. When he died at age 42, Luis da Camara's last act on earth was to give twelve thousand dollars each to seventy people who had never heard of him.

What are the chances that some rich person has picked your name out of a phone book and is planning to give you thousands of dollars? Not good! But we've been named as beneficiaries of a will that's the most astonishing of all time. Its terms and benefits are in the Sacrament of the Altar. "For a will takes effect only at death, since it is not in force as long as the one who made it is alive. . . . This is the blood of the covenant that God commanded for you" (Hebrews 9:17, 20 ESV). Christ forgives quickly. It's in His will.

Through His very body and very blood, Christ also forgives freely. In 2009, hedge fund manager Courtney Wolfe paid 1.68 million dollars to have a meal with billionaire investor Warren Buffet. Put another way—using a McDonald's menu to get perspective—Wolfe spent the equivalent of 560,000 Happy Meals.

How much would you pay to have a meal with a celebrity? How many Happy Meals is George Clooney or Tiger Woods or LeBron James worth? We dine with Jesus freely. There's no fine print. There are no hidden conditions. It's 100 percent forgiveness for all sin for all time. Not because we deserve it but because Jesus loves us. Jesus forgives quickly. It's in His will. Jesus forgives freely. It's in His heart.

In Holy Communion, Jesus also forgives completely. It's in His plan. "Let him return to the Lord, that He may have compassion on him, and to our God, for He will *abundantly pardon*" (Isaiah 55:7 ESV). "Abundantly pardon." Christ is no cheapskate. He's not a nickel-and-dime deity. Christ lavishly forgives your sin, my sin, our ugly sin, our haunting sin, our shameful sin, our damning sin, our every sin.

John the Baptist connects Jesus with Israel's Passover Lamb when he says, "Behold, the Lamb of God" (John 1:29, 36 ESV). Jesus isn't an ordinary Lamb of God. Jesus is the *Passover* Lamb of God. How can we be so sure? John uses the word "Passover" eleven times in his Gospel. He structures his story about Jesus to help us behold, see, gaze, and take note of Christ, the ultimate Passover Lamb, who delivers forgiveness quickly, freely, and completely, for us and for our salvation.

THE TRUMPETS

Attention all trumpet players! Numbers 10:1–10 could very well become your favorite part of the Bible! These verses catalog how different trumpet sounds will direct Israelites once they're on the march. When both of Israel's silver trumpets are sounded, people are to gather around the tabernacle—that is, in the middle of the camp. One trumpet only summons leaders to congregate. "Alarm" trumpet blasts mobilize different parts of the camp. Moses also gives directions for how trumpets will function when the Israelites are living in the Promised Land. And, just like the Passover, the Day of Atonement, and the ritual of the Red Heifer, trumpets are to be "a perpetual statute throughout your generations" (Numbers 10:8).

THE FINAL TRUMPET CALL

The New Testament largely links trumpets with Christ's second coming (Matthew 24:31; 1 Corinthians 15:51–52; Revelation 8–9). The passage 1 Thessalonians 4:13–18 likewise exhorts us to anticipate God's final trumpet blast. Christ's return will happen "with the voice of the archangel and with the trumpet call of God" (1 Thessalonians 4:16a).

Christians in Thessalonica weren't worried about their own departure out of this life. They were concerned about loved ones who had already died in the Lord. Paul assures them that believers who die have only fallen asleep. Jesus likewise taught this before He raised Jairus's daughter (Matthew 9:24). Moreover, that's how Luke describes Stephen's death (Acts 7:60), and it's what Paul affirms in 1 Corinthians 15:51. Thus, the apostle repeats the expression *fallen sleep* two times in 1 Thessalonians 4:14–16a.

When we die, if we die (if Jesus doesn't come again before we die), are we immediately resurrected? No. Our body stays here. But our spirit goes to be with the Lord. We have fallen asleep. These verses confirm this teaching:

> Today you will be with Me in paradise. (Luke 23:43 ESV)
>
> To depart from this body is to be present with the Lord. (2 Corinthians 5:8)
>
> For me to live is Christ; to die is gain. (Philippians 1:21)

When believers die, their spirits go to be with the Lord. And they fall asleep. But not forever. Christ will return with a loud command, with the voice of the archangel, and with the trumpet call of God. Michael is the only angel called an archangel in the Bible (Jude 9; Revelation 12:7). Therefore, when Michael puts his lips to the horn, it's going to be quite a day! Those who have fallen asleep will wake up. If you die trusting in the shed blood of the Lamb and believe God raised Him from the dead, here's God's pledge to you: "The dead in Christ will rise first" (1 Thessalonians 4:16b).

Aristotle called death "The end of everything." A French philosopher, Jean-Paul Sartre, wrote, "Death removes all meaning from life." Another philosopher, François Rabelais, said at the end of his life, "I go to seek a great. . . . Perhaps." Not Jesus. He claims, "I am the resurrection and the life. Whoever believes in Me will live, even though he dies" (John 11:25). Because Jesus lives, you, too, shall live. Guaranteed. Bank on it. It's set in cement.

On the other hand, Christians who are alive when Christ returns will be caught up to be with Jesus. "After that, we who are still alive and are left will be *caught up* together with them in the clouds to meet the Lord in the air" (1 Thessalonians 4:17a). The term "caught up" in the Latin is *rapiemur*. From this comes the English word "rapture." So "rapture" is a biblical idea. The problem is that some Christians distinguish the rapture from the second coming of Christ. This is incorrect. The rapture and the second coming are the same event. They will happen at the same time. If you believe and have been baptized, then you're rapture ready!

Let me put it this way. Let's say I pay fifty dollars for a Bible. I walk out of church, and you come up to me and say, "Reed. Uh . . . Reed? That's *my* Bible." How am I going to respond? "Get a life!" No, I'd be more polite than that. But I might come back and say, "Why do you think this Bible is yours?" What do you need at that point? The receipt.

When Satan approaches, often he whispers, "You're mine because you're a sinner. You're just a dirty rag in God's eyes. After all, I know all about those lying words, that wayward child, that shady business deal. It all means you're all mine. You forever belong to me!" At that moment we can pull out our receipt and say, "I belong to Jesus Christ. He took my sin away, nailing it to the cross. I've got the receipt! I've been baptized!"

"And so we will be with the Lord forever" (1 Thessalonians 4:17b). Have you been to your twentieth high school reunion? Thirtieth? Fortieth? Fiftieth? Sixtieth? Most of us have been to family reunions. Reunions are wonderful opportunities to see friends and talk with relatives.

But can you imagine the reunion at the final trumpet sound? People's bodies reunited with their spirits. Family members seeing one another for the first time in decades, if not centuries. This experience tops everything. I can say with confidence that the most exciting thing in your life hasn't happened yet. I don't care what you've done. You may have landed that dream job, purchased that dream house, and gone on that dream vacation. You may have skydived again and again. This isn't skydiving. This is the opposite! We'll be caught up into this the reunion of all reunions—together with the redeemed from every tribe, nation, people, and language. My best advice? Keep your ears open for the final trumpet call!

WE HAVE LIFTOFF!

Up to this point, Numbers has been like a long prelude to a movie—you know, coming attraction after coming attraction. Yet only nineteen days have passed from Numbers 1:1 to Numbers 10:11. But now? Houston, we have liftoff! God's glory cloud rises. Promised Land, here we come!

It's April/May in 1443 BC, and it's a new day. The Israelites have been camped at Mount Sinai for eleven months and nineteen days—it takes fifty-nine chapters to record it all (Exodus 19–Numbers 10). To give you some perspective, there are 929 chapters in the Old Testament, so about 16 percent of them take place at Sinai. Here are more numbers. Israel breaks camp in Numbers 10:11 and arrives in Moab in Numbers 22:1. Moses condenses Israel's forty years in the wilderness into twelve chapters. Here's a broad outline that shows where we're headed:

Sinai to Kadesh (Numbers 10:12–12:16)

Kadesh (Numbers 13–19)

Kadesh to the plains of Moab (Numbers 20–21)

The plains of Moab (Numbers 22–36)

THE PILLARS OF CLOUD AND FIRE

Israel's departure in Numbers 10:11 launches the nation's first travel narrative in the book. It goes through Numbers 12:16—when the Israelites arrive in Kadesh, in the desert of Paran. Paran is located on Canaan's southern border, a strategic place for God's people to launch their military invasion. How does God lead? Through a pillar of fire and cloud.

We first meet this glory cloud in Exodus 13:21–22, when God directs His people out of Egypt. The cloud in Numbers, however, doesn't escort Israel from the front. Instead, like Exodus 33:7–11, the glory cloud is tethered to the tabernacle.

On the one hand, God's glory cloud reveals His presence—with their own eyes Israelites see it. On the other hand, God veils Himself in the cloud, lest His bare presence overwhelm the Israelites and kill them. Which is it? Reveal or conceal? It's both. Why? People can't see God's unveiled face. He tells Moses, "No one can see Me and live" (Exodus 33:20). God thus covers His full presence. Yet He shows the Israelites enough of Himself to guide them on their way.

Hold on to your hat. In the New Testament, God doesn't give us a pillar of fire and a pillar of cloud. He gives us His Son. "The Son is the radiance of God's glory and the exact representation of His being" (Hebrews 1:3). Old Testament glory was great, but it was nowhere close to being the exact representation of God's being. That's Jesus.

Question: If the fire and cloud covered God's full presence, what covers Jesus—the Second Person of the Trinity—so His presence doesn't destroy us? Flesh and blood. A human body covers Jesus. The great hymn writer Charles Wesley (AD 1707–88) put it this way: "Veiled in flesh the Godhead see, hail the incarnate Deity" (*LSB* 380:2).

There will be a day, however, when God will lift the veil and we'll directly gaze upon Him. That's Paul's promise: "Now we see in a mirror dimly, but then face to face" (1 Corinthians 13:12 ESV). No more clouds, shrouds, curtains, or covers—instead, we will gaze upon the full splendor of our triune God. That's a promise worth living for. That's a promise worth dying for. That's a promise worth waiting for—all our days.

THE ARK AND REST

God not only employs His glory cloud and pillar of fire to lead Israel. His ark also leads His people. "The ark of the covenant of the LORD went before them three days' journey, to seek out a resting place for them" (Numbers 10:33 ESV). When those carrying the ark would let it down, Moses writes that it rested (Numbers 10:36). "Rest" in the Old Testament frequently implies "rest from our enemies" (e.g., Deuteronomy 12:10; Joshua 21:44; Judges 3:11; 5:31).

Rest from adversaries and enemies finds its greatest expression in our Savior. Jesus warmly invites us, saying, "Come to Me, *all* who labor and are heavy laden, and I will give you rest" (Matthew 11:28 ESV). Jesus doesn't only welcome the good people, the religious people, the nice people. No. Jesus offers rest to *all* people.

Christ says, "I carried all your sin to the cross; surely, I will carry whatever frightens you, alarms you, and threatens to undo you. Stop trying to be your own god, and I'll be the only God you'll need. *Stop trying to be your own god, and I'll be the only God you'll ever need!*"

Why would anyone refuse this? I'll tell you why. It boils down to two words: "By myself." When my three children were small, their favorite two words were what? "By myself!" "Let me help you pick this up." "By myself!" "Let me help you put this together." "By myself!" "Let me help you tie your shoes." "By myself!" When we insist, "By myself," we end up carrying our burdens. How does that turn out? We become hard to talk with, hard to listen to, and very hard to live with.

Israel's rest through the ark's leading was grand, but there's a better rest. God promised it. Jesus won it. The Holy Spirit delivers it. We can all leave our heavy burdens at the foot of the cross.

THE ARK OF THE COVENANT

The Israelites begin their march toward Canaan at "the mount of the Lord" (Numbers 10:33 ESV), an expression that only appears again in the Old Testament in Genesis 22:14. What should we make of this connection? Just as God provided a ram in place of Isaac (Genesis 22:13), so He will graciously provide for Israel as they journey to the Promised Land. *Where God guides God always provides*. And one of God's chief provisions is His real presence through the ark of the covenant (Numbers 10:33).

It's easy to confuse this ark with Noah's ark. In Hebrew, though, they're two different words. Noah's is called a *tevah*. Israel has an *aron*. Although *aron* may also indicate a coffin (Genesis 50:26) or a money chest (2 Kings 12:10), most of the time it denotes the ark of the covenant—made out of acacia wood and covered with gold. It housed the Ten Commandments and, in time, also manna and Aaron's rod.

Long after the Israelites entered Canaan, a number of psalms suggest that the ark of the covenant continued to lead God's people into battle. Here are a few verses:

> Lift up your heads, O gates! And be lifted up, O ancient doors, that the King of glory may come in. Who is this King of glory? The Lord, strong and mighty, the Lord, mighty in battle. (Psalm 24:7–8 ESV)

God shall arise, His enemies shall be scattered; and those who hate Him shall flee before Him. (Psalm 68:1 ESV)

Arise, O Lord, and go to Your resting place, You and the ark of Your might. (Psalm 132:8 ESV)

THE ARK AND ISRAEL'S BATTLES

Early on a crisp September morning in 1944, two German spies, near the French-German border, were trying to decide if it was safe to venture into the countryside. The nighttime rumble of tanks had died away, but the Germans still saw American trucks, trailers, cannons, and a few big M4 tanks. What they saw next took their breath away—four soldiers walked over to a monstrous tank and, with one man at each corner, they picked it up!

It was the 23rd Headquarters Special Troops. They were special all right. They specialized in impersonating other troops with inflatable rubber guns, cannons, trucks, and tanks. Couple that with amplified recordings, and the 23rd kept the Nazis fooled throughout much of World War II.

There's another impersonator who, with careful staging and theatrics, keeps us fooled and confused. He goes by several names: Lucifer, the father of lies, the god of this age, the prince of the power of the air, the devil, and Satan. But, like the 23rd Headquarters Special Troops, Satan is all show, no substance. So are Israel's enemies that the ark leads them to attack.

Numbers 13:29 lists the following groups living in the Promised Land: Amalekites, Hittites, Jebusites, Amorites, and Canaanites. Amalekites lived in and around Beersheba (Genesis 14:7). Later Israel defeated them at Rephidim (Exodus 17:8–16). Amalekites regained their power, though, to the point that Israel was told to avoid them (Numbers 14:25).

Hittites were contemporaries with Abraham (Genesis 23), while Jebusites lived in the region of Jerusalem (e.g., 2 Samuel 5:6–7).

Though the term "Amorite" is sometimes employed as a collective title for all the inhabitants of Canaan (e.g., Genesis 48:22; Joshua 24:15), in Numbers, Amorites are distinguished from Canaanites. Israel defeated two Amorite kings, Sihon and Og, who ruled east of the Jordan, from Mount Hermon to the Dead Sea (Numbers 32:33).

And the Canaanites? They lived along the Mediterranean coast as well as by the Jordan River (Numbers 13:29).

The end result? Israel has a lot of enemies! It's no surprise, then, that Moses looks to the ark to save the Israelites from their foes: "Whenever the ark set out, Moses said, '*Arise*, O Lord, and let Your enemies be scattered, and let those who hate You flee before You'" (Numbers 10:35 ESV). Here the command "arise" suggests "attack." Life in Canaan begins through victorious warfare. Israelites will succeed only as God's real presence in the ark leads the way.

I'VE NEVER BEEN THIS WAY BEFORE

You know the sinking feeling. So do I. We say a prayer. Prepare as best as we can. Then step into a decisive situation. We might even mutter under our breath, "I've never been this way before."

Maybe you're terrified at the thought of bringing a new child home or watching your last child leave home. Maybe you're faced with a ministry situation that has your stomach tied in knots. Maybe you're not sure now was the right time to sell your home and make that big move. Maybe you're facing a difficult stretch in your marriage or bills that won't go away. Some of us face a future that's known only to God—it's so painful, so personal, so private. "I've never been *this* way before!"

Israelites understand.

It's tempting to do nothing. God's people could have said, "Let's park the car here! If the wilderness is good enough for snakes and sand, it's good enough for us! After all, this is Mount Sinai, the Mountain of God! All in favor of staying put, say, 'Aye!'"

When faced with enemies, it's easy to tune in to radio station K-FEAR. Satan, the daily host of the program, says, "Take no chances. Say no to courage and yes to caution. Expect the worst. Triple-lock all doors. Protect yourself in a tight radius of won'ts, don'ts, cant's, and quits. Think about every possible peril. Focus on the dangers; worry yourself with 'What if?' Come weal, come woe, make your status quo!"

"The cloud lifted from over the tabernacle of the testimony" (Numbers 10:11 ESV). God tells Moses and crew, "Go!" In fact, God often calls His people to *go*. To Abram He said, "*Go* to the land I will show you" (Genesis 12:1). To Jonah, "*Go* to the great city of Nineveh" (Jonah 1:2 ESV). To the disciples, "*Go*, make disciples of all nations" (Matthew 28:19).

Yet, when God says go, it's in His heart that we never go it alone. He knows a mystical, abstract, vague presence does no good. We need real presence. And real presence is exactly what God delivers. "Whenever the ark set out, Moses said, 'Rise up . . . O Lord'" (Numbers 10:35). "When it rested, he said, 'Return, O Lord'" (Numbers 10:36 ESV). The ark doesn't symbolize God or represent God's presence. In, with, and under the ark is God Himself. *He's a real present God.*

Ultimately the ark of the covenant took on flesh and blood—and a heart. His journey began at Bethlehem, then Nazareth. It continued in the face of kings—Herod and Philip. Then, His final march was south, to Jerusalem, to defeat the satanic coalition that sought worldwide domination. On Thursday, He marched from the Upper Room to Gethsemane, then to the house of Caiaphas. On Friday, with blood dripping from His wounds, Jesus marched to Gabbatha and Golgotha. There they crucified Him. Yet three days later the march went on!

And this victory march continues today. Jesus leads us from victory to victory by His real presence—the Gospel proclaimed, the baptismal deliverance remembered, the body and blood of the Eucharist celebrated.

"This is the feast of victory for our God!" And with hope we await our final journey—the resurrection of the body and the life of the world to come. Our hope is built on nothing more, nothing less, and nothing else than Jesus' blood and righteousness.

Because of cleansing blood, resurrection joy, and the power of Pentecost, we dare to march straight ahead. Paul tells us why. "But thanks be to God, who always leads us in triumphal procession in Christ" (2 Corinthians 2:14). Listen. Do you hear Him? God is calling. God is saying, "Go!" He promises that we will never, ever go alone. "Behold, the ark of the covenant of the Lord of all the earth is going before you" (Joshua 3:11).

MEET HOBAB

Hobab, the "the son of Reuel" (Numbers 10:29 ESV), is Moses' brother-in-law. You may be familiar with Reuel's other name—Jethro, a priest in Midian (Exodus 3:1). Hobab, then, is part of Moses' extended family.

Moses' discussion with Hobab (Numbers 10:29–34) takes place *before* Israel leaves Mount Sinai. (It's a flashback, just like Numbers 7:1–9:14.) The conversation comes between God's gift of His guiding cloud (Numbers 10:11) and His equally gracious gift of the ark (Numbers 10:35–36). That's an important part of this story.

Moses doesn't seem very eager to embrace God's provisions that will lead Israel to Canaan. Instead, he yearns for human help—Hobab's help. Moses wants Hobab to "be our eyes" (Numbers 10:31). No doubt, as a Midianite, Hobab was an expert on the local terrain; he was a pro when it came to traveling in this part of the Sinai Peninsula. But what about God's cloud and ark? Won't they faithfully lead Israel? Aren't they enough? And why does Moses go so far as to insist on Hobab's presence? "Please do not leave us" (Numbers 10:31 ESV). Didn't Moses earlier beg God to go with Israel to the Promised Land? "If Your Presence does not go with us, do not send us up from here" (Exodus 33:15). God's people aren't supposed to be dependent upon someone—a non-Israelite at that.

This is an ominous beginning of the journey.

As events unfold in Numbers, it's going to be like watching cracks in a house's foundation slowly spread. When there are enough cracks, there will be a collapse—always. The first crack? Moses' insistence that Hobab be Israel's guide.

DITCH THE DELUSIONS

Have you seen the movie *A Beautiful Mind*? Russell Crowe stars in a true story about John Nash, a Nobel laureate in economics. Nash suffers from schizophrenia, a fact the audience is unaware of because most of the movie is about Nash's delusions. These delusions include a roommate named Charles, a little girl named Marcie, and an agent of the government named Parcher. These characters turn out to be figments of Nash's imagination.

John Nash lives in a fantasy world until one day he realizes that the little girl, Marcie—who by this time Nash has known for years—has never aged a day. It's at that point that he begins to recover his sanity. In the final scene in the movie, when Nash receives the Nobel Prize for economics, he's asked if he still sees Charles, Marcie, and Parcher. Of course, the audience knows he does because Charles, Marcie, and Parcher are sitting in the front row. Nash replies, "Yes, I see them. But I don't listen to them anymore."

Sitting in my front row every day are three of my delusional companions. Their names? Control, Perfection, and Fear. They seem so real. "Reed! Ditch this Gospel thing. Listen to us; we'll tell you what's really real!"

I see these delusional companions of mine, but I don't listen to them anymore. Why? God's presence is with me. How? Following Babylon's sack of Jerusalem and Solomon's temple in 587 BC, the ark disappeared. But it reappeared in Mary's womb and was born in Bethlehem. Jesus is God's ultimate expression of His presence—covered not in pure gold but in flesh and blood to suffer and bleed for the sin of the world. Is there anyone else worth listening to as we travel through the wilderness to our heavenly Canaan? *I think not.*

CHAPTER 7

COMPLAINING 101: NUMBERS 11

They tested God in their heart by demanding the food they craved. (Psalm 78:18 ESV)

After lumbering your way through Numbers 1–10, you might think that the rest of the book is going to continue with more lists, laws, legislations, and Levites. You may want to close it and not see it for a very long time—perhaps never again! Enough is enough! God gives a command. Moses repeats it. Israel does it. There's no drama. No movement. Nothing grabs you.

Yet throughout Numbers' first ten chapters, there's an undercurrent of looming disaster. Have you seen it? Several warnings of imminent danger appear just under the surface of Israel's lockstep compliance. How so? Anyone coming too close to the tabernacle will die (Numbers 3:10)—like Nadab and Abihu (Numbers 3:4). Levites charged with handling holy things better not touch them, or they'll perish (Numbers 4:15). Kohathites shouldn't look at the tabernacle's sacred objects. If they do, they'll quickly go the way of all flesh (Numbers 4:20). The entire tribe of Levites must camp around the tabernacle "that there may be no plague among the people of Israel when the people of Israel come near the sanctuary" (Numbers 8:19 ESV). Then there are corpses in the camp (Numbers 5:2) as well as a warning that Nazirites shouldn't get too close to dead people, even if it's their parents (Numbers 6:6–7). God offers a second Passover for people who have become defiled by corpses (Numbers 9:6–11). *Where do all these dead people come from?* You're about to find out.

If it's action you're looking for, it's action you're going to get.

Moses negotiated with God to accompany Israel to the Promised Land (Exodus 33:7–11). God consented, but what of the consequences of mixing His holiness with Israel's unholiness—a motif we spent a good deal of time on in Numbers 2–5? God's presence with Israel was a glowing light of love. It was also a powder keg that could explode. With ongoing regularity in Numbers 11–25, Israelites light the fuse. The result? KABOOM!

Buckle up! Here we go!

A PREVIEW OF NUMBERS 11–25

Taxes are due in a few months; gray hair is creeping in; your favorite team is in last place; things took a wrong turn at work; the hard drive just blew up; the car needs new tires; the kids are crabby; and this illustration will go on too long. Let's face it—there's a lot to complain about!

Israel should know. Numbers 11:1–3 is more than a short vignette or a passing description. Instead, it offers a portrait of Numbers 11:4–25:18: complaint, judgment, intercession, and forgiveness. I invite you to say these words out loud (provided no one is around to question your sanity). Complaint, judgment, intercession, and forgiveness. Here's what that looks like:

> Israelites sin by complaining (Numbers 11:1–35; 12:1–15; 13:28–33; 14:1–45; 15:32–36; 16:1–40; 20:2–12; 21:4–9; 25:1–15)
>
> God's anger is aroused in judgment (Numbers 11:1, 20, 33; 12:9; 21:5)
>
> Moses responds by interceding (Numbers 11:2; 12:13; 21:8–9)
>
> God forgives (Numbers 11:2; 12:13; 21:8–9)

Moses sometimes names the rebellion's location, such as, Taberah or "Burning" (Numbers 11:3), Kibroth-hattaavah or "Graves of Craving" (Numbers 11:34), Hormah or "Destruction" (Numbers 14:45; 21:3), and Meribah or "Quarreling" (Numbers 20:13)

Perhaps you're familiar with the term "doom loop." Jim Collin made it popular in his 2001 management book titled *Good to Great*. Doom loop describes a situation when one negative action brings about another negative action, which makes the first problem worse—and on and on it goes. In time, everything is undone. That's Israel in the wilderness. Things go from bad to worse to the point where almost everyone—including Moses and Aaron—die outside of Canaan. It's doom loop, the Israelite way.

There are four different types of negative actions in Numbers 11–25. The first is Israel's failure to trust in God's provision (Numbers 11:1–35; 20:2–12; 21:4–9). In these uprisings, the Israelites forget God's mercies in the past, doubt that He will provide in the present crisis, and disdain His gifts when he does.

The second type of dissent is Israel's unwillingness to trust that God will fight for them (Numbers 13:28–33; 14:1–35). Hadn't He devastated Egypt with ten plagues? Hadn't the Lord hurled Pharaoh's horses and chariots into the Red Sea? Hadn't Moses and Miriam led Israel in a song of salvation? Yes, but in the wilderness, the Israelites developed spiritual amnesia.

There's a third way God's people turn from His guiding—they reject people He places in authority over them (Numbers 12:1–15; 16:1–40). What prompts this? Envy. "I want what you have, and I'll do anything to get it!"

The fourth classification is straightforward. Israel refuses to follow God's commands (Numbers 14:39–45; 15:32–36; 20:2–13; 25:1–15). They defy divine mandates that are clear, concise, and consistent with God's character and will.

How does God respond to this moaning and groaning? "For forty years I loathed that generation" (Psalm 95:10 ESV). God despises whining and whimpering. That's why God sends fire, a plague, an earthquake, and snakes in the book of Numbers. Climactically, He forces the Israelites to live in the wilderness for forty years. Get ready for doom loops on steroids. It's downhill all the way.

PANIC!

Now that we have an overview of Numbers 11–25, let's land the plane, get out, and look at the details. The Israelites had been out of Egypt for a year, a month, and twenty days. That's not very long. Think about how you've felt a year after leaving a place you've lived all your life. Did you miss friends? Relatives? Familiar shopping places and parks? Did your heart keep tugging at you to go back?

After three days—just *three* days into the journey—everything goes south. The Israelites push the panic button. "If there's going to be any trouble along the way, we're going back to Egypt—no questions asked!" Israel's faithfulness in the book's first ten chapters vanishes like the morning dew.

The journey begins with divine fire burning the fringes of the camp (Numbers 11:1). It could've been worse. Since an inferno would've engulfed everyone, we might conclude that this is a slight detour, a small bump in the road. Perhaps the sequence will return with God's commands and Israel's obedience that's so frequent in Numbers 1–10. Don't bet on it. Israelites don't lament. They complain—big time, all the time, even in overtime.

LAMENTS AND COMPLAINTS

Is there a difference between Israel's cries in the wilderness and biblical laments? Yes. They're poles apart. When Job and the psalmists cry out and complain, they also affirm that God is good even though His ways can be difficult to understand. They remember God's covenants and yearn for His deliverance. Conversely, Israel's wilderness generation thought their situation was insurmountable—completely hopeless. Instead of yearning for deliverance, they turned their backs on God.

The expression in Numbers 11:1 translated "the people complained" (ESV) is more literally rendered, "the people complained *among themselves*." God invites us to direct protests toward Him—that's called a lament. Criticizing Him before others? That's called a sin. "When the LORD heard it, His anger was kindled" (Numbers 11:1 ESV). Grumbling and griping *about* God is different from expressing pain *to* God. The former outright rejects the Lord (Numbers 11:20).

Though giving free rein to heartache helps, perpetual whining erodes our faith. If bellyaching about bad breaks was helpful, bellyaching would free us from the need to bellyache. Instead, being critical hardens hearts and solidifies our stubbornness.

On the other hand, trusting God with our disappointments is to turn to Him in prayer. It means looking to God for spiritual nourishment, not to our own resources. Laments are godly prayers; they plead for divine healing and deliverance.

Complaints, however, delete God from the conversation. Their goal is to carp and harp to anyone and everyone—except God. Instead of directing misery to Him, complaints grouse and grumble to anyone within earshot. These caustic outcries are filled with unbelief—Israel's frequent response to their wilderness hardships.

GREAT BEGINNINGS, SUDDEN COLLAPSES

Grumbling didn't make the Middle Ages' list of the seven deadly sins. And no one goes to "Grumbler's Anonymous"—at least I've never met a person who introduced himself by saying, "Hi, my name is Joe Molino from Toledo. I'm in a twelve-step program to recover from my constant negative outlook."

How many people do you know who are actively working to overcome their complaining? "All men are created equal and are endowed by their Creator with certain unalienable rights. First among them is the right to grumble and mumble, even about a deceased great uncle." This sounds like Israel, doesn't it? They go from singing the ark song (Numbers 10:35–36) immediately to grouching and griping. How did things go so badly, so quickly?

The sequence—a great beginning followed by a sudden collapse—appears several times in Holy Scripture. There's the story of creation (Genesis 1–2) followed by Adam and Eve's fall into sin (Genesis 3). Then there's Noah, a righteous man who builds a big boat that saves the human race—along with many birds, reptiles, and animals. Afterward, however, Noah gets drunk and lies naked in a tent (Genesis 9:20–21). Also consider Exodus 25–31, where God gives Moses the blueprint for Israel's tabernacle. What happens next? The Israelites worship a golden calf and Aaron, Israel's high priest, serves as the ringleader (Exodus 32). Before we know it, Aaron has the Israelites declaring that a golden bovine is actually divine!

Next up? Joshua and company take Jericho with ease (Joshua 6) only to stumble and fail in their next battle against Ai (Joshua 7). Here's one more example. Acts 4 ends with an inspiring story of Barnabas's generosity. Turning the page into Acts 5, we read about Ananias and Sapphira—two of the greediest people in the Bible.

What's up with these abrupt changes? How can things shift so dramatically from blissful blessing to downhill drama? The Bible teaches that we live between our new life in Christ and our old life of sin, between what's beautiful in the Gospel and what's ugly in the world. We're simultaneously sinners and saints. One minute we're filled with lofty thoughts. The next minute our minds are in the gutter.

The quick turnabout in Numbers goes from faithful obedience (Numbers 1–10) to mutiny and rebellion in the ranks (Numbers 11–25). The swift undoing begins with all Israel (Numbers 11) and then visits the holy family of Moses, Aaron, and Miriam (Numbers 12). And if that's not bad enough, the wheels fall off the car in Numbers 13–14 with the spy mega-mess and God's one-way ticket to the wilderness for forty years. Yes, there's a glimmer of hope in chapter 15, only to be snuffed out by a major kerfuffle with Korah in Numbers 16. Even Aaron and mighty Moses get sucked into the quagmire in Numbers 20.

None of this comes out of the blue. The book of Exodus includes previews of what to expect in Numbers:

> Why did You bring us out of Egypt? (Exodus 14:11–12 ESV)
>
> This water tastes awful! (Exodus 15:22–26 ESV)
>
> We want food right now! (Exodus 16 ESV)
>
> We're dying of thirst! (Exodus 17:1–7 ESV)

God treats these grievances in the book of Exodus as legitimate. The Israelites are afraid of Pharaoh's horses and chariots; they also need food and water. In the book of Numbers, however, the Israelites grouch and growl about similar needs, but God's responses are very different. Why is that? The Israelites in Numbers have already seen God's power and protection at the Red Sea and Mount Sinai. They've already received pardon for their sin of making a golden calf. God's already given them manna, quail, and water from a rock. "Everyone to whom much was given, of him much will be required" (Luke 12:48 ESV).

Between Sinai and Canaan, the Israelites are in shambles. That's what happens in between. God's people become nostalgic for yesteryear. "Those were the good ol' days!" What follows nostalgia? Embellishment. "We never had it so good as in Egypt!" Weren't the Israelites forced laborers and state slaves? Didn't the empire kill Hebrew baby boys? How could they long to return to the land of the Nile?

SYNOPSIS OF NUMBERS 11:4–35

Have you ever been around children when you tell one of them that, because dinner is in fifteen minutes, they can't have a double-decker chocolate-mint ice cream cone? And that child begins whining? Then, to your shock and surprise, the rest of the children insist on having double-decker chocolate-mint ice cream cones. When? Right now! How could this commotion occur so quickly? Complaining is contagious. It's an infectious disease. It only takes a spark to get a fire going! Need proof? The ominous vignette in Numbers 11:1–3 provides the map for the rest of the chapter. Look at the links.

> Israelites complain (Numbers 11:1; 11:4–6)
>
> Divine anger (Numbers 11:1; 11:10)
>
> Moses in the middle (Numbers 11:2; 11:11–15)
>
> The expression "So the place was called . . ." (Numbers 11:3, 34 ESV)

Numbers 11:4–35 has two interwoven stories—one positive and one negative. Moses' leadership dilemma ends on a happy note. The grumbling ends on a very sour note—there's way too much quail. Psalmists feature the upside to the quail miracle, as well as the downside.

> They asked, and He brought quail, and gave them bread from heaven in abundance. (Psalm 105:40 ESV)
>
> But they had a wanton craving in the wilderness, and put God to the test in the desert; He gave them what they asked, but sent a wasting disease among them. (Psalm 106:14–15 ESV)

Paul, for his part, shines the light on Israel's wanton desires—which he says is Israel's foundational problem in the wilderness. "Now these things took place as examples for us, that we might not desire evil as they did" (1 Corinthians 10:6 ESV).

THE RABBLE

Numbers 11:4–35 reprises Exodus 16 (manna and quail), along with Exodus 18 (leadership help for Moses). That much is clear, but who is "the rabble"? (Numbers 11:4 ESV). The Hebrew word translated "rabble" in the ESV may also be rendered "mixed multitude" (cf. Exodus 12:38). This group didn't consist of full-blooded Israelites. They were Hebrews, with some Egyptian in them (cf. Leviticus 24:10), who held the land the Nile in high regard. "We remember the fish we used to eat for free in Egypt. And we had all the cucumbers, melons, leeks, onions, and garlic we wanted" (Numbers 11:5). Their problem? Nostalgia—it edits out yesterday's pain and its problems.

When we walk down memory lane, it often unleashes its hypnotic power. "Remember when we were seniors in high school? We never had it so good!" But hindsight can be fatally flawed. Before we know it, up is down, in is out, and cold is hot. And if you're part of Israel's mixed multitude? "Life was better when we were in bondage baking bricks! Those were our very best days!"

MOSES' MANNA MELTDOWN

When George H. W. Bush was president of the United States (1989–93), he banned broccoli on Air Force One. It made national headlines. When asked about it, Bush said, "I don't like broccoli and I haven't liked broccoli since I was a child when my mother made me eat it. Now that I'm president of the United States, I'm not going to eat anymore broccoli!" California broccoli growers were offended. To protest Bush's decision, they delivered ten tons of broccoli to the White House.

Moses' problem wasn't broccoli. It was manna. Israelites weren't going to eat anymore manna! On the one hand, God's gift of quail happened all of two times (Exodus 16; Numbers 11). We could compare these events to going out to eat with friends and spending more than we can afford. "I just blew a huge hole in my budget!" On the other hand, manna was a staple in Israelite tents for forty years (Exodus 16:35).

Manna could be prepared in a variety of ways (Numbers 11:8). Surely some industrious Hebrew women developed a church cookbook. "The 365 Ways to Cook Manna." An instant bestseller! Asaph calls manna "the bread of heaven" (Psalm 78:24). This was the original angel food cake!

Who ends up in the middle of the manna mess in Numbers 11? Moses!

Perhaps you've heard about the husband who came home one evening to a cranky wife. Arriving at 6:30 p.m., he spent an hour trying to cheer her up. Nothing worked. Finally, he said, "Let's start over and pretend

I'm just getting home." He stepped outside and, when he opened the door, she screamed, "It's 7:30 p.m., and you're just *now* getting home?"

Moses must have felt like this hapless husband. He couldn't do anything right. His lament is achingly honest. In the Hebrew of Numbers 11:11–15, he refers to himself twenty times. In most crises, Moses has the resolve of granite—but even granite can be worn down by constant dripping. Exasperated and exhausted, Moses asks God to kill him on the spot.

During his manna meltdown, Moses uses female imagery for God—likening him to a mother who gave birth to Israel. It's God's responsibility, not his, to serve as a wet nurse and breastfeed His people. Where is Jethro, who earlier solved Moses' administrative headaches (cf. Exodus 18)?

Do you want a surefire formula for discouragement? Turn the spotlight on yourself. Focus on your angst and anger. Ignore everyone else. Don't pray. Don't read your Bible. Then add a dash self-pity and a tablespoon of "Woe is me." Presto. You're now at the end of your rope.

Yet Moses gets one thing right. Do you notice the difference between Israel's complaining to one another *about* God and Moses' complaining *to* God? The first is a sin. The second God welcomes. "Cast your burden on the Lord, and He will sustain you" (Psalm 55:22 ESV).

BREAKING DOWN THE WALLS

Ancient Romans and Celtics couldn't get along. In AD 55, the Romans scored a series of victories that extended their reach north—all the way to what's now called Scotland. The Celtics fired back with fierce guerrilla warfare. Rome countered. War continued. What do you do when you don't get along? You build a wall. In AD 122, Roman Emperor Hadrian built a wall to separate Romans from Celtics. Hadrian's Wall is still standing today.

There are a lot of walls still standing today. Walls are still standing between husbands and wives, between parents and children, between rich and poor, between young and old, and between ethnicities. We all need some walls to come crashing down. What Moses prays for, God promises, and Peter preaches on Pentecost. The Holy Spirit breaks down our walls.

The Israelites complain to Moses. He becomes so exasperated that he tells God he can't lead the people anymore. "I quit! I'm going back to herding sheep! Sure, they're dirty and dumb, but at least they don't talk back!" God tells Moses to call Israel's seventy elders and to bring them to the tabernacle where God will take some of the Holy Spirit who is upon Moses and put the same Spirit upon the seventy. Then the seventy elders will be quipped to help Moses lead the people. Moses can't carry a ton. But a ton divided among seventy people becomes twenty-nine pounds each. Many hands make light work!

Two of the elders, however, remain in the camp. They don't go to the tabernacle when they're called. Their names? Eldad and Medad. Why didn't they go to the tabernacle? Eldad and Medad built a wall. Chances are, they were upset with Moses. Everyone else was. Why not Eldad and Medad? Perhaps they were complaining about the manna. Maybe they shared the objections of Aaron and Miriam—that Moses had a Cushite wife (Numbers 12:1). Or they were just so fed up with everything that they wanted to go back to Egypt. Whatever the reason, Eldad and Medad simply said, "We don't like what's going on. We refuse to go to the tabernacle. Instead, we're going to build a wall!"

We all build walls. That's what we're supposed to do when we're upset, right? That's what always works when things don't go our way, right? What's the solution to every relational problem? Get out your bricks. Make some mortar. Lay a foundation. Build a wall.

What does God do with Eldad and Medad? "Yet the Spirit rested upon them as well" (Numbers 11:26). No way! God's Spirit rests upon Eldad and Medad. Despite their anger and frustration. Despite their wall. What did the Spirit do? He broke down their wall. How do we know? "They prophesied there in the camp" (Numbers 11:26). Eldad and Medad joined the others. Their wall came tumbling down.

Joshua, Moses' assistant, wants Moses to stop Eldad and Medad from prophesying. Instead of telling them to cease and desist, Moses tells Joshua, "I wish that all the LORD's people were prophets and that the LORD would put His Spirit on them!" (Numbers 11:29). Why is that? Because God's Spirit brings walls crashing down.

What Moses prays for, God promises. "I will pour out My Spirit on all people. Your sons and your daughters shall prophesy, your old men shall dream dreams, and your young men shall see visions" (Joel 2:28). Let's look at the first part of this verse:

I—the power of God

Will—the determination of God

Pour Out—the generosity of God

My Spirit—the presence of God

Upon all people—the universal plan of God

God's Spirit breaks down walls. Do you spot it? Sons and daughters. Old men and young men. They're all together. No barriers. No barricades. No distinctions. Walls come crashing down.

What Moses prays for, God promises and Peter preaches on Pentecost. In the book of Acts, it happened, just as Moses prayed for. Just as God promised. On Pentecost, God pours out His Holy Spirit to do what? Bring walls crashing down. "Parthians and Medes and Elamites and residents of Mesopotamia, Judea and Cappadocia, Pontus and Asia, Phrygia and Pamphylia, Egypt and the parts of Libya belonging to Cyrene, and visitors from Rome, both Jews and proselytes, Cretans and Arabians" (Acts 2:9–11 ESV).

Imagine all the walls. Customs, languages, skin color, young, old, rich, poor, men, women, Jews, proselytes. All the walls between these people came down. How? Spirit-inspired repentance, Holy Baptism, and the forgiveness of sin. "Peter said to them, 'Repent and be baptized every one of you in the name of Jesus Christ for the forgiveness of your sins, and you will receive the gift of the Holy Spirit'" (Acts 2:38 ESV). Walls come down through the salvation purchased and won by Jesus on the cross.

Living in peace with God empowers us to live in peace with people. We can't live in peace with people until we live in peace with God. How important is this? People carrying resentment are twice as likely to have a stroke, three times as likely to have a heart attack, and four times as likely to have unhealthy cholesterol. Researchers also link carrying a grudge to higher levels of diabetes and cancer. There's a physical cost to holding on to hurt.

Who are you alienated from? Are you in a rocky marriage? Do you have a wayward child? What about the people at work? How about those new next-door neighbors? Is there someone at church? Oh, I know. I really do. When we're hurt, when we're offended, what's our first response? "Someone's gonna pay!"

Read the next sentence very closely. *Someone else has already paid.* Someone else has already paid for all your hurt and for all your rejection. His name is Jesus. Jesus paid it. Jesus paid it all. And Jesus paid it all with His own blood. That's how Jesus makes peace. You can put down your bricks now and stop building walls.

What does Christ have to say about all this? "Blessed are the peacemakers, for they shall be called sons of God" (Matthew 5:9 ESV). Our Savior isn't talking about being a peace-faker. "Wrong? Nothing's wrong! Nothing is ever wrong!" It's easy to pretend. Play the part. Put on a face. And Jesus isn't talking about being a peace-breaker. "It's all your fault! You never do anything right!"

Instead, by the Spirit's working in us, Jesus empowers us to be peacemakers. Peacemakers dare to utter the two hardest words in the English language: "You're right." And the three hardest words: "I was wrong." And the four hardest words: "I don't know everything." And the five hardest words . . . Well, you get the idea!

The only other option? Keep building walls. Day by day, year by year, brick by brick—until we're alone and depressed and then do something that causes irreparable damage to ourselves and those we love.

Is there a better way? Yes. What Moses prays for, God promises and Peter preaches about on Pentecost. Walls come tumbling down. If God says He can, He can. If God says He will, He will. The Holy Spirit is for Eldad, Medad, you, and me!

FEATHERS AND ALL

In the final scene of the chapter, God sends a wind that drops a whole bunch of quail into Israel's lap (Numbers 11:31–35). How much is a whole bunch? "Around the camp, and about two cubits above the ground" (Numbers 11:31 ESV). Two cubits is equivalent to three feet deep. Someone must have yelled, "Free food!" Was there any folding of the hands? Bowing of the head? Giving thanks to God? Who's got time to pray when dinner's on the table? "Those who gathered least gathered ten homers" (Numbers 11:32 ESV).

In antiquity, a homer was equal to what a donkey could carry. Ten homers, then, is the equivalent of thirty-three bushels or 4,915 cups. And that's the least amount people gathered. Just imagine how much those who gathered the most collected. A whole bunch of bird!

The Israelites work feverishly for two days to stockpile as much meat as they can. Then, right when they're ready to chow down, God unleashes a plague. "While the meat was yet between their teeth, before it was consumed, the anger of the LORD was kindled against the people, and the LORD struck down the people with a very great *plague*" (Numbers 11:33 ESV). Just when the greedy grabbers began to enjoy their feast, God judged them. Israel has become like its dreaded enemy—Egypt. Moses names the place "Kibroth-hattaavah," or "Graves of craving."

WHAT ARE YOU HUNGRY FOR?

What are you hungry for? I remember asking my children that question when they were little. We'd be going out for dinner so I'd ask, "What are you hungry for?" Abi would say, "I don't know." Jonathan would say, "I don't know." Little Lori Beth Lessing would say, "I don't know."

What are *you* hungry for? Deep down, what do you really want out of life? Be honest. Is it an early retirement with a golden parachute? Better health? A vacation home in Florida?

Jesus addresses our hunger and thirst. "Blessed are those who hunger and thirst for *righteousness*, for they will be satisfied" (Matthew 5:6 ESV). Jesus invites us to hunger and thirst for God's gift of righteousness. What's that? It's God declaring us not guilty of sin when we trust Christ as our Savior. When we hunger and thirst for this righteousness, then we're satisfied.

I know. Sometimes every bone in our body tells us that seeking divine righteousness is a dead end—some kind of spiritual hocus pocus. Then we seek satisfaction in possessions. Do you realize that there are fifty times as many products on the market today as there were twenty years ago? Are people fifty times more satisfied? What do you think?

When possessions become our go-to source of satisfaction, we become like children making mud pies in a cave. We settle for petty things, small things, fleeting things, transitory things. And Jesus? He lavishly gives unconditional, out-of-this-world, everlasting love that money can't buy, that no one can take away.

How do I experience real satisfaction? Recognize my real hunger. "And He humbled you and let you hunger and fed you with manna that He might make you know that people do not live by bread alone, but by every word that comes from the mouth of the LORD" (Deuteronomy 8:3). God let the Israelites get hungry. Problems came to help them recognize that pleasure, performance, and possessions—in the end—don't fully satisfy.

Christ also calls us to live by God's Word; God's Word that declares us righteousness. In my heart of hearts, my deepest hunger and thirst is to know that I'm accepted, valued, treasured, forgiven, loved. *Righteous*.

Do you want to be satisfied? Recognize your real hunger. Also stop eating junk food. "Why do you spend your money for that which is not bread, and your labor for that which does not satisfy?" (Isaiah 55:2 ESV). Do you know about the nardoo plant? The spores of this clover-fern can be made into bread and porridge. But they contain no proteins, no carbohydrates, and no vitamins. People who eat from nardoo plants get their stomachs filled, but they eventually die. Sound familiar? Stuff fills but it doesn't satisfy. In the end, we spiritually die.

There's a better way. Start looking to Christ. Much of what we hear says, "You can find satisfaction inside yourself." When you're physically hungry, do you tell your stomach to feed itself? Of course not. We have to go to an outside source. The same idea applies to our spiritual lives. When we're spiritually hungry, we've got to go to an outside source. "Jesus said to them, 'I am the bread of life; *whoever* comes to Me shall not hunger and *whoever* believes in Me shall never thirst'" (John 6:35 ESV). Bread is the essential food for physical life. Jesus is the essential food for spiritual life.

Don't you love the word *whoever*? Jesus feeds the broken and the burned out. Jesus feeds the overemployed, the unemployed, and the underemployed. Jesus feeds the emotionally starved and the emotionally dead. *Jesus feeds whoever!*

And more satisfaction is on the way. When Christ returns, we'll be completely satisfied. We will feast on the Bread of Life. We will be refreshed with the water of life. The King of glory will come with perfect healing. Then we'll be perfectly satisfied. *Freely! Absolutely! Eternally!*

CHAPTER 8

GREEN WITH ENVY: NUMBERS 12

Put away all malice and all deceit and hypocrisy and envy and all slander. (1 Peter 2:1 ESV)

What would you think if your little brother was elected president of the United States? Some of you might say, "Super! He deserves it!" Others might move to Canada—or rural Australia. Still others would call a tabloid newspaper and negotiate a deal for easy money!

In Numbers 12, Moses is the little brother and Israel's leader. His older sibs—Aaron and Miriam—are tired of playing second fiddle, so they create a diversion. "Look! Moses' new wife is, of all things, a Cushite!"

MOSES' CUSHITE WIFE

What happened to Moses' first wife, Zipporah? Did she die? Did she return to Midian because of family connections there? Who is this Cushite woman? Where did she meet Moses? And why would she marry an eighty-year-old man whose life consisted of nonstop, round-the-clock work with a bunch of hardened ex-slaves traipsing through a God-forsaken wilderness?

Cush was a kingdom south of Egypt. The prophet Jeremiah indicates that its inhabitants were dark-skinned. The ESV has "Ethiopian" in Jeremiah 13:23, but the Hebrew is more accurately rendered "Cushite," which is how the ESV translates the word in Numbers 12:1. I know—translations can be confusing. This is the world I live in!

What's not confusing is that Moses' new wife was a person of color. True, Israelite law forbade marriages with some non-Israelites—but only residents of Canaan (cf. Exodus 34:15–16; Deuteronomy 7:1–3). This much is also clear: It's anachronistic to suggest that Aaron and Miriam were racists. It wasn't until Europeans began mingling with people from Africa—centuries later—that this kind of racial prejudice reared its ugly head. In all likelihood, Moses' new wife was part of the "mixed multitude" (Exodus 12:38 ESV) who left Egypt, the group also described as the "rabble" (Numbers 11:4 ESV). The chief point is that Aaron and Miriam were seeing their influence with Moses diminish due to his new wife being from outside God's covenant community. And they didn't like it!

Have you ever watched the television game show called *Family Feud*? It started in 1976 and is still going strong. Two families compete against each other to win cash and prizes. The original family feud, however, began in Genesis 3 with Adam versus Eve. Families have been feuding ever since.

And families triangulate. "*They* said, 'Has the LORD indeed spoken only through Moses?'" (Numbers 12:2). Who were "they" speaking to? Aaron and Miriam were speaking with each other—not with Moses. That's called triangulation. And just as the Lord earlier listened to Israel's sour grapes (Numbers 11:1), He also hears what's going on now. "The LORD heard them" (Numbers 12:2).

All of God's creatures with ears have a range of hearing. Some can hear low tones; others can hear highly pitched sounds—like dogs. If you've ever used a dog whistle, you know what I mean. But there's no sound too low or too high that God can't hear. God hears everything. He heard Hagar and Ishmael crying and sent His Messenger to minister to them (Genesis 21:16–18). He heard the groaning of the Hebrews under Egyptian oppression (Exodus 2:24). And, if there was ever a passage to convince us that God hears every word, consider what Jesus says: "But I tell you that men will have to give account on the day of judgment for every careless word they have spoken" (Matthew 12:36).

The real issue at hand in Numbers 12 isn't Moses' marriage—that he married a Cushite woman. That's a smoke screen. Moses' marital status isn't the point. Moses' leadership is. "Has the LORD spoken only through Moses? Hasn't He spoken through us too?" (Numbers 12:2). Moses has something that Aaron and Miriam want. What might that be?

God says of Moses, "I speak to him face to face" (Numbers 12:8). Moses enjoyed unmediated communication with the Lord (cf. Exodus 33:11). Both Miriam and Aaron knew that Moses had a unique relationship with God. Moses called down ten plagues against Egypt. His staff parted the waters of the Red Sea. He spent forty days at the top of Mount Sinai, and God gave him the Ten Commandments. Moses would even come out of the tabernacle with his face glowing with the glory of God. It was preposterous for Miriam and Aaron to demand that God give them the same gifts. Still, they turned green with envy.

ENGULFED IN ENVY

It is reported that after his defeat by John F. Kennedy in the 1960 US presidential election, Richard Nixon commented on Kennedy's inaugural presidential address, saying that he wished he could've said something in Kennedy's speech. When asked what part, Nixon replied, "This part: 'I do solemnly swear that I will faithfully execute the Office of President of the United States.'" Richard Nixon wanted something that John F. Kennedy had. That's spelled E-N-V-Y.

What's the leading cause of envy? Here are some hints. It launched in 2004. It's a two-syllable word. Today it has close to three billion monthly users. Any guesses? It's called Facebook. Facebook has created a new kind of envy.

I'm scrolling through my newsfeed, and I see someone from my high school class driving a new BMW. In the next frame, I see someone vacationing in Hawaii—for the 117th time. In the next frame, I see that perfect family of five, so happy, so together, so tanned—so not my family.

Detecting envy is demanding. Defeating envy is difficult. Denying envy is disastrous.

Have you ever caught yourself comparing your life to someone else's? "He has a trophy wife." "She's more beautiful than I'll ever be." "Compared to their home, ours looks like a two-man tent." We're never good enough. Satan knows the feeling. "I will ascend above the heights of the clouds; I will make myself like the Most High" (Isaiah 14:14 ESV).

When I'm dominated by envy, I don't enjoy God's gifts—my life, my home, my job. To be satisfied, I need something bigger, prettier, nicer, more expensive, and more important. What happened to Satan when he envied God? "You are brought down to Sheol, to the far reaches of the pit" (Isaiah 14:15 ESV). There's only one way to go when we get sucked into the world of envy. Down. Way down.

When my life's desire is to become the brightest and the best, I'll always find someone to envy. Why? Because then I'm competing for votes, attention, applause, and affirmation—and there's only so much of that to go around.

I'll put it bluntly. When we compare, we devalue our own worth by measuring ourselves against others, often leading to feelings of inadequacy, envy, and despair—sometimes mildly, sometimes monumentally. Why play a game that we always lose? Luke records two incidents when the disciples asked, "Who matters most?" (cf. Luke 9:46–48; 22:24–27). Let me paraphrase Christ's answer both times: "You're asking the wrong question."

Comparing ourselves with others is a sin we all struggle with—which means we need Gospel rescuing and Gospel redeeming. Envy reveals that I need to pursue satisfaction in the only one who can fill the deepest longings of my heart—Christ Jesus, our Lord.

Here's a place to start. Respect others' callings. God wonderfully gifted Aaron and Miriam and called them into key leadership roles in Israel. He gave Aaron and his descendants the duty of caring for the tabernacle (Numbers 1:47–53; 3:5–39; 4:1–49). God called Miriam to lead the women in singing after Pharaoh's horses and chariots drowned in the Red Sea. She's even termed a prophetess (Exodus 15:20). And Moses? God called him to serve as Israel's leader. He was God's "the-buck-stops-here" man.

Order and authority are important features throughout the book of Numbers. For instance, in chapter 2, God establishes four lead tribes—Judah, Reuben, Ephraim, and Dan (Numbers 2:9, 16, 24, 31). When Israel was on the march, some tribes advanced first and other tribes followed. The nation was moving toward the same goal, so it didn't matter if some were more prominent than others.

Paul makes the same point in 1 Corinthians 12. Some parts of the church are more important than others—but it takes the entire church for it to function properly. We're all part of the same Gospel mission. Jesus is the Head; we're part of His Body, the church. Here's a summary of Paul's discourse on spiritual gifts in 1 Corinthians 12–14: "Don't be obsessed with leading. Be obsessed with loving." The church isn't only a Body; it also consists of stones from the same temple (Ephesians 2:20–21) as well as different branches from the same vine (John 15:5). In every case, Christ is at the center. We're not.

The solution to envy, therefore, isn't to deny differences or pretend we have the same gifts and callings. The solution is to realize that we're on the same team. Do you know how to spell team? Together. Everyone. Achieves. More. Peter forgot all about this.

After Christ rose from the grave, He absolved Peter for denying Him three times. Then Jesus tells Peter how he'll die. Peter turns, looks at John, and asks Jesus about John's death. "Lord, what about this man?" (John 21:21 ESV).

Isn't that just like Peter? So easily distracted. So focused on the wrong thing—in this case, John. Be honest though. How often do you ask Jesus, "What about her?" "What about him?" "What about them?" Who do you compare yourself with? A sibling? A coworker? A friend from high school or college? Your next-door neighbor who owns a boat, camper, three snowmobiles, and a cabin on the lake?

GOD'S RESPONSE TO ENVY

God judges envious people. "As the cloud moved from above the tabernacle, there stood Miriam, her skin as white as snow from leprosy" (Numbers 12:10). Why does God take such a hard line against envy? After all, it's not like Miriam killed someone or robbed a bank or cheated on her spouse. "Come on, God. Be fair. It's just a little envy!"

Don't put this book down, go for a walk, or turn on the television because of what I'm about to say. Are you ready? Here it comes. Envy is blasphemy. "Blasphemy? That sounds way over the top!" Hear me out. Envy is blasphemy because it says, "God, You made a mistake. You don't know what You're doing. If You'd let me run the universe, everything would be so much better." I can't build a life of faith on a foundation that doubts God's goodness and wisdom.

This is what we need to say when we envy: "God, in Your perfect wisdom and sovereignty, You gave that person what You want that person to have. God, in Your perfect wisdom and sovereignty, You gave me what You want me to have." Why is that prayer so important? *I can't build a life of faith on a foundation that doubts God's goodness and God's wisdom.*

Aren't you tired of "If I only had" thinking? "If I only had house like his. If I only had a job like hers. If we only had a bank balance like theirs." Happiness isn't getting what we want. Happiness is enjoying who we have. Whom do we have? Whom do we have that beats envy every time? Every. Single. Time. We have Jesus and His over-the-top devotion and love for us, forever.

WINNING VERSUS SUCCEEDING

God has given each of us gifts. Just not the same gifts He's given others. Here's a verse I've been chewing on for decades but have a difficult time implementing: "When they measure themselves by one another and compare themselves with one another, they are not wise" (2 Corinthians 10:12). When I measure myself and compare myself with others, I'm not being wise. There will always be someone with more money, more property, more stuff, more publications, more members, more awards, more recognition, more achievement—and, since I'm only five-foot-eight, there will always be someone who's a whole lot taller!

We see envy everywhere. Married people envy the freedom of single people. Single people envy the family life of married people. People in one job envy the people who have another job. And the people with the other job envy people who have another job. We envy the looks, the income, the house, the spouse, the children, the parents, the intellect, the athletic ability, and the sense of humor that others have. The list is limitless.

I'm *not* saying, "Don't strive. Don't set goals. Don't try to improve." Do all of that. But when you do, compare yourself today with where you were yesterday and with where God is taking you tomorrow. What do I need to do to up *my* game? That's the question. It's not about competing with others. Focus on self-improvement, not one-upmanship. Choosing this mindset is far more productive, fulfilling, and godly.

In other words, there's a big difference between winning and succeeding. Do you want to win your next half-marathon? That's fine. But most of the time, we're not running a race. Most of the time, there's no need to place first. Most of the time, our best goal is to become the best version of ourselves—confident that Jesus, who began a good work in us, will complete it when He returns (cf. Philippians 1:6).

WE ENVY WHEN WE FORGET WHO WE ARE

Aaron and Miriam became envious of Moses because they forgot who they were. Take a look at Micah 6:4, where God says, "For I brought you up from the land of Egypt and redeemed you from the house of slavery, and I sent before you Moses, Aaron, and Miriam" (ESV). Moses, Aaron, and Miriam—all three—played a part in Israel's exodus from Egypt. All three were at the top of Israel's organizational chart, but Aaron and Miriam forgot who they were. Enter envy.

John Newton (1725–1808), the author of the hymn "Amazing Grace," didn't forget who he was. He prepared this epitaph for his gravestone: "John Newton, clerk, once an infidel and libertine, a servant of slaves in Africa, was, by the rich mercy of our Lord and Savior Jesus Christ, preserved, restored, pardoned, and appointed to preach the faith he had long labored to destroy."

Remembering who we are in God's eyes is an effective way to defeat envy. Think, right now, who you are in Jesus Christ. Baptized. Washed. Cleansed. Chosen. Precious. Loved. Forgiven. Think, right now, what you *will be* in Jesus Christ. Perfect. Glorious. With angels and archangels and all the company in heaven!

GOD JUDGES MIRIAM

The ESV translates Numbers 12:1 (and most other English translations are similar) as, "Miriam and Aaron began to talk." However, the word in Hebrew is better rendered "*she* began to talk." What's the point? Miriam instigates the brouhaha in Numbers 12:1.

"*She* began to talk"! This explains why God punishes Miriam with a skin infection and not Aaron. When Moses later rehearses the events in Numbers 12, he points his accusing finger at Miriam—not at Aaron. "Remember what the Lord your God did to Miriam on the way as you came out of Egypt" (Deuteronomy 24:8 ESV).

Divine anger was kindled in Numbers 11:1, 33—both times there were deadly ramifications. We expect, then, the same results with Miriam and Aaron. Instead, Aaron goes scot-free. And Miriam? God judges her with a skin disease. (For the record, it isn't leprosy, or what's often called Hanson's disease.) The infection, whatever it was, not only impacted skin but also clothing and houses (Leviticus 13–14). Those who had it were forced to live alone and in a state of uncleanness, outside of Israel's camp (Leviticus 13:46). Although Miriam doesn't die from the disease, she looks like a stillborn baby (Numbers 12:12). A stillborn baby has only one hope—to be born again.

BORN AGAIN

When I first got into texting, my daughters would sometimes end their texts with "lol." I was touched by this display of affection—assuming that "lol" meant "lots of love." I began putting "lol" at the end of my texts, thinking I was on the cutting edge of texting. Then, one day, my youngest daughter, Lori, explained to me that "lol" meant "laugh out loud." Who knew? Jargon! "Born again" often sounds like jargon—religious jargon. It means, though, so much more.

Do you know the most quoted Bible verse in America? "God helps those who help themselves." There's a problem with that. It's not in the Bible! God doesn't help those who help themselves. God knows we can't help ourselves. God knows He has to do 100 percent of the work for our salvation. That's why Jesus uses the word "born" eight times in the first eight verses of John 3. What does a child do to be born? Is he in radio communication with his mother, telling her when to push? Does the child place her hands against the top of the womb and push herself out? Here's the point. People are passive when they're born. People don't do a thing. Mothers do all the work. The same is true for our spiritual birth. God does all the work.

In His nighttime discussion with Nicodemus, Jesus tells him, "I tell you the truth, no one can enter the kingdom of God unless he is born of *water* and the *Spirit*" (John 3:5). We're born again by water and the Spirit. What's that called? Holy Baptism.

Water and the Spirit first appear together in Genesis 1:2: "The *Spirit* of God was moving over the *water*." The Holy Spirit moves over water, creating life. Just so, the Holy Spirit moves over water again when we're baptized in the name of the Father, Son, and Holy Spirit. The Holy Spirit is creating new life.

God commanded Moses to banish people who had a skin disease (Numbers 5:2) for seven days (Leviticus 13:5). This is now Miriam's sentence. Moses writes, "Keep her outside the camp for seven days, and after that *she will be accepted*" (Numbers 12:14). "She will be accepted" is one word in Hebrew. And it's a passive verb. Miriam doesn't do anything. God does everything. After her seven-day isolation, "Miriam was brought in again" (Numbers 12:15 ESV). Miriam reenters the community. God gives her a new beginning. God gives her a new life. That sounds like what? Holy Baptism.

Through water and God's Word in Holy Baptism, we're new too! We have new eyes to see God's beauty, a new mind to understand God's Word, a new voice to sing God's praises, new hands for God's service, and new feet to run the race of faith. And most important of all, we have a new heart, pulsating with love for God and for people. Born again is more than just jargon. Born again means we live now *in* Christ and will live forever *with* Christ.

THE DESTROYER OF WORLDS

How did the kerfuffle between Moses, Aaron, and Miriam begin? The first word in the Hebrew of Numbers 12 can be translated "And she said." It began with words. Welcome to the horror show. What's it called? "The Destroyer of Worlds."

On July 16, 1945, the first atomic bomb was tested near Alamogordo, New Mexico. On that day J. Robert Oppenheimer, the bomb's creator, famously quoted an ancient Hindu proverb: "I am become Death, the destroyer of worlds." The nuclear age had begun.

Sometimes our tongues are the destroyer of worlds. The nuclear age continues.

James has a lot to say about this. Forty-six of his letter's 108 verses—or 43 percent of the book—address our use of words. Put another way, two out of every five verses in James have something to say about verbal bombs. Here are some samples:

> We use self-justifying words, accusing God. (James 1:13)
>
> We use flattering words, showing partiality toward the rich. (James 2:3–6)

We use careless words, wishing well toward the poor but not helping them. (James 2:16)

We use superficial words, claiming to have faith. (James 2:17)

We use judgmental words, slandering other people. (James 4:11)

We use presumptuous words, boasting about the future. (James 4:13)

We use negative words, grumbling against others. (James 5:9)

More than a decade ago, the total amount of digital information in the world reached a zettabyte, or one billion terabytes. Huh? A zettabyte is a multiple of the unit byte that measures digital storage, and it's equivalent to one with twenty-one zeros after it. That's a number of words so large that it boggles our minds. Yet words are more than shapes on a screen, sounds from our mouths, or markings on a page. Words do more than convey information. Words have power—to console and crush, to lift up and cast down.

Chapter 3 records James's most sustained discussion on the tongue. It's the most thorough discussion on words in the entire Bible. James begins, "If anyone is never at fault in what he says, he is a mature person, able to keep his whole body in check" (James 3:2). It's immature to be reckless with words, whether they're words on social media, words in texts and emails, or audible words that come from our mouths. A major mark of Christian maturity is that I don't drop verbal bombs. How important is it that we listen to James?

My tongue directs where I go. "When we put bits into the mouths of horses to make them obey us, we can turn the whole animal. Or take ships as an example. Although they are so large and are driven by strong winds, they are steered by a very small rudder wherever the pilot wants to go" (James 3:3–4). What does the tongue have in common with bits in the mouths of horses and ship rudders? All three are small. All three direct where we go.

In the first example, James observes that horse riders place a bit, a relatively small instrument, into the horse's mouth. A 2,500-pound horse is controlled by a one-pound bit. In his next illustration, James invites us to consider something much larger than a horse—a ship. Despite its size (indeed, it's so big that it requires strong winds to move it along the water), a comparatively little rudder guides the ship. The *Queen Mary* has three acres of recreational space. The anchor on the *Queen Mary* is equal to the weight of ten cars. And yet a small rudder directs the huge ship.

Our tongue is like that rudder, like that bit in a horse's mouth. How? It directs where we go. If you don't like the way your life is going, then change the way you talk.

My tongue can destroy what I have. "Likewise the tongue is a small part of the body, but it makes great boasts. Consider what a great forest is set on fire by a small spark" (James 3:5). Once again the apostle points to something that's small—a spark. But a spark can consume what is massive—a great forest. By now James's point is clear: Relative to its size, the tongue wields disproportionate power.

And, just in case we miss his earlier points, James puts it bluntly: "The tongue also is a fire, a world of evil among the parts of the body. It corrupts the whole person, sets the whole course of his life on fire, and is itself set on fire by hell" (James 3:6). In the wrong place, at the wrong time, everything can go up in smoke. Fire consumes the whole forest.

Hell. James says that's where our tongue takes us. In Greek, the word *hell* is *Gehenna*. It's a compound of two words: *ge*, which means "valley," and *henna*, which denotes "Hinnom." Gehenna is the Valley of Hinnom. In the Old Testament, it was Jerusalem's garbage dump. It was also where parents would sacrifice their children, then burn their bodies. Never one to mince words, James says that's where our tongues take us—into a putrid garbage dump where people are scorched. Words out of control consume family members and business partners, as well as brothers and sisters in Christ.

James isn't finished. "All kinds of animals, birds, reptiles and creatures of the sea are being tamed and have been tamed by people, but no one can tame the tongue. It is a restless evil, full of deadly poison" (James 3:7–8). Just think of all the animals we've tamed. Lassie, Trigger, Flipper, Shamu, Benjie, Clyde the orangutan, and Mister Ed. We've tamed "lions and tigers and bears, oh my!" But we can't tame the tongue.

My tongue displays who I am. "With the tongue we praise our Lord and Father, and with it we curse people, who have been made in God's likeness. Out of the same mouth come praise and *cursing*. My brothers, this should not be" (James 3:9–10). James 1:8 and 4:8 both employ the term *double-minded*. Double-mindedness is on full display when it comes to the tongue. We use it to praise our Lord and Father, then we curse those created in God's likeness. The word *cursing* doesn't imply profanity. It means any kind of put-down: being sarcastic, jaded, cynical, or just plain ol' mean.

The heart of our problem, Miriam's problem, and Aaron's problem isn't the tongue. The heart of the problem is the problem in the heart. "The good person out of the good treasure of his *heart* produces good, and the evil person out of his evil treasure produces evil, for out of the abundance of the *heart* his mouth speaks" (Luke 6:45 ESV).

A HEART TRANSPLANT

The first person to receive a heart transplant was Louis Washkansky of Cape Town, South Africa, in December of 1967. He lived for another eighteen days. The first American to receive a heart transplant was Donald Thomas in January of 1968. He lived for eight more months.

I have good news for you! There's a Heart Surgeon who guarantees His work forever. He's competent and kind, trustworthy and true. His office is open 24/7/365. God says, "I will remove from you your heart of stone and give you a heart of flesh" (Ezekiel 36:26). A heart of stone is what we have—hard, unfeeling, callous, dead. A heart of flesh is what God gives—beating, soft, supple, alive.

I know what you're saying, "I'll try some medicine. Or maybe I'll undergo a heart bypass surgery. I'll even lose some weight and begin an exercise regimen. But a heart transplant? Thanks, but no thanks. That's too radical, too evasive, too much!" This is what's killing us. You need a new heart. I need a new heart. We all need a new heart. And Jesus gives it freely.

Though a new heart costs us nothing, it cost Jesus everything. Watch Him walk the via dolorosa, the way of sorrows, on His way to Calvary. Look as Jesus gives His back to those who whip Him, His face to those who beat Him, His head for the thorns, His body and blood for the life of the world.

Heart transplant surgery will change you and your words. I invite you to set up an appointment with your doctor today. He's alive and ready at your beck and call. What does our life look like post op? Our tongues are transformed from hammers that do great harm to scalpels that bring great healing.

LET IT GO

Miriam saved Moses from drowning in the Nile River (Exodus 2:1–10). Now Moses returns the favor. When Aaron asks him, Moses intercedes for Miriam without delay. "Moses cried to the LORD, 'O God, please heal her—please'" (Numbers 12:13 ESV).

Moses could have made Miriam wait a day or two. That would teach her a lesson. "Don't you ever mess with me again!" Moses could've spread the news far and wide: "Come see my stupid sister and what God did to her!" But no. Moses prays for her. There's no "gotcha." No revenge. No bitterness. Just mercy. Moses lets it go.

Ancient Romans in England? Not on your life!

A few years ago, archaeologists unearthed a two-thousand-year-old Roman worship center in Bath, England. Romans had gathered there to worship their gods and goddesses like Neptune, Diana, Apollo, Minerva, and Jupiter. Excavators—digging under this center—unearthed hundreds of two-thousand-year-old clay tablets that had written on them prayers to these gods. Archaeologists called them "curse prayers."

Here's an example: "Docimedus has lost two gloves. He asks that the person who has stolen them should lose his mind and his eyes." No matter how much you love your gloves, this is a bit over the top, don't you think? Here's another curse prayer: "Tie up, block, strike, overthrow, harm, destroy, kill, and shatter Eucherios the charioteer. Let the starting gates not open properly. Let him not pass. Let him not make the turn properly. Let him not come from behind but instead let him collapse, let him be bound, let him be broken up, and let him drag behind. Now. Now. Quickly. Quickly!"

How many "Bless my enemy prayers" on clay tablets do you think archaeologists found? None. Nil. Nada. What does that tell us? Forgiveness was hard yesterday. Forgiveness is hard today. Forgiveness will be hard tomorrow.

We all get stuck in a muddy ditch called revenge. I once talked to a woman who, when she was six years old, was abandoned by her mother. The dad and daughter stumbled through life as best they could. Then, out of nowhere, twenty years later, the mom reappeared, asking for a coffee date with her now grown-up daughter. The mom said, "I'm very sorry for leaving you, but I'd like to reenter your life."

That's it? The daughter is supposed to forgive her long-lost mother? Just like that? Doesn't the mother need to get a little of what she gave? A few years of wondering if she'll ever see her daughter again? Some sleepless nights? A bit of well-deserved suffering and pain?

There are countless ways to settle the score. Silence is a popular technique. Ignore them when they email or text you. Distance is equally effective. When they come your way, walk on the other side of the street. Nagging is another tool for revenge. "Oh, I see you still have fingers on your hand. Funny you never use them to call or text me."

If I can foil one Friday, soil one Saturday, spoil one Sunday, then justice is served and I'm happy—for now. Until I think of that person again. Until I see her again. Until something happens that brings to mind the deed he did. Then I'll demand another pound of flesh. As long as I hurt, she'll hurt. As long as I suffer, he'll suffer. As long as I bleed, she'll bleed. Hurt becomes hate, and hate becomes rage. "What about the parent who abandoned me when I was in college?" "What about my husband who dumped me for a newer model?" "What about the boss who laid me off when my son was dying in the hospital?"

Christ invites us to stop focusing on what they did and start focusing on what He did. "But that's not fair! She doesn't deserve to be forgiven." I agree. I couldn't agree more. None of us is worthy of grace. None of us deserves forgiveness.

Our only other option is what? Hatred. Hatred is like a crack in our windshield. Thanks to a dump truck on I-94 a few summers ago, my window was nicked. In time the nick became a crack. The crack became a winding river. And the winding river became an ugly spiderweb. Hatred makes everything in life look ugly—really, really ugly.

The wisest choice, the only sane choice, is what? Drop the anger. Forgive. Let it go. That's what Moses did with Miriam. More to the point, that's what Jesus does with us.

CHAPTER 9

TWELVE MEN WENT TO SPY ON CANAAN: NUMBERS 13

Perfect love casts out fear. (1 John 4:18 ESV)

CANAANITE TRIBES AND THE ROUTE OF THE 12 SPIES

Numbers 13; Joshua 3:10

One afternoon three turtles went out for a picnic. Soon they felt raindrops. "We can't have a picnic without an umbrella," the first turtle said. "Who will go back for one?" asked the second turtle. Quickly the third turtle was chosen to go get an umbrella. "I won't go," he protested. "As soon as I go, you'll eat all the sandwiches and drink all the turtle-aid." "No way," responded the other two turtles. "We'll wait for you, no matter how long!" "No matter how long?" "No matter how long!" So the third turtle went to get an umbrella.

An hour passed, and the other two turtles sat there, waiting. Then a day, then a week, then two weeks. Three weeks later, one turtle turned to another and said, "Maybe we should go ahead with the picnic." Just then the third turtle popped out from behind the bushes and announced, "If you do, I won't go!"

Numbers 1:3 gives the reason for Israel's first census count in the book: to find out how many Israelite men "are able to go to war" (ESV). In Numbers 2, Moses organizes the twelve tribes into an army. Fast-forward to the end of Numbers 12. Israelites are camped "in the wilderness of Paran" (Numbers 12:16 ESV). The army has arrived at its staging area! Then, for the first time in the book, the term *Canaan* appears (Numbers 13:2). Israel is almost there! The rocket is ready to launch! But it doesn't happen. In Numbers 13–14, almost to a person, each Israelite says, "I won't go!"

Rebellion begins on the fringes of the camp (Numbers 11:1), engulfs the nation (Numbers 11:4–35), then strikes at the heart of Israel's leadership (Numbers 12). What's left? Total anarchy. That's what happens in Numbers 13–14, where, for the first time, we read about the Israelites making concrete plans to go back to Egypt.

THE DEFINING STORY IN NUMBERS

Almost everything from Genesis 12 through Numbers 12 anticipates Israel's entrance into Canaan. Then, just when the nation is ready to march into the Promised Land, their faith fails. Numbers 13–14 tell us about the collapse. It's the book's central and defining story. The two chapters are closely linked to the census reports in Numbers 1 and 26. These twin peaks announce the book's main motif—two generations. Parents who left Egypt and their children. The first failed miserably. The second succeeded overwhelmingly.

Moses ties these two generations to Numbers 13–14. First, he repeats the expression "every one of you twenty years old or more" (Numbers 14:29) that comes fifteen times in chapter 1 (e.g., Numbers 1:3, 18, 20, 36, 45). Second, he composes the second census to end with a summary of the spy disaster (Numbers 26:63–65).

The rest of the Bible has a lot more to say about Numbers 13–14. Moses' final sermon in Deuteronomy refers to Israel's collapse (e.g., Deuteronomy 32:5, 15, 19–20). Then, hundreds of years later, several psalmists reflect on Israel's utter failure (e.g., Psalm 78; 106). Finally, in the New Testament, both 1 Corinthians 10:1–13 and Hebrews 3–4 make much of Israel's unwillingness to follow God's leading into the Promised Land. What was at the heart of one of Israel's greatest debacles? Pride. "We know so much more than God does!"

BLINDED BY PRIDE

Field of Dreams is one of my favorite movies. Kevin Costner plays Ray Kinsella, who turns an Iowa cornfield into a baseball field after hearing the mysterious promise that if he builds it, they would come. Who would come? Well, long-dead major league baseball players—including Shoeless Joe Jackson of the Chicago White Sox. Ray has two problems. First, the baseball players are invisible to almost everyone else. Second, he's going bankrupt because he's used so much farmland to build his field of dreams.

Ray's brother-in-law, Mark, is beside himself. At one point in the movie, Mark yells at Ray, saying he's going to lose the farm; he built a baseball field, and now he just sits there and stares at nothing. But then, Mark sees what Ray has seen all along and does a one-eighty. "Ray! Don't sell the farm! Whatever you do, Ray, don't sell this farm!" Mark had been blind, but now he could see.

What blinded the Israelites from seeing God's power and promises? Pride. They thought they knew more than God—much more. "We're in charge here, and we have a superior plan!" The following verses will give you a feel for what's ahead:

> We are not able to go up against the people, for they are stronger than we are. (Numbers 13:31 ESV)
>
> The land, through which we have gone to spy it out, is a land that devours its inhabitants. (Numbers 13:32 ESV)
>
> Would that we had died in the land of Egypt! Or would that we had died in this wilderness! (Numbers 14:2 ESV)
>
> Let us choose a leader and go back to Egypt. (Numbers 14:4 ESV)

Did the Israelites ever see the light? Sadly, the answer is no. Pride blinded them. Pride blinded them for the rest of their lives.

HISTORIC HEBRON

Moses sends twelve spies on a reconnaissance mission to check out Canaan's inhabitants. He wants a report on their military and fortifications, as well as their land's fertility and food resources. Israel's scouts head north, through the wilderness of Zin, the Negev, and the hill country. They continue northward—as far as Damascus. That's close to five hundred miles round trip, on foot!

Along the way, the spies pass through Hebron (Numbers 13:22). That's like visiting Plymouth Rock, Gettysburg, or Washington, DC. Hebron was one of Israel's most historic places. Hebron was where God reaffirmed His land promise to Abraham (Genesis 13:14–18), where Abraham bought the cave of Machpelah (Genesis 23), and where Abraham (Genesis 25:9) and others were buried (Genesis 35:27–29; 50:13). Hebron was Israel's down payment in the days of the patriarchs. *More land was on the way.*

Thus, Hebron was central to God's promise of Canaan. Surely Israel's scouts remembered. But did it stir their faith? Change their perspective? It did for Joshua and Caleb. The others? Nowhere close.

I SPY

Have you ever played the game I spy? I bet you have. It's a guessing game. One person—the "spy"—chooses something within everyone's sight. Then, the spy says, "I spy something with my little eye, something beginning with . . ." Then she names the first letter of the object.

Ten of Israel's twelve spies return from their mission and say, "I spy something with my little eye, something beginning with *g*." G stands for giants—really big giants!

The book of Numbers didn't need thirty-six chapters. Had the events in chapters 13 and 14 gone as planned, Numbers would have been the shortest book in the Pentateuch—I'd guess about twenty-two chapters. This takes into consideration God's need to issue several more instructions (Numbers 28–30), Reuben's and Gad's territorial allotments (Numbers 32), a list of the nation's itinerary from Sinai to the Promised Land (Numbers 33), and a few more decrees (Numbers 34–36).

TEN WERE BAD AND TWO WERE GOOD

I bet you recognize the words to this song: "Twelve men went to spy out Canaan. (Ten were bad and two were good.) What do you think they saw in Canaan? (Ten were bad and two were good.) Some saw giants big and tall. Some saw grapes in clusters fall. Some saw God was in it all. (Ten were bad and two were good.)"

Israel's ten bad spies, Shammau, Shaphat, Igal, Palti, Gaddiel, Gaddi, Ammiel, Sethur, Nahbi, and Geuel, lived in fear. The two good spies, Joshua and Caleb—lived in faith. The same decision faces us on a regular basis. Will we live in fear? "Some saw giants big and tall." Will we live in faith? "Some saw the Lord in it all."

Here's an acronym for fear: Forget Everything And Run. Forget everything God has promised. Forget your Baptism, forget Christ's forgiveness, forget the Gospel. Forget everything and run. Run for your life!

The second option is to live in faith. Here's an acronym for faith: Forward All Issues To Heaven. *Forward.* Don't hold on to it or obsess over it. *All.* Not some, not most, not a lot. All. All your nightmares. All your worry. All your future plans. *Issues.* Issues like past regrets, past sin, past mistakes. *To Heaven.* Where God is. After all, He made heaven and earth. One of the most important questions we answer every day is this: Will I live in fear or live in faith?

God commands Moses, "Send men to spy out the land of Canaan that *I am giving* to the people of Israel" (Numbers 13:2). Is there a question mark in this sentence? Does God say, "That I might give"? "That I could give"? "That I may give if you show Me you're worthy?" No. God says, "I am giving." And the Bible keeps saying this:

> The land the Lord promised them on oath. (Numbers 14:16)
>
> The land I promised on oath to their forefathers. (Numbers 14:23)
>
> The land I am giving you. (Numbers 15:2)

In spite of God's intent, "Some saw giants, big and tall!" How did the ten spies only see difficulties and dilemmas? Closely read these two verses. "We went into the land to which you sent us" (Numbers 13:27). "The land we explored" (Numbers 13:32). Now compare these passages with the three cited above. Do you recognize the difference? For Shammau, Shaphat, Igal, and the others, Canaan was the land where God sent them. Canaan was land they explored. Canaan wasn't the land God had promised to Abraham, Isaac, and Jacob—as a gift. Canaan wasn't the land God had been steering the nation toward for the last five hundred years. It makes sense that the ten spies lived in fear; they thought they knew better than to trust divine promises. Pride does that every time.

The Roman poet Horace once wrote, "It is sweet and fitting to die for one's country." What noble words. What great conviction. But what a hard act to follow! During the Battle of Philippi in 42 BC, Horace ran from the battlefield—even tossing his shield by the wayside as he fled. It's easy to spout off pious sentiments. It's much harder to follow through in the heat of the battle.

Look at Israel's ten faithless spies. They not only ignore God's promises to the patriarchs; they also become overwhelmed by massive obstacles—large, fortified cities (ancient Canaanite cities had walls thirty to fifty feet high and fifteen feet thick), Amalekites (on the southern border), Hittites (around Hebron), Jebusites (in Jerusalem), Amorites (in the hills), and Canaanites (along the Mediterranean coast and valleys).

Yet these ten spies had witnessed God's power in Egypt; they saw locusts gobble up crops and flies buzz through Pharaoh's court. Right before their eyes God turned the chest-thumping Egyptians into lightweights and losers. Now, within sight of their goal, these spies forget it all.

We get it. Giants show up in our boardrooms, waiting rooms, living rooms, and conference rooms. Fear ties stomachs in knots. Fear sets faith on the shelf. Fear twists everything out of perspective. When fear pushes us hard, we give up convictions and turn into cowards. Fear's favorite question is "What if?" "What if I don't make the team? What if I don't make the sale? What if they don't like me? What if I fail *again*?"

It's happening all around us. The land of the Stars and Stripes has become the land of the dismayed and doomed. And it's costing us mucho dinero. We spend over three hundred billion dollars each year on fear-related issues that require surgeries, therapists, rehab centers, and medications. Since 1994, Americans have more than doubled their usage of Valium and Xanax.

Frequently we're visited by fear of the future. Another word for that is chronophobia. Chronophobia? It's a compound of two Greek words: *chrono* means "time" and *phobia* means "fear." Will my children be okay? My grandchildren? Will I have enough money? Will I stay healthy?

What about my job and investments and the bad actors in Russia, Iran, China, and elsewhere? Fear of the future prompts us to make dreadful decisions, form dreadful habits, and get into dreadful relationships.

We can stay in bed, but that may make us one of the half million Americans who end up in the emergency room each year for injuries sustained while in bed. We can cover our windows, but that may make us one of the ten Americans each year who accidentally get stuck on the cords of their venetian blinds. Chronophobia experts tell us that fear of the future leads to risk-lock: a condition that—like gridlock—leaves us unable to do anything or go anywhere. Then what do we do when faced with an obstacle? Forget everything and run!

Where do we run? Some run for another drink. Others run for more work. Still others run for more fantasy, more vacations, more money, more illicit sex. You name it, and we've probably run to it. And in every case, what happened? After a quick rush, all we had was dust in our hands and dirt in our hearts.

There's a story about a thief who was captured and sentenced to death by a general in the Persian army. This general had the strange custom of giving condemned criminals a choice between a firing squad and opening a big, black door. As the moment for execution drew near, the thief was brought to the Persian general, who asked, "What will it be: the firing squad or the big, black door?" The thief hesitated. It was a difficult decision. He chose the firing squad. Moments later, shots rang out, confirming the execution. The general's aide asked, "What lies beyond the door?" "Freedom," replied the general, "but people prefer the known to the unknown." Why? It's called fear.

God calms our fears, often not by removing our problems but by showing us grace and mercy in Jesus. Finally, a place for our fears. At the foot of the cross, at the feet of Jesus, in the presence of our Savior, who says, "I carried all your sin. I will certainly carry whatever frightens you. Stop doubting and believe."

EXAGGERATIONS

We all exaggerate. "This weighs a ton!" "I was dying of laughter." "He runs like the wind!" None of this hurts a soul. So what if someone says, "I could eat a horse"? Big deal.

On the other hand, sometimes we exaggerate when we don't want to do something. "It's too cold out! And the stores will be too crowded! And besides, the lines will be too long!"

A deadly exaggeration epidemic ran rampant among the Israelites. They exaggerated how good the food was in Egypt and—in the same sentence—disregarded Pharaoh's tyrannical oppression, saying that the seven-course meals were always free (Numbers 11:5). Now they overemphasize Canaan's military strength and underemphasize the land's abundance (Numbers 13:23–33).

Fear causes us to distort reality and blow things out of proportion. Scared stiff, we understate God's power and overstate our hardships. Doubt and dread coax us into misrepresenting the facts. The facts? "God is giving us this land" (Numbers 13:2).

Here's another exaggeration. It's a doozy. "The land devours its inhabitants" (Numbers 13:32). Really? Valleys and mountains and hills and plains sit down for a meal and eat people? This sounds like a Hollywood horror movie. "The Return of the Human-Eating Humus!" Come on. Who are these people kidding?

That's what fear does. We begin seeing a monster behind every corner and a boogeyman under every bed. A spark becomes a raging wildfire. A cough and a sniffle become the sentence of death. Any setback becomes the end of the world.

Israel's faithless scouts go further: "We saw the Nephilim" (Numbers 13:33 ESV). Wait a minute. The Nephilim last appeared before the worldwide flood, Noah's ark, and the rainbow. And now they've returned? The heroes of old, the men of renown, are back? (Cf. Genesis 6:4.) How could they? Everyone but Noah and his family were wiped out by the flood.

When I was a child, my dad would occasionally take me into downtown Denver. While not Chicago or New York, to a little six-year-old, Denver appeared to be the largest city on the planet. What did my dad do? Give me a map? Loan me his compass? Challenge me to dodge the traffic, weave my way through the crowds, and find my way home by myself? Instead, he reached out and said, "Reed, hold my hand." God does the same for us. From His tender heart, He says, "I will uphold you with My righteous right hand" (Isaiah 41:10 ESV).

The next time you're faced with a daunting challenge, resist the urge to fabricate and overstate. Stay calm. Trust your heavenly Father. For Him, no problem is difficult, no pain is too deep, and no life is too far gone. And this, my friend, is no exaggeration.

"HONEY, I SHRUNK THE LORD"

Honey, I Shrunk the Kids is the name of a 1989 movie that I've seen 681 times—and counting! An inventor with his electromagnetic shrinking machine accidentally reduces his kids to a quarter of an inch. Then he unintentionally throws them out with the trash.

"Honey, I shrunk the Lord!" That's what happened to the ten spies. "We seemed to ourselves like grasshoppers, and so we seemed to them" (Numbers 13:33 ESV). When we shrink the Lord, we shrink ourselves. "We've become like tiny bugs. Giants will step on us and squash us to smithereens!" Canaan is doom and gloom and a huge darkroom.

On the other hand, Joshua and Caleb have great faith in their great God. They saw grapes from clusters fall. They saw the Lord in it all!

None of the twelve spies disputed that the land was flowing with milk and honey. None of them denied that there were fortified cities. None of them discounted the fact that Canaanites represented a formidable force. The twelve did, however, disagree on where to put the "but."

Everything goes swimmingly through Numbers 13:27. But in Numbers 13:28, the ten spies utter the word *but*. And this derails the entire train. Kissing cousins to *but* include *on the other hand*, *along with that*, and *nevertheless*. *But* becomes the nail in the coffin for the adults who left Egypt. "They told Moses, 'We came to the land to which you sent us. It flows with milk and honey, and this is its fruit. *But* . . ." (Numbers 13:27–28). But the people are powerful. But the cities are fortified. But they make us look like grasshoppers. It's true! Everything in Canaan is doom and gloom and a gigantic darkroom!

It was Thanksgiving weekend 2024, and my two sons-in-law invited me to go cross-country skiing with them on Cameron Pass in northern Colorado. I'm not a bad cross-country skier in Minnesota. But Colorado? At ten thousand feet above sea level? When two feet of snow fell the night before? When the windchill is minus five? When I'm with two accomplished skiers half my age?

Going uphill was difficult. Going downhill was nearly impossible. The trail was barely three feet wide. One slip, and I'd find myself buried in two feet of snow. My sons-in-law, AJ and Adam, assured me that I'd make it. They told me that the goal was to be mentally tough. From twenty to thirty yards away I could hear them yelling, "Reed! It's all in your mind!"

Joshua and Caleb aren't intimidated by the other spies. These heroes of faith understand that Canaan's occupants aren't the problem. Note where Joshua and Caleb place their "but." "Do not fear the people of the land, for they are bread for us. Their protection is removed from them, *but* the Lord is with us; do not fear them" (Numbers 14:9). When it comes to stepping (or skiing) out in faith, the real barrier is always in our mind.

COURAGEOUS CALEB

Caleb has no doubt that God will give Israel the land. "Let us *go up* at once and *possess* it, for we are well able to overcome it" (Numbers 13:30). Caleb is echoing earlier promises that God made to Abraham and Moses:

> I am the Lord who brought you out from Ur of the Chaldeans to give you this land *to possess*. (Genesis 15:7 ESV)

> The LORD said to Moses, "Depart; *go up* from here, you and the people whom you have brought up out of the land of Egypt, to the land of which I swore to Abraham, Isaac, and Jacob." (Exodus 33:1 ESV)

Caleb had read his Bible!

While the ten frantic scouts agreed the land abounded in fruitfulness, Caleb trusted God's faithfulness. The ten were correct when they assessed that things looked impossible. They were incorrect when they forgot who was on their side—the Lord, Ruler of All, the Most High God, who made heaven and earth. Do you see the stark difference? The world is either governed by God or it's an empty stage, with no director.

What instilled such confidence in Caleb? Here it is: "Perfect love casts out fear" (1 John 4:18 ESV). God's perfect love forgives our past. No need to fear that. God's perfect love directs us today. No need to fear that. God's perfect love has secured our future. No need to fear that.

Jesus is God's final, definitive, ultimate, conclusive, and most amazing expression of perfect love. He lived a perfect life. He died a perfect death. He rose again with perfect victory. Jesus delivers perfect peace, perfect joy, perfect power—all for you!

What will it be? Fear or faith? The ten frightened spies say, "We're weak. We'll always be weak." Joshua and Caleb say, "We're weak, but we're getting stronger!" The ten say, "We're victims of our circumstances." Joshua and Caleb say, "We're victorious in spite of our circumstances!" The ten say, "This is a difficult time. We'll never make it!" The two say, "This is a difficult time. God will get us through it!" The ten lament, "We can't." The two confess, "We can do all things through God who strengthens us!"

The suspense builds. Will the Israelites be encouraged by the report of the land's fertility? Will they recall God's promises about the land that He gave to Abraham, Isaac, and Jacob? Will faith overcome their fear? Stay tuned.

CHAPTER 10

SHIPWRECKED: NUMBERS 14

They did not remember His power—the day He redeemed them from the oppressor, the day He displayed His signs in Egypt. (Psalm 78:42–43)

From 1962 to 1988, the Chevy Nova was a wildly successful American car. But the Nova didn't sell well in Mexico. Why? When Chevrolet executives discovered the answer, it was embarrassing. In Spanish—which, of course, is what people speak in Mexico—*Nova* means what? "No go."

When offered life in Canaan, the Israelites say, "No go!" In four verses (Numbers 14:1–4), they slam the door on everything God had done for them. It takes about thirty seconds to read Numbers 14:1–4. In thirty seconds, everything went kaput—God's promises to Abraham and Sarah, Joseph's leadership in Egypt, Moses and the burning bush, the Red Sea and Mount Sinai, water, manna, and quail. Everything. Dismissed, denied, discarded, disowned, and down the drain.

This wasn't just a small debate. It was wholesale mutiny. "All the congregation . . . all the people" (Numbers 14:1, 2). The rebels raise their voices and complain—not to God but to Moses and Aaron. "Back to Egypt" becomes the mantra of the moment (Numbers 14:3–4). In total dismay, Moses and Aaron fall on their faces (Numbers 14:5). Get used to it. Either Moses or Moses and Aaron fall flat on their faces again in Numbers 16:4, 22, 45; 20:6.

Joshua and Caleb join Moses and Aaron—tearing their garments in great grief (Numbers 14:6). Joshua then offers a stirring sermon on God's faithfulness and power to defeat Israel's enemies. "If the LORD is pleased with us, He will lead us into that land, a land flowing with milk and honey, and He will give it to us" (Numbers 14:8). Was anyone moved? Yes. The entire congregation was moved to stone them to death!

Factor God out of any equation, and the result is outright hysteria.

God renders His verdict—it's a life sentence. Everyone twenty years old and older, with the exception of Caleb and Joshua, will die in the desert. Adults who witnessed God's mighty hand and outstretched arm in the exodus must sojourn in the wilderness for forty years—one year for each of the forty days the spies spent in Canaan (Numbers 14:29–35). God got Israel out of Egypt in a flash. It will take forty arduous years to get Egypt out of Israel.

The real issue isn't the size and strength of Canaan's inhabitants and it's not the power and size of Israel's army. The bottom line is God's faithfulness. Can He be trusted when things look impossible? The vote is unanimous. "*All* the congregation said to stone them with stones" (Numbers 14:10 ESV). End of discussion. Case closed. "Get your stones! Prepare to launch!"

FORGETTING THE GOSPEL

Faithless Israelites cry out, "Why is the Lord bringing us into this land, to fall by the sword? Our wives and our little ones will become a prey" (Numbers 14:3 ESV). Look how far the people have fallen! They're saying the Gospel God—who rescued them out of Egypt—is now only the Law God. He plans to kill them, their wives, and their children in the wilderness. The same twisted logic appears in one of Christ's parables.

Jesus begins, "For it will be like a man going on a journey, who called his servants and *entrusted* to them his property. To one he gave five talents, to another two, to another one, to each according to his ability. Then he went away" (Matthew 25:14–15 ESV). This parable has two key words. The first is "entrusted." When we put money in a bank, we don't outright give our money to the bank. We entrust our money. Just so, when God entrusts His servants with money, He doesn't unequivocally give it to them. He entrusts it to them.

God owns the money. The servants manage the money. The first two servants agree. In Matthew 25:20, 22, both use the word "entrusted." The third servant? He refuses to admit that the master "entrusted" money to him—even though, in his response to his master, he uses three times as many words as the first two servants. Thirty-one compared to ten, and he still doesn't say "entrusted." This, however, isn't the most revealing thing he said.

Check out this next verse: "He also who had received the one talent came forward, saying, 'Lord, I knew you to be a *hard* man, reaping where you did not sow, and gathering where you scattered no seed'" (Matthew 25:24). Here's the second important word in the parable: *hard*. Honestly? Reaping where he did not sow and gathering where he scattered no seed. Really? This is Jesus? He's "hard"? Not even close, ever.

This is Jesus. God in the flesh. Betrayed, abandoned, forsaken, bloodied, crucified, dead, and buried. He did it for you—for you and for your salvation. This is astounding. This is astonishing. This is most certainly true!

And this is Gospel throughout the Bible. It's more than just black letters on white paper. The Gospel is vibrant and neon and in living color. It provokes wonder and amazement. The Gospel can be applied from a thousand angles—always instilling hope in our hearts.

The temptation is to, like Israelites in Numbers 14 and the third servant in Matthew 25, ignore the Gospel. Twist the Gospel. Make it into a new Law. Then what? God laments.

GOD LAMENTS

What's God's response over Israel's unwillingness to walk by faith? He laments. "How long . . . how long?" (Numbers 14:11 ESV). Hold on. God grieves? God aches? God feels sorrow? Yes. God feels heart-piercing sorrow (Genesis 6:6), deep pain (Exodus 3:7), and the affliction of His people (Isaiah 63:9). All the more so in Christ Jesus, who weeps over Lazarus (John 11:35) and feels great dread in Gethsemane (Luke 22:44).

God doesn't view Israel's rejection of Canaan with detached objectivity. He doesn't take it in stride and let bygones be bygones. There's more to God than rational reflection and critical analysis. God has emotions.

To be sure, the triune God is sovereign and utterly removed from us. The cherubim cry out, "Holy, holy, holy is the Lord of hosts; the whole earth is full of His glory!" (Isaiah 6:3 ESV). Yet, at the same time, our God is personal and relational. He has feelings. He isn't a stoic chess player who moves pieces on a board. Neither is God a cerebral scientist executing an experiment. God is an abandoned Lover, a frustrated Father, a covenant Partner whose heart breaks over His wayward people.

Note, for example, Judges 10:11–13—a record of God's frustration with Israel. He concludes, "I will deliver them no more" (Judges 10:13). Yet God can't give up on Israel that quickly. Judges 10:16 states, "He became impatient over the misery of His people." God's heart is disposed toward mercy. The book of Jeremiah is replete with descriptions of God's merciful emotions. Jeremiah 31:20 is representative. The Lord calls Ephraim His dear son and darling child, saying, "My insides are turbulent for him." God is far from being an unmoved mover. He's anything but indifferent and standoffish.

When the Israelites throw everything overboard in Numbers 14, God doesn't stay on the sidelines. He shows up in glory—just in the nick of time. (God fully steps into the fray two more times in Numbers—in chapters 16 and 20, both also turning points in the book.) Here, in Numbers 14:12, He repeats His earlier offer to Moses: "Say your goodbyes to Abraham's offspring because I'm going to start over with you and your descendants" (cf. Exodus 32:10).

Moses won't have any of it. Instead, he lays out two arguments—the same ones he employed after the golden calf fiasco. First, Moses appeals to God's mission to the nations (Numbers 14:13–16). If God wipes out Israel, other nations will conclude He wasn't able to keep His promise to Abraham and give Canaan to His people. In his second argument, in Numbers 14:17–19, Moses cites Exodus 34:6–7, divine words that forgive Israelites for constructing and worshiping the calf. Moses' strategy in Numbers 14? If God did it once at Sinai, He'll do it again in Paran—absolve His stiff-necked and stubborn people.

And He does! That's the good news. The bad news? "I will strike them with the pestilence" (Numbers 14:12 ESV). The last time that happened was in Exodus 9:15. The target then? Pharaoh and the Egyptians. "Because you doubt My power, just like Pharaoh and his minions, I'm going to judge you as I judged them—with the pestilence!"

What's the difference between Exodus 32 and Numbers 14? After the golden calf upheaval, God allowed the Israelites to proceed to the Promised Land. In Numbers? God slams the door shut—for forty years. And His mind is made up. To prove it, God employs the expression "declares the LORD" (Numbers 14:28 ESV), a solemn oath that can't be revoked. While "declares the LORD" is a frequent expression in prophetic books (e.g., it appears 162 times in Jeremiah), it only occurs again in the Pentateuch in Genesis 22:16—God's solemn pledge to bless Abraham. Both times, God means business.

Let's place the events in Exodus 32 and Numbers 14 side by side:

Israelites sin on a massive scale.

God executes judgment.

God threatens to wipe Israel off the map and begin again with Moses.

Moses intercedes—reminding God of His mission to the world.

Gospel promises win the day.

GOSPEL PROMISES

God's forgiveness doesn't appear out of the blue in Numbers 14:20. Moses reminds Him of Israel's creed—God's gift to Israel after the golden calf apostasy. What did God do after His people broke the First Commandment on Mount Sinai? Scold? Shame? Berate? Reject? Condemn? Turn His back on the whole wretched mess? No. He cries out, "The LORD! The LORD!" (Exodus 34:6). This is the first and only time in the Old Testament God Himself repeats "the LORD." By revealing His name, God pledges fidelity and forgiveness for rebel sinners.

Within Exodus 34:6–7, the Lord's steadfast covenant love exists side by side with His slow-burning anger. Yet because God's Gospel characteristics come first in these verses—and are more numerous—they become Israel's hope and confidence, even in the nation's darkest hour. In fact, the confession in Exodus 34:6–7 appears again, with slight variations, in sixteen other passages (Numbers 14:18; Deuteronomy 4:31; Psalms 78:38; 86:5, 15; 103:8; 111:4; 112:4; 116:5; 145:8; Joel 2:13; Jonah 4:2; Habakkuk 1:3; Nehemiah 9:17, 31; 2 Chronicles 30:9). "Where sin abounds, grace abounds all the more" (Romans 5:20). God's tenacious love absolves Israel—even in the nation's most rebellious moments. This is the central teaching in Holy Scripture. The exodus deliverance. Conquest and kings. Gethsemane and Galilee. Crucifixion and resurrection. "Suffered under Pontius Pilate . . . the third day He rose again from the dead" (Apostles' Creed). *God is for us, forevermore.*

FORTY

Have you ever been delayed? Let me restate that. Have you ever tried fixing a riding lawnmower? Getting gunk out of a bathroom drain? Repairing a broken window on your front porch? Helping your daughter with her Calculus II homework?

The book of Deuteronomy opens with a reference to the first day of the eleventh month in 1406 BC; that's thirty-nine years, eight months, and ten days after Israelites left Sinai (Deuteronomy 1:3). It took almost forty years to do what could've been done in roughly a year and a half. That's what I call a major league delay! Numbers chronicles the events that occurred during Israel's detour of all detours:

> Numbers 1–10 depict events that fall within a two-month period.
>
> Numbers 11–24 document the next thirty-nine years in and around Kadesh or Kadesh-barnea (the terms are synonymous)—located in the desert of Paran northeast of Mount Sinai and south of the Promised Land, probably modern Ain Qudeis.

Numbers 25–36 concentrate on what happened in the thirty-eighth year after the exodus.

Forty is a prominent number in the Bible. The forty days of rain washed away unrepentant people (Genesis 7:12). Elijah's forty days of running takes him out of Jezebel's reach (1 Kings 19:8). God gives Nineveh forty days to repent (Jonah 3:4). The forty days of Jesus' temptations clarify how God accomplishes salvation (Matthew 4:2; Luke 4:2). Christ shows Himself bodily alive during forty days of the joyful Eastertide (Acts 1:3). In each of these cases, forty days or years brings about a clean slate, a fresh start, a new beginning.

For Israel, God's punishment of forty years fits the crime. Those who didn't want to enter Canaan will get what they wanted. They'll die in the wilderness, while the next generation will inherit the Promised Land. God doesn't cancel His plans with Israel. Instead, He stakes everything on Israelites under twenty years old. This generation will arise—phoenixlike—out of their parents' ashes. "The little ones" will inherit the land (Numbers 14:31 ESV).

Isn't this just like God? The promise isn't to the high and mighty. Instead, God's rule and reign belongs to children (cf. Matthew 19:14). Little ones will possess Canaan. Didn't God's missional program begin with a childless couple—Abraham and Sarah? Didn't He use an eighty-year-old has-been named Moses to rescue Israel from Egypt? Didn't Jesus say that the first will be last and the last first? And doesn't the Bible state that God opposes the proud but gives grace to the humble?

Israel's adults who left Egypt are remembered for two massive moral failures: building and worshiping the golden calf and their unwillingness to enter the Promised Land. These are the only sins singled out when Moses reviews Israel's time in the wilderness (Deuteronomy 1:22–45; 9:12–25). And these are the only transgressions that provoke God to threaten to annihilate His people and begin anew with Moses (Exodus 32:10; Numbers 14:12).

Why is God so upset after the revolt in Numbers 14? Because He looks back and recalls that, since leaving Egypt, the Israelites have tested Him "ten times" (Numbers 14:22 ESV). Ancient Jewish rabbis compiled this list:

The Red Sea (Exodus 14:11–12)

Marah (Exodus 15:23)

The Sin Wilderness (Exodus 16:2)

Twice at Kadesh (Exodus 16:20, 27)

Rephadim/Massah/Meribah (Exodus 17:2–7)

Sinai (Exodus 32:1–35)

Taberah (Numbers 11:1)

Kirbroth Hattaavah (Numbers 11:4–34)

Kadesh in Zin Wilderness (Numbers 13:1–14:45).

NEVER RESCUED

Do you remember these words? "Just sit right back and you'll hear a tale, a tale of a fateful trip that started from this tropic port, aboard this tiny ship."

Gilligan's Island was produced by Sherwood Schwarz. The show recorded ninety-six episodes from 1964 to 1967. Gilligan was played by Bob Denver. Alan Hale was the Skipper. Every episode can be summarized with four somber words—shipwrecked, but never rescued.

What does Israel's shipwrecked look like? "Then all the congregation raised a loud cry, and the people wept that night. And all the people of Israel grumbled against Moses and Aaron. The whole congregation said to them, '*Would that* we had died in the land of Egypt! Or *would that* we had died in this wilderness!'" (Numbers 14:1–2 ESV). What a happy group of people!

Have the words "would that" ever helped you? Would that I had more money. Would that I could lose weight. Would that I could leave home, go home, find a new home. Sometimes we feel like we're just one relationship, one promotion, one election away from the good life. Would that! Where did that get the Israelites? Shipwrecked, but never rescued.

I call it unbelieving Christianity. That sounds like an oxymoron. You know, words that appear to contradict each other. Short sermon. Government efficiency. Jumbo shrimp. Unbelieving Christianity? It's unbelief in the congregation—and I intentionally use the term *congregation*. Stephen, in his defense before the Sanhedrin, reported in Acts 7, describes the Israelites in the wilderness as "the congregation" (Acts 7:38 ESV). A congregation is supposed to be a place where believers gather. Shockingly, it can become the reverse. A place where the deadly virus of unbelief spreads and spiritually kills. I see it. So do you. "He hears the words of this sworn covenant, blesses himself in his heart, saying, 'I shall be safe, though I walk in the stubbornness of my heart'" (Deuteronomy 29:19 ESV).

Church unbelief is worse than the world's unbelief. Why is that? Because the lack of a true and living faith is hidden by appearing to be a Christian. Church unbelief is deceptive in a way that naked unbelief isn't. This is what makes unbelieving Christianity so pernicious and why Stephen warns us about it. Unbelief causes greater damage in the church than it does in the world because it can be disguised in the church.

Israel in the wilderness wasn't a community of atheists. It wasn't even a community of polytheists. These people despair over the report of the ten scouts: "Why is the Lord bringing us into this land, to fall by the sword?" (Numbers 14:3 ESV). The unbelieving Israelites still call on the Lord. They still say that God had brought them to the borders of Canaan. Here's the question of the day: After all they had seen and experienced, how could these people invoke God's name yet have no confidence in the power of that name to save them?

In Numbers 14, the Israelites preview unbelieving Christianity. It may look like faith. Sound like faith. Smell like faith. Talk like faith. But it's not faith. "We must pay much closer attention to what we have heard, lest we drift away from it" (Hebrews 2:1 ESV).

Hebrews was written to warn a community that was drifting into unbelieving Christianity. Spiritual indifference was rampant. Apathy reigned. Recipients of Hebrews (probably residents in Rome who were Jewish converts to Christ) were tempted to become rebellious and unbelieving—like Israel in the wilderness (Hebrews 3:16–19). They weren't progressing into Christian maturity (Hebrews 5:11–6:2).

The author of Hebrews, therefore, urges people to remain faithful to their Christian confession (Hebrews 3:1; 4:14; 10:23). He points out the danger of losing confidence in God's promises (Hebrews 3:6) and falling away from the faith (Hebrews 3:12).

LOOKS CAN BE DECEIVING

Five hundred years ago, a fifteen-year-old Incan girl got dressed in her finest clothes and went on a hike up a snowcapped mountain in Argentina. She made it to the 22,000-foot summit but never came back. In 1999, her frozen body was discovered. Because of the cold dry air on the top of the mountain, the girl was incredibly well preserved. Her clothes looked brand new. Her internal organs were intact. There was still blood in her heart and lungs. Her hair was still combed. Now housed in Argentina's Museum of High Altitude Archaeology, a computerized climate control system ensures that the child, called *La Doncella*, or "The young woman," still looks very much alive. But she has been dead for five hundred years.

The same fate threatens us. The Christian hike up the mountain may become dull and dreary—much like Israel's journey in the wilderness. Then, before we know it, we're spiritually cold and frozen. On the outside, it looks like we're very much alive. We come to church, sing the songs, pray the prayers. On the inside? Our faith is slowly dying. We're headed toward unbelieving Christianity.

It's easy for me to come to church and never consider the possibility that Israel in the wilderness might be a picture of my life. "Not one shall come into the land where I swore that I would make you dwell, except Caleb the son of Jephunneh and Joshua the son of Nun" (Numbers 14:30 ESV). What is Paul's warning when he reviews Israel's failures in the wilderness? "Let anyone who thinks that he stands take heed lest he fall" (1 Corinthians 10:12 ESV).

Did you ever see the episode where the castaways on *Gilligan's Island* were just about to get off the island, then, right at the last minute, Gilligan did something to spoil it? Did you see that one? Oh, wait a minute, that was every episode. It didn't matter what they did. It didn't matter what they tried. At the end of the thirty-minute show, they were still stranded on that deserted island. Shipwrecked, but never rescued.

Israel remained in the wilderness for forty years. They spun their wheels. They went nowhere. They ended up going in circles. Their lives were lived in vain, for no purpose, for no lofty goal. "God, save me from such a dismal destiny!"

In February of 2020, David Ayres was sitting in the stands with his wife at a hockey game. Just after the referee dropped the puck, the starting goalie for the Carolina Hurricanes, James Reimer, was injured. Then Petr Mrazek, the Hurricanes second-string goalie, got hurt. The next thing the forty-two-year-old David Ayres knew, he was skating onto the ice. Ayres was a third-string goalie who had never played a second in the NHL. He allowed goals on the first two shots. Then he stopped the next eight shots as Carolina defeated the Toronto Maple Leafs 6-3.

Caleb and Joshua were also willing to get into the game. "The Lord will lead us into that land, a land flowing with milk and honey, and will give it to us" (Numbers 14:8). "The Lord will lead . . . the Lord will give!" Look what's in store for us! A land flowing with milk and honey!

The Holy Spirit—working through God's Word and Sacraments—empowers us to get out of the stands and skate onto the ice. God will see to it that we live as "more than conquerors through Him who loved us" (Romans 8:37 ESV). Let's do everything we can to reject and renounce unbelieving Christianity.

MORE DRAMA

There's still more drama in Numbers 14. Moses announces, "Your children shall be shepherds in the wilderness forty years and shall suffer for your *faithlessness*" (Numbers 14:33 ESV). The word translated as "faithlessness" more literally means "prostitution." There's a huge difference! Sexual infidelity is more personal. It's what a rejected husband might say to his promiscuous wife—or vice versa. Israel's refusal to trust God was more than walking out of a business transaction or falling behind on mortgage payments. It was an intimate event—God's heart was broken. That's why Moses likens Israel's actions to prostitution—the nation abandoned her Husband, Yahweh, and "jumped in bed" with another "man," called "Faithlessness."

That not all. The ten rebellious spies then die from a divinely sent plague (Numbers 14:36–37). Those who lead others to sin bear a greater responsibility; therefore, they suffer a greater judgment. And it's an ominous sign, pointing to what will happen to the entire cohort of adults who left Egypt. They will all die in the wilderness—with the exception of Caleb and Joshua.

We might think that by this time the Israelites would have been sufficiently humbled. But no. A group decides to take matters into their own hands and—without the ark or Moses (Numbers 14:44)—they launch an attack on Canaan. But it was too late. The train had left the station. The ship had already sailed. Israel had its opportunity and missed it. The battle against the Canaanites was an outright disaster. Fittingly, the place of the military trouncing was called "Hormah," a term that means "Destruction" (Numbers 14:45).

These three events—spiritual prostitution, God's judgment against the ten timid spies, and military catastrophe—serve as a prelude to Numbers 15–25. Everything will go to the dogs until the first generation of Israelites mentioned in Numbers lies dead and buried in the wilderness.

THE END ISN'T THE END

But it's not the end! God meets Israel's faithlessness with His faithfulness, their cowardly actions with His dauntless love. God is still devoted to His people. God turns His heart toward Israel, and mercy triumphs over judgment. God will stick with Israel through thick and thin.

One of the Hebrew words Moses uses in Numbers 14:18–19 is *hesed*—translated "steadfast love" in the ESV. There's more to *hesed* than meets the eye. It's shorthand for God's unconditional, whatever-it-takes commitment to keep His covenant promises. *Hesed* is God rolling up His sleeves and pushing heaven and earth for the sake of His people. It's a shepherd leaving ninety-nine to find the one. It's the father running toward his wayward son, then dancing to the music. *Hesed* is this same Father giving His sinless Son for all people of all time in all places.

Because of God's *esed*, when everything looks like it's over, it's not over. The end is never the end. The failure of Israel's adults will lead to their children entering Canaan under Joshua.

What God says to Israel's apostate adults is of monumental importance: "But your little ones, who you said would become a prey, I will bring in" (Numbers 14:31 ESV). *New life will rise out of the old.* That's a superb description of Holy Baptism. How so?

When we were baptized, we died—that's what Paul teaches in Colossians 2:12–13. Death isn't something in our future. It's something in our past. We were too far gone for God to rehabilitate us. We were totaled, thoroughly corrupted and enslaved to sin. Rather than trying to do some repair work, God killed us.

God killed the old me so He could make the new me. That's why Paul writes, "Since you *have been* raised with Christ " (Colossians 3:1). Paul doesn't write, "Since you *will be* raised with Christ." When we were baptized, we were raised from the dead. One moment, we're dead to Jesus and alive to sin. The next moment, we're dead to sin and alive to Jesus. One moment, we're controlled by sin and hostile toward God. The next moment, we're clothed in Christ's righteousness, a member of God's family, and at peace with our Creator.

Death leads to life. After the shipwreck in Numbers 14, this is Israel's only hope. It's our hope as well—all our days.

CHAPTER 11

KORAH'S COUP: NUMBERS 15–17

Do nothing from selfish ambition or conceit, but in humility count others more significant than yourselves. (Philippians 2:3 ESV)

Here's the storyline of Numbers 10–15. After almost a year at Mount Sinai, "the cloud lifted from over the tabernacle of the testimony" (Numbers 10:11 ESV). The Israelites were on their way! After three days, they experience "misfortunes" (Numbers 11:1 ESV). What kind of misfortunes? We're not told. The rest of Numbers 11 gives us some clues. The chapter describes Israel's complaining and lack of appreciation—to the point that Moses breaks down and wants to die. And if all this isn't bad enough, in the next chapter, the nation's inner circle of leaders can't get along. Moses, Miriam, and Aaron square off. Then the car drives off the cliff. Israel's long-awaited entry into the Promised Land is delayed—for forty years (Numbers 13–14).

But the Gospel still stands! The Gospel is about God's grip on us, not our grip on God. Check it out. "*When* you come into the land you are to inhabit, which I am giving you" (Numbers 15:2 ESV). "*When* you come into the land to which I bring you . . ." (Numbers 15:18 ESV). Not "if." "When." God doesn't say, "I hope you make it to the land . . . someday."

"Someday" often expresses unfounded optimism, pie-in-the-sky dreams. Here I would cite the Minnesota Vikings as Example A. At the end of every mediocre season, with four Super Bowl losses in their rearview mirror, Viking fans inevitably say, "Well, maybe . . . someday."

When it comes to Canaan, God doesn't say, "someday." God sticks to His promises made to the patriarchs—Abraham, Isaac, and Jacob. In fact, the laws and ordinances in Numbers 15 are intended to guide Israel *when* they live in Canaan. If that's not affirming enough, the last verse of the chapter reiterates the core Gospel announcement in the Old Testament: "I am the LORD your God, who brought you out of the land of Egypt to be your God" (Numbers 15:41 ESV).

After the abounding good news in Numbers 15, you'd think things might get better. Instead, Numbers 16 describes a fight to the finish. In one corner is God, Moses, and Aaron. In the other corner is Korah and company, whose chief accusation is that there's no way Moses is the nation's only mediator (Numbers 16:3, 13, 28–29). In fact, truth be told, both Moses and Aaron have gone way "too far" (Numbers 16:3 ESV).

Why the upheaval? Numbers 15 describes God talking to Moses—and *only* Moses (Numbers 15:1, 17, 22, 23, 35, 36, 37). Count the verses. Seven times God initiates a conversation with Moses. God speaks with Moses exclusively. And Aaron? God puts him in charge of receiving sacrifices and making atonement (Numbers 15:25, 28, 33). This explains the otherwise out-of-the-blue revolt in Numbers 16.

For the children to whom God promised the land (Numbers 14:31), Numbers 15 is affirming and hopeful. For their parents—typified by Korah and clan—it's too much Aaron and way too much Moses. These malcontents want to turn God's plan upside down. Instead of leaving Egypt and entering Canaan, they want to leave Canaan and enter Egypt.

TWO STORIES IN NUMBERS 16

Leaders don't always get a lot of respect—especially when results don't match expectations. Think NFL coaches of last-place teams, US presidents overseeing stagnant economic growth, and generals of losing armies. Also think Moses and Aaron.

Numbers 16 contains two stories. Both center on Israel's rejection of Moses and Aaron. God judges Korah, Dathan, and Abiram—and all who take issue with divinely appointed leaders (Numbers 16:1–40). The chapter's second story describes the entire nation's rebellion against Moses and Aaron (Numbers 16:41–50), who end up getting it coming and going!

The first, and much longer part of Numbers 16, is about Korah's grievance that every Israelite is holy, not just Aaron and Moses (Numbers 16:1–3). Korah's second point of contention is that Moses is a sorry excuse for a leader (Numbers 16:12–15). Korah never sought a conversation or reconciliation with Moses. Korah's only intention? Cancellation. Full stop.

God's first reproof demonstrates that Moses is the nation's appointed leader (Numbers 16:25–34). God's second judgment shows that He chose Aaron and his descendants to be Israel's priests (Numbers 16:35–40). Separation from willful sinners is a motif in both parts (Numbers 16:24, 26, 45). That's the big picture. Now let's look at the details.

THE GUNFIGHT AT THE OK CORRAL

The gunfight at the OK Corral is the most famous standoff of the American Wild West. The shootout happened at about 3:00 p.m. on October 26, 1881. It lasted only a minute. US Marshall Virgil Earp—along with his brother Wyatt Earp and Doc Holliday—took the field against Billy Claiborne and two sets of brothers, the Clantons and the McLaurys.

Who are the key players in Numbers 16?

The first is Korah, a fourth generation Levite (Exodus 6:18, 21, 24). Korah is a son of Izhar, Kohath's son, and thus part of the Levitical clan that oversaw the tabernacle's most holy things (Numbers 4:4). Not content with that, Korah wants a promotion. He yearns to become a priest.

Joining Korah are Dathan and Abiram, who are from the tribe of Reuben—as is On. All four men are movers and shakers. They mobilize two hundred and fifty other well-known leaders. Their protest? "The entire nation is holy, not just Aaron and Moses!" They're not entirely off base, which is how most conflict arises—with half-truths. In this case, these disgruntled men assert, "For all in the congregation are holy, every one of them, and the Lord is among them" (Numbers 16:3 ESV).

They're right. God called the Israelites "My holy people" (Exodus 19:6). And God does tabernacle among all Israel—rich and poor, male and female, Levite and non-Levite. However, only Aaron and his sons are ordained into the priesthood (Leviticus 8). And only these ritually holy priests have access to the Holy Place and Most Holy Place (Numbers 3:10).

Korah and crew needed to reread their Bible! They also needed a class titled "Intro to Biblical Leadership." Had they enrolled in the course, what would they have learned? Being a leader has nothing to do with wielding authority. It has everything to do with serving others. Since they rejected this basic biblical truth, the New Testament book of Jude describes Korah and his ilk as self-serving, waterless clouds, fruitless trees, wild waves, and wandering stars (Jude 12–13). These are not the kind of people we want serving on our church boards and committees!

Shared status (God's people) doesn't imply shared function (serve as priests). "Any *outsider* who came near was to be put to death" (Numbers 3:38 ESV). "Outsider" here denotes anyone not directly related to Aaron. Not content with what God says, Korah, Dathan, Abiram, and On refuse to stand down. The die is cast. Either you're for Moses and Aaron (God's representatives), or you're with Korah and company. It's the Old Testament's version of the gunfight at the OK Corral. Who will come out on top?

UP!

What word makes our hearts beat? Our spirits soar? What word causes us to get a quiver in our liver and an ocean of emotion? The word has two letters. Any guesses? U–P. That's right, *up*. Upscale. Up and coming. Upper class. Upwardly mobile. Rise up against the odds, the crowd, or whatever else gets in your way. Our world offers us a simple one-word solution to every problem: *up*!

What do we learn from Korah? Up is our greatest enemy. Down is our greatest friend. Up—pride—is our greatest enemy. Down—humility—is our greatest friend.

Korah goes up. "One day Korah son of Izhar, a descendant of Kohath son of Levi, conspired with Dathan and Abiram, sons of Reuben. They incited a rebellion against Moses, along with 250 other leaders of the community, all prominent members of the assembly" (Numbers 16:1–2). All priests were Levites, but not all Levites were priests. Korah is a Levite, but he isn't directly related to Aaron so he isn't allowed to serve as a priest.

And Korah wants to be a priest. Korah yearns to be in charge. Korah longs to go up. Dathan and Abiram are from the tribe of Reuben. The Levite-priest issue doesn't apply to them, but they piggyback on Korah's complaint their own unhappiness with Moses. Korah, Dathan, Abiram, and On—along with 250 Israelite leaders—want more control. They all want up. "They united against Moses and Aaron and said, 'You have gone too far! The whole community of Israel has been set apart by the LORD, and He is with all of us. What right do you have to act as though you are greater than the rest of the LORD's people?'" (Numbers 16:3).

MILD-MANNERED MOSES

Did Moses get up one morning and say, "Today I'm going to appoint myself leader over Israel"? Is that how it happened? I don't think so! There was a burning bush. And the voice of God. And holy ground. And Moses took off his sandals. This is a divine call if I've ever seen one! Then Moses said . . . "Send someone else!" Moses is far from being full of himself. He has several character flaws, but pride isn't one of them.

Once Moses is God's top man, he's more than happy to delegate authority to others (Exodus 18). He also shares the Holy Spirit's presence and power with Israel's seventy elders (Numbers 11:24–29). Was Moses self-seeking? Did he flaunt his authority? Did he thumb his nose at underlings? Not even close! Moses never hoarded power. He gave it away.

Incidental verses in Scripture are often as profound as well-known promises. Here's one of those easily overlooked texts: "*The man* Moses was very meek, more than all people who were on the face of the earth" (Numbers 12:3 ESV). This verse doesn't call Moses "Israel's savior and judge," "the one and only," or "the nation's eminent intercessor." Moses is just "the man." We wouldn't ever think of comparing Moses with a blowfish.

Blowfish love to look bigger than they really are. That's why they fill their stomachs with water and blow themselves up. Blowfish fish have a toxin level 1,200 times more deadly than cyanide. There's enough poison in one blowfish to kill thirty people.

Korah and his cronies are blowfish. They're trying to look bigger than they really are. Here's what these blowfish say: "Isn't it enough that you brought us out of Egypt, a land flowing with milk and honey, to kill us here in this wilderness?" (Numbers 16:13). Whoa! Egypt is the Promised Land? Egypt is where God's people lived in abundance? Egypt is where Israelites had it made? Lived on easy street? Were awash in peace and prosperity?

We lose our perspective when we aspire to go up. Then we begin to call bad "good," lies "truth," darkness "light." And Egypt "a land flowing with milk and honey."

The lines are drawn. Korah and his 250 combatants are on one side. Moses and Aaron are on the other. Every man takes his censer, puts fire in it, and stands at the entrance of the tent of meeting. Then the glory of the Lord appears. What happens to Korah and his 250? The group of blowfish that wanted to go up? "The earth opened its mouth and *swallowed* the men" (Numbers 16:32). The Red Sea swallowed the Egyptians (Exodus 15:12). Now the earth swallows Israel's rebels. What's the connection? God reckons Korah and his tribe to be just like Pharaoh's army—out to destroy Israel. Up is our greatest enemy. Down is our greatest friend.

Moses goes down. Three times in Numbers 16, Moses falls flat on his face before the Lord (Numbers 16:4, 22, 45). "Moses. Haven't you heard? Down is the language of losers, the lazy, the left-behind, and the low-achievers." Down and out. Downscale. Downsize. Down in the mouth. Downhill. Downhearted.

But Moses? He's willing to go down—way down. "Moses was very *humble*" (Numbers 12:3). The Hebrew word translated "humble" means "the lowest of the low." There's no other word in Hebrew that goes lower. And before God? Low is the only place to go. "God opposes the proud but gives grace to the humble" (1 Peter 5:5 ESV).

THIS POINTS TO JESUS

Moses' movement down foreshadows Jesus, who was as up as anyone could ever be. "Who, though He was in the form of God . . ." (Philippians 2:6 ESV). Jesus isn't a junior partner with God. Jesus isn't a sort of vice president of the universe. Jesus is a full-fledged member of the Godhead, equal with the Father in every way—from eternity past. We confess this in the Nicene Creed. Jesus is "one substance with the Father."

Then Jesus took His first step down. "[He] did not count equality with God a thing to be grasped, but emptied Himself, by taking the form of a servant" (Philippians 2:6–7 ESV). Jesus never stopped going down. The Creator of all things, He owned nothing. The King of kings, He washed feet. The Son of God, He became a servant. A servant? Really? You can almost hear the angels crying out, "That's far enough, Jesus. That's far enough!"

But the Savior continued to go down. How did Jesus die? "And being found in human form, He *humbled* Himself by becoming obedient to the point of death, even death on a cross" (Philippians 2:8 ESV). In Paul's Greek, "humbled" denotes a reversal of status. Christ went from being totally up to being totally down. "Who for us men and for our salvation came *down*." That's the way the Nicene Creed puts it. Jesus came down to suffer. Down to bleed. Down to die.

By dying on a cross, Jesus violated every tenet of our system. He subverted everything we hold near and dear. Jesus turned everything upside down. The least are the greatest and the greatest are the least. The exalted are humbled and the humbled are exalted. And death is the way to life. Check this verse out: "I have been crucified with Christ. It is no longer I who live, but Christ who lives in me" (Galatians 2:20 ESV).

When I was six years old, my family was vacationing in Glenwood Springs, Colorado, with its famous hot springs and swimming pool. My dad decided it was time for me to jump off the high dive. It's a ritual of sorts, isn't it? For a child to trust a parent who coaxes them to jump off the high dive for the first time. And we need coaxing. We don't want to go down!

Moses (and all the more, Jesus) calls us to go down. Down to love. Down to give. Down to forgive. Down to humbly serve all the people God places in our lives.

DIVIDED TEAMMATES

In 2013, Richie Incognito and Jonathan Martin were teammates on the Miami Dolphins football team. They had every reason to work well together—but they didn't. It wasn't even close. Incognito harassed and bullied Martin. He went so far as to call Martin a racial slur in a voicemail that was played by every media outlet in the country. Incognito also threatened to kill Martin. Then Incognito claimed it was all just locker room talk. It's the way guys have fun in the NFL. Apparently, no one told Martin. He left the Miami Dolphins, fearing for his life.

Incognito and Martin had much in common. Consider all the reasons they had to live well together. Both were football players and on the same team. Both were starting offensive linemen. Both were big dudes. Both were millionaires. Yet somewhere along the way, one or both of them began to treat the other like an enemy—in this case, like the other guy was a New England Patriot! Incognito and Martin forgot what? *Together is so much better.*

Korah and clan forgot this too. So did members in the church founded by Paul in the Greek city of Philippi. Consider, for example, that the apostle writes this: "I plead with Euodia and I plead with Syntyche to agree with each other in the Lord" (Philippians 4:2). Euodia and Syntyche are forever etched in God's Word because they didn't get along with each other. Ouch!

Holy Baptism unites us with Christ. Holy Baptism unites us with each other. It's a package deal. We get Jesus. We get people. Paul has much more to say about this in Philippians.

TOGETHER IS MUCH BETTER

How does unity begin? "Do nothing out of selfish ambition" (Philippians 2:3). There's a part of me (it might be in you too) that tries to outdo others. What's it for you? Is it about who has the coolest car? Who lives in the nicest house? Who makes the most money? Remember that game you played when you were a kid called king of the hill? We've taken that same idea and transferred it into our adult arena. "I'm *the* king of *this* hill!"

In some marriages, husbands and wives needlessly compete with each other. It begins in wedlock and now it's stuck in deadlock. I heard a woman once say, "I was married by a justice of the peace. Since then, I've had neither justice nor peace!" Husbands and wives compete to be king of their hill called home. "I call the shots around here, and your job is to obey me. Am I making myself clear?"

Paul continues. "Do nothing out of . . . *vain conceit*" (Philippians 2:3). "Vain conceit" is having an exaggerated opinion of myself. Guess what? If I eliminate this, I'll solve most of my problems. In America, however, we've elevated conceit to an art form. Can you imagine a best-selling book called *Looking Out for the Other Person*? Ha!

Men, the next time you come home and your wife says, "Why didn't you text and tell me you were going to be late for dinner?" I suggest you say, "Honey, I'm sorry. I was only thinking of myself." After your wife is shocked and stunned, then she comes to her senses, say to her, "Next time, I'll think about you."

Anytime I'm critical of another person, I destroy unity. But let's admit it. Criticizing others makes us feel better. We build ourselves up by putting others down. I must warn you. Belittling is like a drug. It's easy to become addicted, then we need our daily dose. Give it time, and it will destroy every relationship we have.

Sometimes we can be like donkeys. Say what? When donkeys are in danger, they form a circle with their faces outward. Then they begin kicking their rear legs inward and end up kicking their fellow donkeys. How smart is that? Yet that's what we do. We get nervous and anxious and worried, so we end up kicking one another with biting sarcasm and deadly doses of cynicism.

Humility is the cure. "In humility consider others better than yourselves" (Philippians 2:3). This is countercultural stuff! I saw a bumper sticker a few years ago that said, "I bet I'm twice as humble as you are." That pretty much misses the point!

The apostle exhorts us, "Each of you should *look* not only to your own interests, but also to the interests of others" (Philippians 2:4). Note the word *look*. The Greek verb is related to the noun *skopos*, a word that appears in words like "telescope" and "microscope" and "horoscope." The verb denotes looking intensely at something or someone. Can you name the three greatest interests of your husband, or the three greatest interests of your wife? What about your children or grandchildren?

If we're going to live together in unity, we need Christ's help. Jesus isn't competitive, conceited, or critical. Jesus is considerate. Jesus scopes out our greatest need. And what would that be? Full, free, and forever forgiveness, especially for our soured relationships. How did Jesus do it?

Paul has something to say about this too. He points us to the cross. From Christ's cross, we're forgiven. From His cross, we're loved. From His cross, we're washed and cleansed. And Holy Baptism delivers these gifts to us, uniting us to Christ and His people.

What if we dismiss Paul? We'll find ourselves on a desert island—friendless, lifeless, and hopeless. Is that the way we want to live? Is that the way we want to die? Is there a better way? You bet! Philippians 2:1–11. Read it. Mark it. Inwardly digest it.

TWO PLACES

To make sense of Numbers 16:23–40, we need to remember that Israelite tribes camped separately—thus, Korah the Levite was in a different place than Dathan and Abiram, who belonged to the tribe of Reuben.

Moses invites Korah and the other rebels to take censers. Korah is ready for the challenge in front of the whole congregation and—most importantly—God Himself (Numbers 16:19). God sees this as a national rebellion (because of the presence of Israel's leaders) and wants to consume everybody. Moses' intercession convinces God to judge only those who sinned—the three ringleaders Korah, Dathan, and Abiram.

This section of Numbers 16, therefore, goes back and forth between two different places. The narrative camera, for example, shifts quickly in Numbers 16:32. "The earth opened its mouth and swallowed them up, with their households [Reubenites aligned with Dathan and Abiram] and all the people who belonged to Korah [two hundred and fifty] and all their goods" (ESV). God sent a plague the next day and struck down 14,700 additional people. Had it not been for Aaron making atonement (Numbers 16:46), there would have been many more casualties.

DIVINE WRATH

I can almost hear you say under your breath, "Thank God I live in New Testament times and not during the days of the Old Testament! I've got Jesus and mercy. So long, Moses and the Law!"

Not so fast. In Christ, God intensifies *both* divine love *and* divine judgment. The Savior's teachings about loving our enemies, turning the other cheek, and going the extra mile are absolutely important. But so are His acts of retribution and condemnation. Here are four New Testament examples:

Christ announced punishment against unrepentant cities (e.g., Matthew 11:23–24; 24:37–39; Luke 10:13–15).

> Christ drove out money-changers from the temple (John 2:15).
>
> Christ destroyed unbelieving Israelites in the wilderness (Jude 5).
>
> Christ threatened to kill people in Thyatira if they persisted in following a Jezebel-like prophetess (Revelation 2:23).

Divine vengeance appears not only in Deuteronomy 32:25 but also in Romans 12:19. God curses enemies of the cross (Philippians 3:18), for His wrath is against every form of evil and wickedness (Romans 1:18). While Paul pens 1 Corinthians 13—his famous chapter on love—in the same letter he calls down a curse to all who don't love Jesus (1 Corinthians 16:22). Paul's curses appear again in Galatians 1:8–9. The apostle also believes God will repay Alexander the coppersmith who did him great harm (2 Timothy 4:14), while Peter tells Simon the magician, "May your silver perish with you" (Acts 8:20 ESV). John compares Christ's return at the end of time to a rider on a white horse who judges and makes war (Revelation 19:11). He will rule the nations with an iron scepter (Revelation 2:26–27; cf. Psalm 2:9).

God's judgment and indignation, in both the Old and New Testaments, are intended to drive us into the arms of His mercy. And that mercy is most vivid when Christ cried out, "My God! My God! Why have You forsaken Me?" (Matthew 27:46; Mark 15:34). God's wrath and anger? Jesus took it—Jesus took it all for us. These hymn lyrics aptly summarize God's Good Friday love and wrath: "What wondrous love is this that caused the Lord of bliss to bear the dreadful curse for my soul, for my soul, to bear the dreadful curse for my soul!" (*LSB* 543:1)

GOD'S CHOICE OF AARON

Numbers 17 confirms God's choice of Aaron to serve as Israel's high priest—and in a much less dramatic way than in chapter 16. Calmly and peacefully, Israelite leaders gather twelve staffs—one from each tribe—and place them before the tent of testimony (Numbers 17:1–6). The next day, only Aaron's staff sprouts, with blossoms bearing almonds (Numbers

17:8). Buds and blossoms could happen overnight. But almonds? I don't think so. Who's the rightful high priest? Aaron.

Is there anywhere else in the Bible where we encounter a small tree with almond flowers? Indeed, there is. It's in Exodus 25:31–40, where Moses describes the tabernacle's lampstand—a beautiful source of light, standing before the Lord's presence. The lampstand and Aaron, both stand before the Most Holy God. "This is the Word of the Lord" (e.g., *LSB*, p. 156).

God confirms His choice of Aaron in Numbers 18 where three times this phrase appears: "The Lord said to Aaron" (Numbers 18:1, 8, 20). God only directly speaks to Aaron one other time, in Leviticus 10:8. What's God up to? He's affirming Aaron's role as Israel's high priest. In doing so, the Lord maintains these spheres of holiness emanating from the tabernacle:

Aaron, the high priest

The priests

The nonpriestly Levites

Israel's twelve tribes

Unclean Israelites and all non-Israelite people

LIVING IN A SPITE HOUSE

Moses intercedes for the Israelites several times in the book of Numbers (Numbers 11:2; 12:13; 21:7). Others catch on. Two times Aaron follows suit (Numbers 16:22, 47–48), and on one occasion, Phinehas intercedes along with Moses (Numbers 25:7–13). We probably wouldn't blame Moses if, overcome with spite, he finally lets Israel have it. "Enough is enough!"

One of the strangest stories of spite involves a wealthy businessman named Hyman Sarner and an eccentric contractor by the name of Joseph

Richardson. Both lived in New York City in the 1880s. Richardson owned a narrow strip of land—five feet wide and over one hundred feet long. Sarner owned a normal-sized lot next to Richardson's. Sarner wanted to build an apartment that fronted the street, so he offered Richardson one thousand dollars for his meager plot. Richardson was offended by the amount and demanded five thousand dollars. Sarner refused, and Richardson called Sarner a tightwad. Things went downhill from there.

Sarner concluded that the land would remain vacant and instructed an architect to design an apartment building with windows overlooking the street. When Richardson saw the finished building, he resolved to block the view. No one was going to enjoy a free look over his property! Richardson proceeded to build a house that was five feet wide, 104 feet long, and four stories high. The house was so narrow that only one person at a time could use the staircase. The largest table in any room was eighteen inches wide. People called the building the spite house.

In 1897, Richardson died in his spite house. Both the house, along with Sarner's apartment building, were bulldozed in 1915 to make way for a new apartment residence at 129 East 82nd Street, which still stands today.

If anybody had a reason to live in a spite house, with large amounts of animosity and resentment, it was most certainly Moses. At the top of Moses' list of people who offended him was Korah. Then, there were Dathan, Abiram, and On. Add the ten faithless spies as well as almost every other Israelite. We wouldn't be shocked if Moses decided to build a spite house at Mount Sinai and live in it the rest of his life! Why didn't he?

At least four times in the Old Testament, Moses is called "the servant of God" (1 Chronicles 6:49; 2 Chronicles 24:9; Nehemiah 10:29; Daniel 9:11). What does God's servant do? He intercedes for his enemies. He blesses those who curse him. He doesn't return evil for evil. Moses refuses to respond with revenge. By showing mercy to those who hurt him, Moses previews the world's greatest act of forgiveness. If anybody had good reason to live in a spite house, with large amounts of animosity and resentment, it was *the* Servant of God, Jesus, our Lord.

At the top of Christ's list was Judas, who betrayed Him with a kiss. Then there were the chief priests (Annas and Caiaphas) and Jewish scribes. Together they paid Judas thirty pieces of silver, sent temple soldiers to arrest Jesus, brought His case before Pilate, and stirred the crowd to demand that Jesus be crucified.

And don't forget the Roman soldiers. They brutally whipped Jesus at Gabbatha, placed a crown of thorns on His head, blindfolded Him, dressed Him in a purple robe, struck Him in the face, spit on Him, and finally, with three nails, crucified Christ at Calvary.

Add to the list Pontus Pilate, who found Jesus innocent. Yet, because of Jewish pressure, the Roman governor sentenced Jesus to die. Pilate then publicly washed his hands of the bloody mess. How double-minded can you get?

That's quite a list, wouldn't you agree? But it's not complete. There are other notorious sinners that Christ could have had spite toward. Brace yourself. You're on the list. So am I. Our sin sent Jesus to the cross—our pride and our pettiness nailed Him to a tree.

The soldiers hoisted Jesus up, and the cross swayed forward, then back, until it was secured with wedges at the bottom. Then the soldiers callously gambled to decide who would get the Savior's garments. At that point, what did Jesus say? "Father, forgive them, for they know not what they do" (Luke 23:34 ESV). God's servant intercedes for His enemies. Christ is the Bible's greatest insister and intercessor:

> Who is to condemn? Christ Jesus is the one who died—more than that, who was raised—who is at the right hand of God, who indeed is interceding for us. (Romans 8:34 ESV)
>
> Consequently, He is able to save to the uttermost those who draw near to God through Him, since He always lives to make intercession for them. (Hebrews 7:25 ESV)

> For Christ has entered, not into holy places made with hands, which are copies of the true things, but into heaven itself, now to appear in the presence of God on our behalf. (Hebrews 9:24 ESV)
>
> My little children, I am writing these things to you so that you may not sin. But if anyone does sin, we have an advocate with the Father, Jesus Christ the righteous. (1 John 2:1 ESV)

Jesus refuses to live in the spite house. How about you?

Oh, I know. It's easy to hold on to anger and resentment. He treated you like trash. She left you when you needed her the most. They let you down in the most crucial moments of your life. Besides, we feel better when we replay all of *their* failings and foibles. But does it work—for the long haul? How many ways can I say, "No, it doesn't"? Nursing our hurts erodes our relationship with Jesus and others. Our best option? Our only sane option? Forgive.

Forgiveness may not change the person who wronged us, but I promise you this: Forgiveness will change us. Forgiveness leads us out of darkness and into light. Forgiveness is letting go of our hatred and hurt so we can live and love again. Is forgiveness easy? No. Quick? Seldom. Painless? I don't think so. But stay the course. *Stay the course.*

CHAPTER 12

LOOSE LIPS SINK SHIPS: NUMBERS 20

They made his spirit bitter, and he spoke rashly with his lips. (Psalm 106:33 ESV)

"Loose lips sink ships." The United States War Advertising Council used this expression on posters during World War II. The government wanted to persuade citizens to refrain from sharing military information that could fall into enemy hands.

Moses' loose lips in Numbers 20 sink more than ships. They torpedo and capsize his entire future. Because Moses spoke rashly, he died on Mount Nebo, outside of Canaan. A rap song for Numbers 20 might include these lyrics: SAY IT AIN'T SO! MOSES IS A NO-GO?

REVIEW

It's easy to get lost in this part of the Old Testament, so let's step back and do some review. The Israelites travel from Egypt to Mount Sinai (Exodus 12:37–19:1) and stay at Sinai for almost a year (Exodus 19:2–Numbers 10:10). God leads His people from Sinai to Kadesh (Numbers 10:11–21:35), then from Kadesh to the plains of Moab—where Israel will camp from Numbers 22:1–36:13, throughout the book of Deuteronomy, as well as Joshua 1:1–2:24. Joshua finally leads Israel into Canaan (Joshua 3). Where are we now? In Kadesh for two more chapters.

Now that we've got the geography down, what about some chronology? Moses methodically cites dates from Numbers 1:1–10:11:

> The second year after the exodus, the second month, the first day (Numbers 1:1, 18)

> The second year after the exodus, the first month, the first day (Numbers 7:1; cf. Exodus 40:17)
>
> The second year after the exodus, the first month (Numbers 9:1)
>
> The second year after the exodus, the second month, the twentieth day (Numbers 10:11)

Then what? There are no dates until Numbers 20:1—though here Moses only writes "in the first month." The first month of what year? Why the lack of precision? Because every year seemed the same. Every day seemed the same. Time stood still. Isn't that how we feel when we're going nowhere in particular?

Most commentators think that, beginning in Numbers 20, the Israelites are in their fortieth year after the exodus. That makes sense. The clock is ready to strike midnight. The parents are almost dead, and their children are about to enter Canaan. Miriam's death announces this changing of the guard.

MERIBAH 2.0

The Israelites are on the plains of Moab, ready to conquer the Promised Land. Then tragedy strikes—three times. Numbers 20 begins with Miriam's death and concludes with Aaron's passing. Their deaths are grim reminders that no one over twenty, except for Joshua and Caleb, will enter the Promised Land. Sandwiched between Miriam's and Aaron's deaths is the account of Moses' anger. This, too, doesn't end well.

Moses is between a rock and a hard place—though this time the rock is real! The Israelites are still disgusted with their manna. Though the requests in Numbers 20:5 are different from those in Numbers 11:5, the complaint is the same. "We're sick and tired of manna!" It's Meribah 2.0. Moses was in Meribah forty years earlier—both places in Exodus 17:7 and Numbers 20:13 are called Meribah. The word means "quarreling." That's fitting!

The Hatfields and the McCoys are at it again! Same song, second verse. They sing a bit louder and a little bit worse! "Why have *you* brought the assembly of the LORD into this wilderness" (Numbers 20:4 ESV). The enterprise wasn't Moses' harebrained concoction. Moses wasn't the one who brought Israel out of Egypt and into the wilderness. You'd think that by now the Israelites would know that they were participating in God's plan. God was the one who rescued them from Pharaoh's house of slavery and led them into the wilderness.

Moses falls on his face again. He does this—with or without Aaron—in Numbers 14:5, 10; 16:4, 22, as well here in Numbers 20:6. If we read the earlier accounts, then we know what to expect this time: divine judgment against stubborn Israelites followed by Moses' intercession and God's deliverance. This time, though, the pattern is broken. Let's see how additional events in Exodus 17:1–7 and Numbers 20:2–13 are different.

Here's a comparison of the two Meribahs. First, in Exodus 17, Moses takes the lead; in Numbers 20, both Moses and Aaron are in view. Second, in Exodus 17:5, Moses uses the staff he had employed earlier to strike the Nile. However, in Numbers 20:9, Moses takes the staff "from before *the* LORD" (ESV). Whose staff is this? We don't know for sure. Numbers 17:6–7 gives us this information. Chiefs from each of Israel's twelve tribes placed their staffs "before the LORD." Aaron's staff was also included. Then this: "Moses took the staff from before the LORD . . . and struck the rock with his staff twice" (Numbers 20:9, 11 ESV). Now Moses uses either one of the chieftains' staffs or Aaron's—not his own.

JUST LIKE LEON LETT

Leon Lett was a fierce defensive tackle who helped the Dallas Cowboys win three Super Bowls (1993, 1994, 1996). Unfortunately, for most NFL fans, these aren't the memories they have of Lett. Instead, two recollections of spectacular failure stand out.

The first blunder occurred in Super Bowl XXVII against the Buffalo Bills. Lett recovered a fumble late in the game. People call it the "Fumble

Rumble." Lett was on his way to a touchdown, but as he approached the end zone, he slowed down and stretched out his arms to celebrate. Just seconds before he crossed the goal line, Don Beebe of the Buffalo Bills came racing from behind to slap the ball out of Lett's hands. The ball bounced through the end zone, resulting in a touchback. It cost Lett his Super Bowl touchdown.

Then, during the next season in 1993, the Cowboys were leading the Miami Dolphins 14-13 toward the end of the game. The Dolphins attempted a forty-one-yard field goal to win it. A Cowboy player slipped through the line to block the kick. Lett's teammates jumped and shouted with glee.

According to the NFL rule book, the ball was dead. But Lett didn't know that. He tried to recover the football, and, in his attempt, he fumbled it and kicked it back into play. The Dolphins recovered the loose ball and attempted another field goal. This time, the kick sailed through the goalposts. The final score? Miami 16, Dallas 14.

Do you ever feel like Lett? Did you almost score, only to fumble it away? Was it a sale, a customer, a dream, a business deal, a relationship? Have you ever put harmful words back in play? Or a negative attitude? Or a toxic idea? We can all relate with Lett. So can Moses.

THE WORST DAY OF MOSES' LIFE

Have you ever squeezed too much toothpaste out of its tube? Did you try to clean it up? I bet you didn't try putting the excess toothpaste back in the tube. We all know that's impossible. Something else is also impossible: taking words back once they're spoken. Moses knows. Here are his words: "'Hear now, you rebels: shall *we* bring water for you out of this rock?' And Moses lifted up his hand and struck the rock with his staff twice" (Numbers 20:10–11 ESV). Where does Moses mention God? Why does he refer to "we"? Why does he lift up his hand? And why in the world does Moses strike the rock—not once but twice? How does God respond? First, in mercy. He provides water for His people. Second, in anger. God disciplines Moses and Aaron. Neither will enter Canaan.

Hold on! God's punishment doesn't fit the crime! For years (count them, *forty*), Moses and Aaron put up with Israelites—a bunch of Oscar the Grouch soundalikes. Then, in a moment of weakness, they lose their temper, and it's over? No milk and honey? No view of the Mediterranean Sea? No carefree days in Jerusalem, Jericho, or Joppa? Don't the ungrateful Israelites have anything to do with this?

Yes, they do. Moses later points this out, not once but three times (Deuteronomy 1:37; 3:26; 4:21). Psalm 106:32–33 concurs. "They angered him at the waters of Meribah, and it went ill with Moses on their account, for they made his spirit bitter, and he spoke rashly with his lips" (ESV). We don't know the exact nature of Aaron's sin, but God points out this: "You [both] rebelled against My command at the waters of Meribah" (Numbers 20:24 ESV).

This all needs some unpacking. First, God doesn't bar Moses from the Promised Land because Moses got angry. Rather, it's what Moses did with his anger that got him in trouble. Feeling resentment and acting on it are different. Allowing his anger to get the best of him, Moses disobeyed God's clear commands—and this in sight of his fellow Israelites. What's more, in their animosity, both Moses and Aaron substituted themselves for God. "Shall *we* bring water for you out of this rock?" (Numbers 20:10 ESV).

What else sank Moses' ship? God commands Moses, "*Tell the rock* before their eyes to yield its water" (Numbers 20:8 ESV). So what does Moses do? "He said to *them*" (Numbers 20:10 ESV). Moses spoke to people, not the rock. Bad mistake! And if this wasn't terrible enough, though God said nothing about raising a hand and striking the rock, Moses does both.

By raising his hand, Moses aligned himself with pagan magicians who manipulated gods by incantations and actions (cf. 2 Kings 5:10–13). Earlier though, when he was in Egypt, Moses demonstrated that miracles didn't happen because of a magical incantation but instead because of God's power (e.g., Exodus 7:15–20; 8:1–6). Even when Pharaoh asked Moses to implore God to stop a plague, Moses did so in private, after leaving Pharaoh's presence (Exodus 9:28–29).

Moses continued this approach in the wilderness. He would announce a coming miracle, but when the time came, he didn't say anything. This is the pattern, for instance, in the miracles of manna, quail, and water (Exodus 16–17).

Put the last four paragraphs together, and what do we have? Moses placed himself in the same place as the Israelites who refused to enter Canaan. Connections between Moses' sin and the debacle in Numbers 13–14 are as follows:

Both fail to trust God.

Both fail to enter Canaan.

Both events happen in Kadesh (Numbers 13:26; 20:1).

In both instances, unbelief is the chief sin (Numbers 14:11; 20:12).

Both acts of unbelief are followed by Israel's failed plans (Numbers 14:39–45; 20:14–21).

God held Moses, Israel's leader, to a higher standard. James warns, "Not many of you should become teachers, my brothers, for you know that we who teach will be judged with greater strictness" (James 3:1 ESV). In Moses' case, "greater strictness" means he will die outside of Canaan.

FINISHING STRONG

If there was ever a surefire candidate for the ministry, it was Moses! Trained in Pharaoh's court, he received the finest education money could buy. As an adult, Moses was bold and courageous, a visionary and a leader. Check out his "can-do" attitude in Exodus 2:11–22, where mighty Moses doesn't back down from anyone—not from Egyptians, Israelites, or Midianites.

And yet . . . Moses had a problem with anger. It was in anger that he killed an Egyptian taskmaster for beating a fellow Israelite (Exodus 2:11–12). Forty years later, Moses "went out from Pharaoh in hot anger" (Exodus 11:8 ESV). Later still, when Moses descended from Mount Sinai and saw the Israelites worshiping a golden calf, he smashed the Ten Commandments (Exodus 32:19). Moses' anger also got the best of him at Meribah 2.0. Afterward, God reminded him with these words: "You rebelled against My word in the wilderness of Zin when the congregation quarreled, failing to uphold Me as holy at the waters before their eyes" (Numbers 27:14 ESV).

What's your besetting sin? What keeps tripping you up? I pay too much attention to what people think about me. I worry if they'll still like me—especially when I make a mistake, forget a deadline, or miss the mark. No one likes abandonment and rejection, but these twin terrors too often dictate my words and actions. "The fear of man lays a snare, but whoever trusts in the LORD is safe" (Proverbs 29:25 ESV). I don't want my "fear of man" to trap me emotionally, spiritually, or financially. I long to finish strong—trusting wholeheartedly in the Lord my God.

ZAP!

A few years ago, I was sitting outside on a warm summer evening. I kept hearing a constant, "Zap! Zap! Zap!" It was the sound of bugs hitting a bug zapper. A light attracts them. They fly toward it. Then they get zapped. You'd think bugs would see the tray littered with dead bugs. You'd think some bug would say, "Wait a minute! I'm not going to blindly follow my desires toward that light!" You know what? Bugs don't do that. And you know what else? Neither did Moses.

Moses disregarded God's clear command: "Take the staff, and assemble the congregation, you and Aaron your brother, and tell the rock before their eyes to yield its water" (Numbers 20:8 ESV). Instead, Moses flies toward other lights, deadly lights—these lights that we've just considered. "He said to *them*, . . . 'Shall *we* bring water for you out of this rock?' And Moses *lifted up his hand and struck the rock* with his staff twice" (Numbers 20:10–11 ESV). Ugh, ugh. Triple ugh. The result? "Zap!" Moses loses life in the Promised Land.

It's easy as pie to begin. It's tougher than nails to finish.

Sadly, there are other people in the Bible who ran well for a while but later in life stumbled and fell. David, who wrote seventy-three psalms, was probably in his fifties when he committed adultery with Bathsheba and then arranged to have her husband, Uriah, killed in battle (2 Samuel 11). King Solomon, who had extraordinary wisdom and brought unprecedented prosperity to Israel, allowed his many wives to turn his heart toward other gods (1 Kings 11:3).

Then there's King Asa. He began by doing "good and right in the sight of the Lord his God" (2 Chronicles 14:2). Asa made a number of godly reforms in Israel. But in the thirty-sixth year of his reign, rather than relying on God, Asa stripped the silver and gold from the temple and hired a foreign king to fight his foes. When a godly prophet confronted him, rather than repenting, Asa became angry and put the prophet in prison (2 Chronicles 16:1–11).

The godly King Jehoshaphat likewise made many reforms but later allied himself with wicked Ahab and his evil son, Ahaziah (2 Chronicles 19:2; 20:35). King Joash, for his part, began by repairing the Jerusalem temple but later rejected God, served idols, and murdered the son of the man who raised him (2 Chronicles 24). King Hezekiah restored worship in Judah and saw God bring amazing victories for His people, but late in life, he nonchalantly showed Babylonian envoys Judah's treasures, setting the stage for a Babylonian invasion (2 Chronicles 29:2, 36; 30:26; 32:22).

We're great at beginning. We're full of unbridled enthusiasm, high energy, a never-say-die attitude. Like hot knives into butter, we tear into new projects, new jobs, new classes, and new relationships. But as time goes on, we tend to become weary, fatigued, impatient. Then we're tempted to zoom toward different lights, dazzling lights, deadly lights. Lights of pride, prestige, and prominence. "Zap" goes the joy of our salvation. “Zap” goes our commitment to prayer. “Zap” goes our zeal for God’s Word. Then one day we find ourselves in a tray littered with dead bugs.

I have good news for you! One greater than Moses is here (cf. Hebrews 3:3). Jesus was also surrounded by lucrative lights. Jesus began strong. Jesus also finished strong. And for Him it was tougher than nails—literally. In addition to the nails, there was scourging, mocking, spitting, beating, slapping, sweating, and bleeding. Still, Jesus finished strong—in spite of the kiss of betrayal, His friends running for cover, and His countrymen clamoring for His death. Jesus finished strong in spite of His Father’s abandonment.

The sky is dark. Two others are dying beside Him. Jesus takes a deep breath and announces, “It is finished” (John 19:30 ESV). The blood? Poured out. The curse? Removed. The sacrifice? Completed. Death? Defeated. The veil? Rent asunder. Paradise? Restored forevermore. “It is finished!” Was this a cry of defeat? *By no means.*

So today, just now, lackluster finishers like us get no “zap” from on high. Instead, because of Christ’s finished work on the cross, we receive a Father’s welcome, a Shepherd’s embrace, and a Friend’s infinite love. By God’s grace, let’s strive to make these words our last testimony to the world: “I have fought the good fight, I have finished the race, I have kept the faith” (2 Timothy 4:7 ESV).

CHRIST, OUR ROCK

I once bought some furniture at an IKEA store in Chicago. As you probably know, IKEA is “the king of ready-to-assemble furniture.” It took me a year to put it all together! Making sure that A connects to B. Bolting C into D. Sliding E over to F. And hoping, even if I forgot to attach L, M and N, that my brand new furniture wouldn’t look like it was ready for a garage sale.

As we’ve learned, in both Exodus 17 (Meribah 1.0) and Numbers 20 (Meribah 2.0), God gives the Israelites water from a rock. We may quickly pass over this fact. Paul doesn't. He writes, "For they drank from the spiritual Rock that followed them, and the Rock was Christ" (1 Corinthians 10:4 ESV). Of course, Christ wasn't literally a rock. He didn't turn into a boulder or a mineral unearthed from a quarry. What, then, does Paul mean? Be warned. There is some assembly required!

Part A. The context of Paul's statement in 1 Corinthians 10:4 indicates that God and Jesus are unified. Note how the apostle describes the bronze serpent narrative of Numbers 21: "We must not put *Christ* to the test, as some of them did" (1 Corinthians 10:9 ESV). Christ? The account in Numbers 21 mentions God and the Lord, but not Christ. For Paul, God, the Lord, and Christ are synonymous terms. If you've seen one, you've seen the other.

Part B. Consider Deuteronomy 32. In this chapter, Moses often refers to God as Israel's "Rock" (Deuteronomy 32:4, 15, 18, 30, 31). It was the Rock—that is, the Lord—who brought salvation to Israel (Deuteronomy 32:15) and gave her birth (Deuteronomy 32:18).

Our next piece, part C, is pivotal. God was present when Moses struck the rock at Meribah 1.0—the event recorded in Exodus 17:1–7. When the people complained, God instructed Moses, "Behold, *I will stand before you* there on the rock at Horeb, and you shall strike the rock" (Exodus 17:6 ESV). How did God stand before the rock? Through His glory cloud (e.g., Exodus 13:21–22; 14:19, 24). When Moses struck the rock, his rod passed through the cloud. At that point, God took Israel's punishment for their grumbling and in return gave them life-giving water.

Two senses of "rock" (a literal rock and God, our Rock) appear in Psalm 78. Asaph, the psalm's author, writes that when Israel grumbled against God, Moses struck the rock and water gushed out (Psalm 78:20). Later, Asaph says, the Lord judged His unthankful people and "they remembered that God was their rock" (Psalm 78:35 ESV). Whew! Parts A, B, and C are a lot. I know! The point? *When Moses strikes the Rock, he strikes God.*

On Good Friday, John stands at the foot of Christ's cross and adds part D. John describes a Roman soldier taking his spear and splitting our

Savior's side. "There was a sudden flow of blood and water" (John 19:34).

Here it is! Water flowing from the Rock! A gushing river of life surging from the Rock! Living water flowing from the Rock, who cried out, "I thirst" (John 19:28 ESV). Here is Jesus—the Rock of Ages—crushed and cursed by the sin of the world. The end? On the third day Jesus rose from the dead—bodily, permanently, and victoriously. Peter links Good Friday with Easter when he calls Jesus the *rejected* stone as well as our *living* Stone (1 Peter 2:4).

How does water, coming out from our Savior's side, purge and purify the gunk and goo in my heart? Through the Sacrament of Holy Baptism. Like a conduit or pipe, Baptism connects us to the Rock of living water. Baptism delivers the gifts of Christ's cross and crucifixion. Guilt is gone, the debt is paid, sin is forgiven, and hell is vanquished.

Our building task is now complete. Parts A, B, C, and D fit together beautifully. Christ, our Lord and God, was present in the wilderness to quench Israel's physical thirst. Christ, our Lord and God finally in the flesh, is present in Baptism to satisfy our spiritual thirst. Our response? "Oh come, let us sing to the LORD; let us make a joyful noise to the Rock of our salvation!" (Psalm 95:1).

EDOMITES

The fastest way from Kadesh (where the Israelites are camping) to Canaan was through Edom. That's why Moses sends messengers to Edom's king requesting safe passage through his land. This encounter between the Israelites (descendants of Jacob) and the Edomites (descendants of Esau) reprises an earlier meeting when Jacob returned home to Canaan and Esau met him with great kindness (Genesis 33). In Numbers 20:14–21, however, there's nothing close to brotherly love coming from Esau's family to Jacob's. Instead, Edom's king tells the Israelites, "Take a hike—just not on my land!"

The Edomites should have leaped for joy at the opportunity to help a fellow family member. Instead, they reject Moses' request and slam the door shut in his face. The Edomite king even threatens to confront Israel with a sword (Numbers 20:18). How nice is that? Moses gets the message and decides not to pursue things further. He leads Israel around by another way (Numbers 20:21). Edom's harsh treatment of God's people primes the pump for several prophetic oracles that target the land of Esau.

Oracles against Edom include Isaiah 34; Jeremiah 49:7–22; Ezekiel 25:12–14; 35:1–12; Amos 1:11–12; Obadiah 1–21; and Malachi 1:2–5. These prophecies depict Edomites as cruel, spiteful, and vindictive. In fact, Doeg the Edomite is one of the most ruthless men in the Old Testament. He boasts of his evil (Psalm 52:1), while David likens his tongue to a sharp razor, full of deceit and lies (Psalm 52:2–4). With bloodthirsty cruelty, Doeg kills eighty-five Israelite priests (1 Samuel 22:18–19).

Following the events in Numbers 20, Edom becomes a bitter pill to swallow. Who tried to kill baby Jesus? King Herod, an Edomite.

MOURNING AARON'S DEATH

Aaron's death on Mount Hor and God's appointment of Eleazer (Numbers 20:23–29) anticipate not only the passing of the old Israel and the birth of the new. They also foreshadow Moses' death and the designation of Joshua to be his successor (Numbers 27:12–23; Deuteronomy 34:1–12).

In the Old Testament, seven days was the normal amount of time for grieving the loss of a loved one (Genesis 50:10; 1 Chronicles 10:12). The Israelites grieve Aaron's death for thirty days (Number 20:29). Thirty days? Wouldn't one day be long enough? Shed a tear then get on with things? Have a meal and get back to the routine? Weep for a moment, then put it all behind you? Why rehearse the hurt for a whole month? Is this the best use of time—especially when you're trying to get somewhere as important as the Promised Land? Isn't it better to ignore pain? Put on a happy face? Saddle up and keep riding? Swallow hard and slog on? What do we call these responses to death? Denial.

There are countless ways to live in denial. Overeating, overdrinking, overworking, overexercising, overspending, overachieving, and overproducing. Over time, where does this take us? Further and further from God's healing mercy.

Here's what we learn from Israel's thirty-day lament for Aaron. Name pain. Lament loss. Face failures. Refuse to stuff it down. It may seem paradoxical, but we need to experience grief in order to alleviate grief. There's no other way forward.

What if we insist on whitewashing the mess? Pain will grow until it crushes and kill us. Is that putting it too strongly? Not at all. "When I kept silent, my bones wasted away through my groaning all the day" (Psalm 32:3). God invites us to weep over life's disasters and allow Him to redeem them. Then what? We boldly announce these words to the world: "Those who sow in tears will reap with shouts of joy" (Psalm 126:5).

MOSES IN THE PROMISED LAND

Did you know that Moses finally made it into the Promised Land? That's right. Moses made it on the day Christ was transfigured on a mountain with Peter, James, and John. Elijah was there too (cf. Luke 9:30). What looks like it's over isn't over—not when God is involved. It's the way His kingdom works.

Soldiers paraded Jesus from Pilate's courtyard to Calvary. At the end of the march, Jesus was stripped and executed. It was ugly, vile, and barbaric, but it wasn't over. On Easter morning, Jesus showed Himself alive. Heaven's best took hell's worst and triumphed. The master of death couldn't destroy the Lord of Life. Paul puts it this way: "In all these things we are more than conquerors through Him who loved us" (Romans 8:37 ESV). That's true for Moses, me, and you!

CHAPTER 13

IN THE WAITING ROOM: NUMBERS 21

As Moses lifted up the serpent in the wilderness, so must the Son of Man be lifted up. (John 3:14 ESV)

Numbers 20 is a slow-moving disaster. It's a horrible, terrible, no-good, and very sad part of the book. Miriam dies. Her brothers, Moses and Aaron, forfeit life in the Promised Land. Edomites—long-lost relatives—deny the Israelites passage through their land. Then Aaron dies. In fact, since Numbers 14—when God's people rejected the Promised Land—there has been little good news. But in Numbers 21, Israel finally turns a corner. The sun begins to shine. There are four scenes in Numbers 21. They all end on a positive note:

Israelite forces defeat a Canaanite king of Arad in the Negev (Numbers 21:1–3).

Though Israelites rebel, they confess their sin and God heals them (Numbers 21:4–9).

On their march toward Canaan, God's people sing two victory songs (Numbers 21:10–20).

Israel defeats Sihon, king of the Amorites, and Og, king of Bashan (Numbers 21:21–35).

Things are starting to look up!

TAKING OUR ENEMY SERIOUSLY

On July 11, 1804, Alexander Hamilton, one of the founding fathers of the United States, underestimated his enemy. It happened on the

New Jersey side of the Hudson River. Aaron Burr, the country's sitting vice president, challenged Hamilton to a duel. (Yes, they did things like that in those days!) Hamilton had insulted Burr long enough, so, on that day, the two were ready to shoot each other at ten paces. Hamilton fired first and, by all accounts, aimed high to strike a branch in a tree. He figured that Burr would do the same. Case closed. However, Burr took aim, shot straight, and killed Alexander Hamilton. Don't underestimate your enemy. It could cost you your life!

Israel underestimated its enemy, a Canaanite king who apparently governed an area named Arad—about 130 miles south of Jerusalem. In round two of the battle, however, Israelites took their foe seriously, making a vow to the Lord (Numbers 21:2). Then what? Once God is involved, the Israelites gain a victory over the Canaanites (Numbers 21:3). The first battle at Hormah ended in defeat (Numbers 14:45). This, the second battle at Hormah, results in a come-from-behind triumph. Hormah, which means "destruction," now announces Canaan's destruction, not Israel's. God's people are now within striking distance of their long-anticipated goal, the Promised Land! Their lesson? Don't underrate your enemy. And don't try to fight battles on your own. Ask for divine help. "With God we shall do valiantly; it is He who will tread down our foes" (Psalm 60:12 ESV).

Then there's another bump in the road. Because the Israelites have to detour around Edom, they become impatient. Who hasn't been frustrated with, of all things, an unexpected detour? And at the worst possible time! People begin recycling their same old laundry list of complaints. There is, however, one difference. This time around, the Israelites complain to Moses *and* God. Though only a slight improvement, this is the right direction. God's now involved!

IN THE WAITING ROOM

There I was. In the waiting room. My doctor's waiting room. The receptionist took my name, recorded my insurance information, then blandly intoned, "Have a seat in the waiting room." I did. I took a seat next to a man thumbing through an old *Time* magazine and across from a woman blindly staring into space. We were there to do what? Wait. We weren't in the examination room or the consultation room or the operation room. No. We were in the waiting room. It's like watching grass grow. Why? We're Americans! We rush headlong into the next big thing. I'm writing this chapter the day after the Super Bowl. What are sports fans talking about? In two days, pitchers and catchers report for spring training!

We live in an instant gratification society. When do we want things? N-O-W! We place an order and find it on our doorstep the next day. We send a message across the ocean, and people get it almost instantaneously. We have 24/7 access to endless information. "Wait? I don't have time to wait! What do you think? That I'm just going to sit here and twiddle my thumbs?"

Are you waiting for a baby to be born? Or a course to be completed? Or a hot and humid summer to end? This isn't what I'm talking about. The most difficult waiting times are when we don't know when the waiting will end.

GOD'S DELAYS AREN'T GOD'S DENIALS

God's delays aren't God's denials. When we're stuck in the waiting room, God's delays are never His denials. Bank on it.

Israelites are delayed. Edom's refusal to let them pass through their territory means God's people have to take a roundabout route. Whatever its exact course was, we know that it was south from Mount Hor because Israel was forced to go around Edom (Numbers 20:20–21). It looked like they were returning to where they started, the Red Sea! This quickly leads to impatience. The Israelites have had it with both God and Moses. "It's true," Israelites lament. "God's delays must be God's denials!"

Israelites are a bunch of type A personalities! Type A personalities are frequently impatient, under stress, and feel that they never have enough time. Type A people are obsessed with sales made, articles written, forms completed, clients contacted, books published—you name it. They're driven by one word: *more*.

Everyone has some form of a type A personality—others (like me) have just drank more of the Kool-Aid. When we're forced to take a different route, learn a new software program, stay late at work—anything that gets in the way of our agenda—what's our response? "Now is the absolute worst possible time for this to happen! I'm ruined!"

Do you notice yourself in Israel's impatience? "They [the Israelites] began to speak against God and Moses. 'Why have you brought us out of *Egypt* to die here in the wilderness?' they complained. 'There is nothing to eat here and nothing to drink. And we hate this *horrible* manna!'" (Numbers 21:5).

Egypt? Again? The Israelites still want to return to Egypt? For what? Egyptian food! Since seeing Pharaoh in their rearview mirror, how many times did the Israelites long for the land of the Nile? Let's count them: Exodus 14:11; 16:3; 17:3; Numbers 11:4–6; 14:2–3; 16:13; 20:3–5; 21:5. *Eight times!* Don't they remember the whips and bricks and Pharaoh's endless bag of tricks?

While the events in Numbers 21 sound just like Israel's earlier grievances, there's something new. This time they call God's gracious gift of manna "horrible." Come on, people! Just think what you can do with manna. You can slice it, dice it, bake it, broil it, cook it, smoke it, flavor it, salt it, or even freeze it for another day.

When we have to wait, we're much like these Israelites. We're tempted to forget God's power, God's promises, God's provisions. Then we make things sound worse than they really are. What does God do with His people? Judgment comes swiftly in the form of snakes—or, as Moses calls them, "*fiery* serpents" (Numbers 21:8). The word *fiery* likens the snake bites to a burning sensation upon the skin.

Thomas Lawrence writes about poisonous snakes in the Sinai wilderness. Thomas Lawrence? That would be the famous Lawrence of Arabia. In his 1927 book titled *Revolt in the Desert*, he describes an entire valley in the Sinai wilderness creeping with horned vipers, puff adders, cobras, and black snakes. He walked with two sticks, beating the snakes back. That's difficult to get my mind around! "Then the people [Israelites] came to Moses and cried out, 'We have sinned by speaking against the Lord and against you. Pray that the Lord will take away the snakes'" (Numbers 21:7).

CONFESSION

When we hear the word *confession*, we might envision backroom interrogations, Chinese water torture, or CIA waterboarding. In the Bible, however, confession normally suggests admitting sin. How did this go for Israel in the book of Numbers? The nation's only confession of sin in chapters 1–20 was shallow (Numbers 14:40). How come? In the next verses, Moses writes that they set out to take Canaan despite his warning that it would end in failure (Numbers 14:39–45). But now, in Numbers 21, for the first time in the book and after almost forty years (!), God's people come clean. They honestly and repentantly confess their sin.

Here are a few things that confession isn't. It's not telling God something that He doesn't know. (God knows everything already.) Confession isn't complaining about my sorry lot in life. Confession isn't blaming and pointing fingers at others. That's what confession isn't. Here's what confession is.

> Create in me a clean heart, O God, and renew a right spirit within me. (Psalm 51:10 ESV)
>
> Father, I have sinned against heaven and against You and am no longer worthy to be called Your son. (Luke 15:21)
>
> God, be merciful to me, a sinner! (Luke 18:13 ESV)

Here's my confession: In church, it's easy for me to fast-forward through confession. Say the words. Sound the syllables. Complete the sentences. Then get on with things. When I wake up to what I'm doing,

I realize that I'm a hypocrite. A two-faced pretender. I've preached sermons about people like me—people who just go through the motions, say the right words, but their hearts are galaxies from God. "Dear Jesus, I confess my lack of confession!"

Let's slow down. Admit our sin. Return to the Lord. Need a verse? Romans 3:23: "All have sinned and fallen short of the glory of God" (ESV). Need forgiveness? Gaze upon Christ. Fix your eyes on His five wounds. That's right—be mesmerized, captured, stare.

Staring is pretty easy. As a child, I must have been an Olympic-class starer. My mom would often say, "Reed, stop staring!" We don't have to go to college or read a book to learn how to stare. Anyone can stare. But stare where? Not at ourselves. Not at the media. Not at our smartphone. Jesus says, "Stare at Me. I sweat drops of blood for you. Stare at Me. I was crucified and buried for you. Stare at Me. I'm alive for you. Stare at Me. I hear your confession, and I love you and forgive you!"

SALVATION

Make sure you don't stare at the snakes. And don't look around to find a way out of the snakes. And don't look within yourself to find a solution for all the snakes. Look up. Look up to the snake on the pole. "Then the LORD said to Moses, 'Make a fiery serpent and set it on a pole, and everyone who is bitten, when he sees it, shall live'" (Numbers 21:8 ESV). Don't just glance. Don't just glimpse. Gaze. Pay close attention. Israelites don't have to crawl to the snake, make promises to the snake, or do anything to get the snake's attention. God's command is singular: "Look."

If we want to be distressed, look within. If we want to be defeated, look back. If we want to be distracted, look around. If we want to be saved, forgiven, and loved, stare—stare at Jesus. Fix your eyes on Jesus. This is how Hebrews 12:1–2 puts it: "Let us run with endurance the race that is set before us, looking to Jesus, the founder and perfecter of our faith" (ESV).

MOSES' MISFORTUNES

How do you deal with life's setbacks and disappointments? There are several options. *Fight*. Let people have it. Give them a piece of your mind. Throw verbal missiles. Don't respond to phone calls or texts. Another option is *flight*. Run. Duck. Avoid. Change the subject. Numb yourself with binge drinking, binge shopping, binge eating—you name it. Still another way to respond to a negative situation is to *freeze*. Get stuck. Replay the situation repeatedly. Rehearse the hurt in every conversation. Reiterate and recapitulate till you're blue in the face.

Moses faces a lot of headaches in Numbers. That's putting it mildly! How does he respond? Fight? Flight? Freeze? Moses doesn't become aggressive. Moses doesn't run away. And Moses doesn't get stuck in a rut. Most of the time, Moses takes his problem to God.

Surrounded by snakes and people screaming, Moses prays. God then tells him to make a bronze (or copper) snake and put it on a pole. Anyone who stares at it will live. This isn't magic. This is looking to where God has placed His promise. The Wisdom of Solomon—a first-century BC intertestamental book—states, "For he who turned toward it was saved, not by what he saw, but by you, the Savior of all. . . . It is you who delivers from every evil" (The Wisdom of Solomon 16:7–8).

Up to this point in the Bible, God has used a number of creatures to save His people. He covered Adam and Eve with animal skins, provided a ram in place of Isaac, and delivered forgiveness and atonement in Israel's divine worship through bulls, goats, rams, and lambs. Now God uses a snake. And, just around the corner in Numbers 22, He'll rescue Balaam through a talking donkey. When you have heaven and earth at your disposal, you can use anything or anyone anytime or anywhere!

JESUS AND THE BRONZE SNAKE

Jesus uses the story of the bronze snake in a conversation with a Jewish teacher named Nicodemus. "As Moses *lifted up* the serpent in the wilderness, so must the Son of Man be *lifted up*, that whoever believes in Him may have eternal life" (John 3:14–15 ESV). These verses serve as a prelude to the most famous verse in the Bible, John 3:16: "For God so loved the world, that He gave His only Son, that whoever believes in Him should not perish but have eternal life" (ESV). What a humbling, staggering, knee-buckling promise! And it's connected to snakes!

Jesus links the "lifting up" of the bronze serpent with His being "lifted up" on the cross (cf. John 8:28; 12:32). Do you notice what the bronze snake and Jesus have in common? Death and life—with the accent on their life-giving power to all who stare, to all who believe. Note what Jesus says in John 12:32–32: "'I, when I am *lifted up* from the earth, will draw all people to Myself.' He said this to show by what kind of death He was going to die" (ESV).

GOD IS LOVE

God isn't a gotcha god. God is the Gospel God. "God so loved . . ." Love isn't peripheral to God. Love isn't tangential to God's character. A commitment to sacrificially give, come what may, is central to what makes God God.

When we hear "God is love," we often think, "That means God loves us." Yes. That's true. God loves us. But God doesn't need us to love. Before creating us, God wasn't in heaven thinking, "I'll create people so I can become a loving God." No. John doesn't write, "God *became* love." John writes, "God *is* love" (1 John 4:8, 16 ESV). We don't really understand this unless we understand the Trinity.

There is one God. And this one God has always existed as three persons—Father, Son, and Holy Spirit. For all eternity, Father, Son, and Spirit have loved one another. For all eternity, they have a commitment to sacrificially give, come what may. And that's why we say God is love. God is love because God is a Trinity.

Imagine if we worshiped a single-person god. One god who eternally exists as one person. For all eternity, this god sits on his throne in solitary confinement. What can we say about this god? Prior to creating us, he didn't have anyone to love. So, we can't say that this god *is* love. Instead, we have to say that this god *became* love. Love isn't intrinsic to this god.

Now, contrast this god with the God of the Bible—the Father, Son, and Holy Spirit. For all eternity, the members of the Trinity have loved one another, listened to one another, cared for one another. And in an explosion of love, the triune God creates us. And in an explosion of more love, the Father sent His Son to be lifted up, high upon a cross.

GOD TURNS CURSES INTO BLESSINGS

What was once cursed, the snake, becomes a blessed means of salvation. Nehemiah makes the same point when referring to the events in Numbers 22–24—Balaam's attempt to curse Israel. Nehemiah writes, "They did not meet the people of Israel with bread and water, but hired Balaam against them to curse them—yet our God turned the curse into a blessing" (Nehemiah 13:2 ESV). Paul employs the same logic when he writes, "Christ redeemed us from the curse of the law by becoming a curse for us—for it is written, 'Cursed is everyone who is hanged on a tree'" (Galatians 3:13 ESV). God's specialty? He reverses curses! He turns them into blessings!

Isn't this Joseph's story? Seized by his brothers. Thrown into a pit. Sold to Midianites on their way to Egypt. Then enslaved, falsely accused, imprisoned, forgotten, and abandoned. Twenty years later, though, Egypt's pharaoh elevated Joseph to the second most powerful position in the land. When his brothers finally show up, what does Joseph say? "You meant it for evil, but God meant it for good" (Genesis 50:20). God uses evil for good. That's also Paul's point. "For those who love God all things work together for good" (Romans 8:28 ESV). God takes the seemingly random threads of life and knits them together, making our lives beautiful, symmetrical, ordered, and Christlike. There's hope!

Isaac Watts (1674–1748) affirms this hope. In his 1719 Christmas hymn titled "Joy to the World," Watts writes, "He comes to make His blessings flow far as the curse is found" (*LSB* 387:3). Where is the curse found? It's found in wars and weapons, want, and worry. The curse is found in your life and mine. The curse seeps into our homes, weaves its way into our heads, and sometimes makes life a living hell. In the end, the curse kills everything and everybody. But not forever!

"He comes to make His blessings flow far as the curse is found." God's blessings are more powerful than the curse! When Christ returns, God will uncurse creation. He will restore our lives and heal our hearts. Indeed, God has already begun this work. Joy to the world! The Lord has come! Joy to the world. The Lord will come again to make everything perfect and pristine—forever!

ISRAEL AND NEIGHBORING NATIONS

Israel's cadence picks up speed after the bronze serpent story. God's people zero in on the Transjordan—the land directly east of Canaan. There they meet Sihon, king of the Amorites, as well as Og, king of Bashan. Israelite victories are sweet. Three songs are sung. Progress is being made. Momentum fills the air!

Recall Genesis 12:3, where God says He'll curse those who curse Abram and his descendants. This verse provides background for the second half of Numbers 21. Moses sends messengers out to Sihon to say, "Let me pass through your land" (Numbers 21:22 ESV). Instead, Sihon rises up in defiant anger. The Israelites soundly defeat him—along with Og, king of Basham. Both kingdoms become part of the Promised Land.

If Sihon and Og hadn't taken the wrong attitude toward Israel, they could have maintained their land. Instead, God's curse came upon them because they cursed Israel, just as God had promised Abram. This points to what God will do against all of the Canaanites.

The book of Numbers presents three categories of nations:

The elect nation of Israel.

> Non-elect nations like Edom and Moab that Israel doesn't go to war with (Numbers 20:14–21), to whom their first response was to offer peace (Deuteronomy 20:10–15).
>
> Anti-elect nations, Ammonites and Canaanites, that God commands Israelites to annihilate (e.g., Numbers 21:1–3, 35)—but only when Israel is *entering* the Promised Land.

When did God place Canaanites in the non-elect category? When Noah cursed Ham's son named Canaan (Genesis 9:18–27). The Lord reaffirmed this when He appeared to Abram in a dream—where "Amorites" become synonymous with "Canaanites" (Genesis 15:16). In Leviticus 18 and 20, God again repeats His curse on Canaan. These chapters catalog a number of Canaanite sins, including incest, sexual abuse, and sacrificing children to false deities. God therefore mandated severe action against the inhabitants of Canaan—both as judgment for sin as well as to keep His people from being led astray by their perverse practices (e.g., Numbers 7:2–6; 20:16–18).

I'm sure there were some in Israel who said, "Can't we all just get along? Can't we bring Canaanites into our fold and then change them?" God's answer? "No, you can't. You can kill them or be killed by them. There's no middle ground." If the Israelites fail to remove Canaan's population, all will be lost (Numbers 33:55–56). Moses bluntly says, "They shall *trouble* you" (Numbers 33:55 ESV). The same verb translated "trouble" appears in Numbers 25:18, where the ESV renders it with "harassed" in the context of Israelite men having sex with Moabite prostitutes. The last thing Israel needs are multiple reruns of *that* botched situation.

It was March 24, 1989, off the Alaskan coast. The captain of the *Exxon Valdez* oil tanker barked out orders to a second mate. But the orders were vague. A mistake was made. Then it happened. The *Exxon Valdez* ran aground. The oil tanker dumped eleven million barrels of crude oil into one of the most scenic bodies of water in the world. Oil blackened everything—from the surface of the sea to beaches to otters to sea gulls. The only option was to clean up the spill lest it pollute more of the environment. That's God's mandate to Israel. "Clean up the pagan pollution so it doesn't destroy you."

That's why God commands Israel to bulldoze the Canaanites and their idol shrines (e.g., Numbers 33:52; Deuteronomy 7:5; 12:2–3). Any remaining inhabitants will become "barbs," "thorns," and "trouble" (Numbers 33:55 ESV). The sum and substance of this teaching? Either the Israelites will defeat the Canaanites or the Canaanites will defeat the Israelites.

HOW WELL DID THAT GO?

For the most part, the Canaanites got the upper hand against the Israelites. Note, for instance, that the book of Judges begins with the tenfold repetition of the phrase "did not drive them out" (Judges 1:19, 21, 27, 28, 29, 30, 31, 32, 33; 2:3). Israel's failure to drive out the Canaanites sets the tone for the rest of Judges as the author evaluates Israel's spiritual condition by using the sevenfold refrain (with variations), "The sons of Israel did evil in the LORD's eyes; they forgot the LORD and served the Baals and Ashteroth" (Judges 2:11; 3:7, 12; 4:1; 6:1; 10:6; 13:1). Gideon's father even has an altar to Baal in his backyard (Judges 6:25).

The Promised Land, completely free from adversaries, remained an elusive goal throughout the Old Testament. Even David and Solomon couldn't drive out Israel's enemies—the Philistines. The Hebrew Scriptures end with the book of Malachi, where the prophet documents Israel's ongoing failure and inability to secure the entirety of Canaan.

Just like He calls the Israelites in the book of Numbers, God calls us to refuse any compromise with evil and wickedness. The Christian faith isn't the bland leading the bland or the nice leading the nice. No. The Christian faith is a battle. A war is going on. It's a battle of opposing powers. There are eternal consequences with casualties, traitors, and triumphs. David's confession is ours as well: "The battle is the LORD's" (1 Samuel 17:47). And that spells what? *Victory*.

ISRAELITES VERSUS CANAANITES

Let's take a step back from God's call to arms and ask a question. What are we to make of God's command to judge, drive out, and in many cases kill Canaanites? This doesn't sound like Jesus—not even close! How do these Old Testament mandates comport with New Testament admonitions like "Love your enemies" (Matthew 5:44), "turn the other cheek" (Luke 6:29), "Walk the extra mile" (Matthew 5:41), and "Bless, and do not curse" (Romans 12:14)? If genocide and ethnic cleansing are morally wrong in the twenty-first century AD, wasn't it also wrong in the fifteenth century BC? How are the atrocities of our day, done in the name of religion, different from killing Canaanite men, women, and children?

One option is to discard these parts of Israel's Scriptures. Get an X-Acto knife and remove all the holy war verses. Such a decision, however, asserts that sections of the Old Testament are pre-Christ, sub-Christ, or anti-Christ. And, if we marginalize Israel's battle texts, then we can't affirm with Paul that all of Israel's Scriptures are "profitable for teaching, for reproof, for correction, and for training in righteousness" (2 Timothy 3:16 ESV). Neither can we agree with the apostle when he wrote, "Whatever was written in former days was written for our instruction" (Romans 15:4 ESV).

What's more, negating parts Israel's Scriptures drives a wedge between the testaments that overlooks the fact that, while "the LORD is a man of war" (Exodus 15:3 ESV), so is Jesus. Christ "judges and makes war," is "clothed in a robe dipped in blood," and out of His mouth "comes a sharp sword with which to strike down the nations" (Revelation 19:11–15 ESV). The only way to hold the historic Christian faith is to affirm that all of Genesis through Malachi is God's Word—then look to the New Testament for how to appropriate Israel's holy war texts. What do we learn there?

First and foremost, we don't take the sword to our enemies. Period. End of discussion. There's a huge discontinuity between the war texts in the Old Testament and our new life in Christ. We are never called upon to resort to physical violence (cf. Matthew 26:52). *Never*. However, we are in a battle, though not with "flesh and blood" (Ephesians 6:1a ESV). Rather, our fight is "against the rulers, against the authorities, against the cosmic powers over this present darkness" (Ephesians 6:12b ESV). These supernatural enemies are conquered with "the sword of the Spirit, which is the Word of God" (Ephesians 6:17). Our prayer? "Lord, keep us steadfast in Your Word!"

CHRIST, OUR CONQUEROR

While growing up, I was enamored with a television show called *Davy Crockett*. The theme song included these words: "Davy, Davy Crockett, king of the wild frontier." Crockett is most famous for his death at the Alamo in 1836, when he found himself with a small group of men facing three thousand enemy soldiers.

Texas had declared independence from Mexico. Mexico responded by sending in an army led by General Santa Anna. Davy Crockett and others at the Alamo faced a decision: They could either fly the white flag, flee, or fight. Colonel W. B. Travis drew a line in the dirt with his sword and challenged those who were willing to stay and fight to step across the line. Crockett did, knowing it meant death.

Long before that, Jesus stepped across the line to fight our enemy, also knowing that it meant certain death. That was a dark day. It was the darkest of all days. The sinless Son of God hung between heaven and earth, taking upon Himself the full brunt of all sin for all people of all time.

But then Peter and John ran to the tomb. The angels appeared to the women. The Emmaus disciples hurried back to Jerusalem. Christ is alive! Can our enemies—sin, Satan, and death—defeat us? No, Jesus gained the victory over this toxic trio. What about failure? Jesus is greater than our failures. Panic? Jesus calms our fears and heals our wounds.

Abandonment? Jesus will never leave us nor forsake us.

You name it, and it can't defeat us. Nothing can separate us from God's love in Jesus Christ. In Romans 8:38–39, Paul lists ten enemies: death, life, angels, rulers, things present, things to come, powers, height, depth, and anything in creation. Ten. It's a complete number. It's Paul's way of saying that Christ defeated all enemies—every single one. The Gospel is unbreakable. God's promises are indestructible. Our victory is eternal!

CHAPTER 14

BALAAM AND BALAK: NUMBERS 22

You have some there who hold the teaching of Balaam, who taught Balak to put a stumbling block before the sons of Israel. (Revelation 2:14 ESV)

In 2006, two movies were made about the World War II Battle of Iwo Jima. Both were directed by Clint Eastwood. The first movie was called *Flags of Our Fathers* and was released in October of 2006. The second movie was called *Letters from Iwo Jima* and was distributed in December of 2006. Why did one director make two movies about the same historical event and release them two months apart?

Flags of Our Fathers was a movie about the fight from an American perspective. *Letters from Iwo Jima* was a movie about the battle from a Japanese perspective. No movie director, that I'm aware of, has ever done something like this before or since. Leave it to Clint Eastwood!

The book of Numbers exhibits the same idea. Chapters 1–21 tell the story of Israel's journey from Moses' perspective. Chapters 22–24 look at Israel from the perspective of two foreign leaders—Balak and Balaam.

Numbers 22:1 indicates that Israel is camped on the cusp of the Promised Land—the plains of Moab. Then the viewpoint abruptly changes. Moses isn't mentioned for the next three chapters. The spotlight instead turns to a famous divination expert named Balaam. Fittingly, ancient Jewish rabbis called Numbers 22–24 "The Book of Balaam."

The uniqueness of these chapters, however, isn't a talking animal (Numbers 22:28). After all, a reptile spoke in the Garden of Eden (Genesis 3:1). Instead, what makes Numbers 22–24 unique is that, for an extended time, the focus switches away from Israel and into the enemy's camp. This happens in the Bible elsewhere (for example, Judges 7:13–14; Matthew 26:3–5)—but never for such a long time.

Let's meet the main characters in Numbers 22–24—Balaam and Balak. It's easy to get these two mixed up. Balaam and Balak evoke the same kind of confusion that comes with Elijah and Elisha, Jehoiakim and Jehoiachin, James and John, Peter and Paul. We begin with Balaam.

A SEER OF THE GODS

Of all the people and nations mentioned in Numbers 22–24, Balaam takes center stage—hands down. Our knowledge about Balaam was enhanced by an archaeological discovery in 1967 at Tell Deir 'Alla (biblical Succoth) in the Jordan Valley, which was part of ancient Ammon. The fragmentary plaster revealed an inscription dating to about 750 BC. It describes Balaam as "a seer of the gods." This extrabiblical writing solidifies Balaam's international renown. Why, he's still on the Ammonite radar over six hundred years after his encounter with Israel on the plains of Moab. That's what I call an enduring legacy!

What exactly does it mean that Balaam was "a seer of the gods"? Ezekiel 21:21 is helpful. This verse describes Nebuchadnezzar, a Babylonian king, attempting to predict the future by shaking arrows, consulting idols, and studying livers. There you have it. Arrows, idols, and livers. Sound bizarre? That's because it is. God condemns it in Deuteronomy 18:10: "There shall not be found among you anyone who . . . practices divination or tells fortunes or interprets omens, or a sorcerer" (ESV).

Why does God use Balaam? Here's a pagan fortune teller who makes his living by doing things like examining animals' entrails (especially the liver), studying patterns produced by pouring liquids onto oil or flour, detecting the direction of smoke, and casting lots. Balaam is an Ammonite soothsayer, a non-Israelite, and, as we'll see, craven and corrupt at his core.

Balaam isn't the only nonconformist God uses. There are, for instance, non-Israelite sages in the book of Proverbs—Agur (Proverbs 30:1–33) and Lemuel (Proverbs 31:1–9). Also consider Cyrus II, king of Persia, whom God calls "My shepherd" as well as My "anointed" (Isaiah 44:28; 45:1 ESV). Then there's Nebuchadnezzar, who is called God's "servant"

(Jeremiah 25:9 ESV). And don't forget Caiaphas (a high priest we met earlier), who prophesied of Jesus that it "is better for you that one man should die for the people, not that the whole nation should perish" (John 11:50 ESV). While Balaam is similar to these men, he's also different—and in a number of ways. Consider the following:

God speaks to him directly (Numbers 22:9–12, 20).

His donkey talks (Numbers 22:22–30).

Balaam utters four predictive poems about Christ (Numbers 23:7–10, 18–24; 24:3–9, 15–24).

God puts His words into Balaam's mouth (Numbers 23:5, 16).

Balaam speaks by direct inspiration of God's Spirit (Numbers 24:2).

Balaam calls the Almighty "the Lord my God" (Numbers 22:18 ESV).

Through Balaam, God turned Balak's curses into blessings (Deuteronomy 23:4–5; Joshua 24:9–10; Nehemiah 13:2; cf. Micah 6:5).

Though Balaam is never called a prophet, his words are prophetic blessings on Israel and predictions of future people and events.

Add this to the mix. In the New Testament, Peter condemns Balaam for his greed—writing about "the way of Balaam, the son of Beor, who loved gain from wrongdoing but was rebuked for his own transgression; a speechless donkey spoke with human voice and restrained the prophet's madness" (2 Peter 2:15–16 ESV). Another apostle of Jesus, John, also denounces him: "But I have a few things against you: you have some there who hold the teaching of Balaam, who taught Balak to put a stumbling block before the sons of Israel, so that they might eat food sacrificed to idols and practice sexual immorality" (Revelation 2:14 ESV). Balaam would be killed by Israel for being "the practitioner of occultic arts" (Joshua 13:22). He also counseled Midianite women to lead God's people astray (Numbers 31:8, 16). Balaam's quite a character!

Why are three chapters devoted to Balaam and his oracles? I can answer that question with one word: *Jesus*. Balaam's oracles go back to God's promises of a Savior to Adam and Eve (Genesis 3:15), Abraham and Sarah (Genesis 12:1–3), and Jacob and Judah (Genesis 49:8–12). Balaam's visions also point forward to Jesus. "I see Him, but not now; I behold Him, but not near: a star shall come out of Jacob, and a scepter shall rise out of Israel" (Numbers 24:17 ESV). Jesus is this star. Indeed, Jesus is the bright morning star (Revelation 22:16).

Jesus. That's why God uses Balaam, whose messianic predictions play an important role in the Bible's portrait of our Savior. God uses a crooked pencil to write straight lines!

BALAK, KING OF MOAB

Balaam would never have appeared in the Bible had it not been for Balak, a king of Moab. Balak is the second key person in Numbers 22–24. His country had recently lost territory to Sihon—a fact celebrated in Sihon's victory song (Numbers 21:26–30). Israel subsequently defeated Sihon. Where did this put Moab and its king, Balak? On high alert! Balak quickly urged his neighboring Midianites to form a coalition with him and fight the advancing Israelites.

As a sidenote, let me underscore that Moab (a nation) and Midian (a nomadic tribe) are allies (Numbers 22:4, 7). This partnership helps us understand Numbers 25 (Israel's worship of Baal prompted by Moabites and Midianites) and Numbers 31 (Israel's vengeance against Midian).

But for now, Israel must be stopped. How? Not by meeting them on the battlefield. Israelites would knock out the Moabites and Midianites in the first round. If God's people can't be stopped by hook, the only other option is by crook. Balak therefore sends messengers 370 miles away to hire the hexer Balaam, who lived along the Euphrates River in a place called Pethor. Moab to Pethor. That's about four hundred miles, or the distance between Baltimore and Boston. Balak wants Balaam as a gun for hire. The target? Israel.

BALAAM'S TALKING DONKEY

Balaam's donkey is perhaps the most puzzling part in this story. In all three encounters between Balaam and the Lord's Messenger, Balaam's donkey sees (Numbers 22:23, 25, 27) what Balaam, the "seer," can't see—the Messenger trying to kill Balaam. The donkey's vision is twenty-twenty. And Balaam's? He's as blind as a bat. The donkey is more of a prophet than the prophet! Rembrandt's 1626 painting titled *Balaam and the Ass* captures the irony.

Balaam strikes his donkey three times until the beast refuses to go further. She made a fool of him, Balaam says, and he wished he had a sword to kill her. God, who opened the mouth of the donkey (Numbers 22:28), now opens the eyes of the seer, who sees the Messenger and how his donkey saved his life.

And if this isn't strange enough, God had told Balaam to go with Balak's envoys in the first place (Numbers 22:20), but He quickly becomes livid with Balaam (Numbers 22:22a)—to the point of sending His Messenger to take Balaam out (Numbers 22:22b). Jacob had a similar experience when, on his way back to Canaan, the same Messenger (this time in the form of a man), wrestled with Jacob all night (Genesis 32:22–23). Moses had an encounter like this as well. Finally obedient to God's call, Moses returns to Egypt, only to meet God, who tries to kill him on the way (Exodus 4:24). Joshua, for his part, is stopped in his tracks by the Messenger, who has a drawn sword in his hand (Joshua 5:13). Why does God do an about-face—from sending people to putting roadblocks in their way? We're not told. "Oh, the depth of the riches and wisdom and knowledge of God! How unsearchable are His judgments and how inscrutable His ways!" (Romans 11:33 ESV). This is a lesson I repeatedly need to learn. I'll break it down for you. First, there is a God. Second, I'm not Him. Our best response? "Have Thine own way, Lord; have Thine own way!"[4]

---

4 Adelaide A. Pollard, "Have Thine Own Way, Lord," 1906, Hymnary.org (accessed February 24, 2025).

GOD'S MESSENGER

Who is the Messenger that the donkey saves Balaam's life from? He's Christ Jesus, our Lord. It seems strange to think of Jesus as present and active before His birth in Bethlehem, but time and space restrictions don't apply to Him. Long before Jesus became flesh in Mary's womb, He was present in the world as the "Angel/Messenger of the Lord." The term appears fifty-seven times from Genesis 16:7 to Zechariah 12:8. The Messenger doesn't pop up sporadically or occasionally. He delivers and rescues throughout the Old Testament.

This might be confusing to you—especially because English Bibles consistently employ the word *angel*—as in "angel of the Lord." More literally, however, the Hebrew word means "messenger," which describes what an angel *does* rather than what an angel *consists of*. Every angel is a messenger, while Jesus is *the* Messenger. He's no angel. Jesus is God the Son—the Second Person of the Holy Trinity.

The Messenger first appears to Hagar near the spring on the way to Shur after she fled from Sarai's mistreatment (Genesis 16:7). He makes a promise only God can make: "I will surely multiply your offspring so that they cannot be numbered for multitude" (Genesis 16:10 ESV). Hagar then realizes that she has seen God (Genesis 16:13). And she's right! Jesus says, "Whoever has seen Me has seen the Father" (John 14:9 ESV).

The Messenger of the Lord appears several times in the book of Judges. He admonishes Israel for unfaithfulness, saying, "I brought you up from Egypt and brought you into the land that I swore to give to your fathers" (Judges 2:1 ESV). Later the Messenger appears to Samson's mother and father. On this occasion, Manoah confesses, "We have seen God" (Judges 13:22 ESV). The Messenger is unlike angelic beings in the Old Testament. He displays divine attributes, actions, and names. He's even worshiped.

There are, however, several important clarifications. In the Old Testament, the Messenger takes the form of a man. In the New Testament, the Messenger, Jesus, takes the flesh of a man. From Genesis through

Zechariah, the Messenger appears as a man but is not yet a part of humanity. When He becomes incarnate, the Messenger keeps His deity while becoming a human being—for us and for our salvation.

There you have it—the cast of characters. Balaam, Balak, a donkey, and the preincarnate Christ, God's Messenger. We're ready now for action.

THE CAMP

Three times on their way to Canaan, the Israelites stay in one place for a considerable amount of time. For almost a year they camp at Mount Sinai to receive the Ten Commandments and build the tabernacle. Then God's people stay in Kadesh while Moses sends twelve spies to check out Canaan. Now, in Numbers 22, the Israelites are on the Plains of Moab. And Balak, the king of Moab? He's having a nervous breakdown.

First, Balak knows what the Israelite army did to the Amorite kings Sihon and Og (Numbers 21:21–35). Second, he's well aware of the number of Israel's soldiers, as recorded in the census list in Numbers 1. "This horde will now lick up all that is around us, as the *ox* licks up the grass of the field" (Numbers 22:4 ESV). Balak gets it half right. The ox isn't the nation; it's the nation's God, the one true God who made heaven and earth. "God brings him out of Egypt and is for him like the horns of the wild *ox*" (Numbers 24:8 ESV). Forget lions and tigers and bears. God is like an ox, and He's on Israel's side.

Balak's first group of messengers arrive at Balaam's house together with "fees for divination" (Numbers 22:7 ESV). Balaam asks for a night to get an answer from the Lord. The next morning, Balaam stays put, refusing to curse the Israelites, for "they are blessed" (Numbers 22:12 ESV)—a motif that runs throughout Numbers 22–24 and is derived from Genesis 12:2–3. Balak's first delegation returns home empty-handed.

The king doesn't give up. He charms his way into Balaam's heart through offers of more money—a strategy that proves to be effective. Balak's second contingent isn't only made up of more and better officials (Numbers 22:15), but it's offer is more lucrative than the first one.

Even though Balaam can name his own price (Numbers 22:17), his reply appears to be very honorable. It's the kind of response an Israelite might say (Numbers 22:18).

The fact that Balaam asks for still another night shows he's hoping God will give him a green light. Surprisingly, the Lord lets Balaam go (Numbers 22:20). Is this a change of heart on God's part? No. Instead, God is judging Balaam. Recall that Israel's request for meat ended up with it coming out of their noses (Numbers 11:18–20). Sometimes God judges people by giving them over to what they want (Romans 1:24, 26, 28). Wasn't this what the father did to his prodigal son (Luke 15:12)?

The movement in Numbers 22 goes back and forth—building tension along the way. By the end of the chapter, we know Balaam is a good-for-nothing prophet for hire who has a surface relationship with God, no matter what else he may claim.

GOD'S COVENANT WITH ABRAHAM

A story is told of a monastery in Portugal, perched high on a three-thousand-foot cliff and accessible only by a terrifying ride in a swaying basket. The basket was pulled by several monks using a single rope. One day, an American tourist visited the site and understandably became nervous when the basket reached the halfway mark up the cliff because the rope looked old and frayed. Hoping to relieve his fear, the tourist asked the monk in charge, "How often do you change the rope?" The monk replied, "Whenever it breaks!"

With the hall-of-fame hexer Balaam ready to curse Israel, it looks like the rope is going to break. God's people will be doomed!

Not so! Why is that? The covenant. God tells Balaam in a dream, "You are not to curse these people, for they have been blessed!" (Numbers 22:12). In Genesis 15, God establishes a covenant with Abram. The patriarch kills and slices three animals in half—a heifer, a goat, and a ram (Genesis 15:9–10). Then Abram falls into a deep sleep, and God—in, with, and under a smoking fire pot and flaming torch—passes between the slain animals (Genesis 15:12–17).

What does this signify? God is confirming His earlier promises to Abram in Genesis 12:2–3. The Lord will make Abram into a great nation, bless him, make his name great, so he may be a blessing. And then God said, "I will bless those who bless you, and him who dishonors you I will curse" (12:3 ESV). This covenant rests upon God's faithfulness (He passed through the dead animals), not Abram's (he slept through it). Genesis 17:7 solidifies this interpretation. Sealed in circumcision, it's an everlasting covenant. It will never be broken.

When we hear Balak say to Balaam, "Come now, curse this people for me" (Numbers 22:6 ESV), we know it won't work. No one can oppose God's covenant with Abraham and his descendants. When the Lord sets His saving blessing on His people, no one can defeat it. The enemy might be a broken childhood, a dead-end job, a cancer-ridden body. It might be the blues, the blahs, or bad blood between you and your brother. But God's purposes will never be defeated—never! Check out, again, Nehemiah's amazing words: "They [Moabites] did not meet the people of Israel with bread and water, but hired Balaam against them to curse them—yet our God turned the curse into a blessing" (Nehemiah 13:2 ESV). God reversed Balaam's curse. That's exactly what He did with the bronze serpent (Numbers 21:8–9). The serpent, once cursed (Genesis 3:14), becomes God's means of forgiveness. Déjà vu!

Numbers 22–24 is brimming with reversals. Balaam, the expert in all things spiritual, is outwitted by a donkey. Moabites want to defeat Israel, but in the end, Israel will defeat the Moabites—along with the Midianites. Balak hires Balaam to curse, but all Balaam can do is bless. God is working to bring about His saving purposes for Israel and for the nations—whatever it takes.

GOD'S COVENANT IN CHRIST

Balaam's curses turn into blessings because of God's covenant with Abraham and his offspring. Jesus fulfills this covenant in His blood, seals it in the Holy Spirit, and delivers it to us in the Gospel, Holy Baptism, and the Holy Supper. We need this. Oh, how we all need this covenant security! Why? Because life gives lemons to young people, old people, sane people, crazy people, good people, bad people, all people.

You've been tossing and turning since 1:00 a.m. Now it's 3:30 a.m. In five hours, you'll be walking into one of the greatest challenges of your life. Are you ready? Are your ducks lined up? Have you contacted the right people? Is this even the best thing to do? What awaits you at 8:30 a.m.?

a new job

a divorce attorney

a family intervention

a meeting with a funeral director

an estranged sibling

In times like these, we need to know that nothing can remove from us God's covenant blessings in Christ. Do we believe this? If the heavenly Father says He can, He can. If the heavenly Father says He will, He will. Paul spells it out. "God will supply every need of yours according to His riches in glory in Christ Jesus" (Philippians 4:19 ESV).

BALAAM'S PREDICTIONS

Predictions can be made with great fanfare. Here are a few:

In 1876, the president of Western Union, William Orton, dismissed the telephone as a "toy" when Alexander Graham Bell offered to sell him the patent for one hundred thousand dollars.

In 1903, the president of Michigan Savings Bank warned Henry Ford's lawyer Horace Rackham to protect his money. "The horse is here to stay, but the automobile is only a novelty—a fad."

"There's no chance that the iPhone is going to get any significant market share." That's what Steve Ballmer, the CEO of Microsoft, said in 2007.

Predicting the future is difficult—unless you're Balaam. He has a direct line from God, who enables him to see the coming Messiah.

In Balaam's first oracle, he alludes to God's promises to Abraham, Isaac, and Jacob (Numbers 23:10; cf. Genesis 13:16; 28:14), which includes the promise of Christ's coming. Balaam's second oracle is about Israel's king (Numbers 23:21; cf. Genesis 17:6, 16; 35:11). He also refers to the messianic Lion of Judah from Jacob's prophecy (Numbers 23:24; cf. Genesis 49:9; Amos 1:2; Revelation 5:5). In his third oracle, Balaam speaks of the greatness of Christ (Numbers 24:7) and connects the messianic Lion of Judah to God's promise to the patriarchs (Numbers 24:9; cf. Genesis 12:3; 49:9). Balaam's final oracle speaks of the Messiah as "not near" (Numbers 24:17 ESV). When he arrives, however, the Messiah will be a star from Jacob (cf. Matthew 2:2; Revelation 22:16) and will wield a royal scepter (cf. Genesis 49:10) to defeat Israel's enemies (cf. Genesis 49:9; Revelation 19:11–21). John aptly summarizes Balaam's predictions: "The testimony of Jesus is the spirit of prophecy" (Revelation 19:10 ESV). Indeed!

STILL WAITING

Is this you sometimes? "Things aren't moving fast enough! Oh, that my life would be more like a James Bond movie or a J. R. R. Tolkien novel, where action careens from one thrilling adventure to the next. If I sit still and wait, I'm doomed to a life of insignificance and mediocrity. Who wants that? And what's God doing about it?"

Much of life consists of waiting. Waiting to get married or start a family or land that job or get that raise or go on that dream vacation or retire. "Then I'll really start living!" But in between? We've been there. Done that. And have way too many T-shirts.

Israel's march to Canaan comes to a halt in Numbers 22–24.

They were *still* between Egypt and Canaan. Did it that mean God wasn't working? Wasn't involved? Didn't care?

In 1996, Yasuko Namba of Japan set a goal. She wanted to be the oldest woman, at age 47, to climb Mount Everest. And she made it! Namba stood at the top of the world, and all of Japan cheered her on. Later that afternoon, though, as she began her descent, Namba was caught in a terrible blizzard. As the icy winds blew, she succumbed to exhaustion and froze to death.

What was Namba's fatal mistake? She set the wrong goal. It had been to summit Everest. But successful climbers know that the goal is never to get to the top. It's always to get back to the bottom.

Too often I set the wrong goal. It's to see God at work, sense His leading, feel His presence. How does that work for me? I become frustrated, antsy, and full of fear—sometimes I sink into deep despair. "God will never answer my prayer!"

Here's a better goal: Trust that God is working, even when everything is at a standstill, even when time moves as slow as molasses, even when demons and devils mock our faith, even when nothing seems to change.

Jesus carried the sin of the world to Calvary. And Jesus carries all our fears—every single one of them—including our fear of the future. Behind the scenes in Numbers 22–24, God is protecting Israel and turning curses into blessings. He's doing the same for us. So, we faithfully wait.

CHAPTER 15

A STAR IS BORN: NUMBERS 23–24

> I am the root and the descendant of David, the bright morning star. (Revelation 22:16 ESV)

Solomon writes, "A feast is for laughter. Wine gladdens the heart. And money is the answer to everything" (Ecclesiastes 10:19). Don't you love that? Money is the answer to everything. You've got a problem? Solomon has the solution—money!

Solomon is speaking in hyperbole. He's exaggerating. Here's what he means: Although money isn't *literally* the answer to every problem, money does solve a lot of problems. Car repairs? Medical bills? Mortgage? Heat? Water? Money meets tangible needs. And money solves intangible needs like happiness and peace of mind. Need to get out of the upper Midwest for the winter? Need a lake house? Need a more exciting life? What's the answer? Money!

Money is an essential part of life. And yet, beware! The only word money has in its vocabulary is M-O-R-E. More! Money talks. What does money say? "Always get more!" Don't believe me? Then consider Balaam.

BALAAM'S BELIEFS

Recall what we learned from Numbers 22. Is Balaam an honest man, checking with God as to what he should do? Or is Balaam holding out for more cash to pad his pockets? The rest of the Bible makes it clear that Balaam is a prophet for hire. He's looking for the right price—the highest price.

Balaam shows us money's dark side. Money definitely has a bright side. But money also has a dark side. What's money's dark side?

The belief that money is *literally* the answer to everything. Look what the New Testament says about Balaam:

> They have followed the way of Balaam, the son of Beor, who loved gain from wrongdoing. (2 Peter 2:15 ESV)
>
> Woe to them! For they walked in the way of Cain and abandoned themselves for the sake of gain to Balaam's error and perished in Korah's rebellion. (Jude 11 ESV)

Numbers 24:25 appears to end Balaam's story. Turn the page, however, to the next chapter. What do you see? Israelite men engaging in idolatry and sexual immorality—and it was all Balaam's idea (Numbers 31:16). Balaam would never give up the chance to dip his hand into Balak's deep pockets.

Balaam isn't the only person tempted by quick money. Listen to the radio. "You can make a hundred thousand a year in as little as two hours a week, working from home." "You can earn millions from real estate without any money down." "You don't have to wait. You don't have to work. You can have everything you want right now!"

Have you ever watched children eating pizza? Some take a piece and eat it before taking another. But others stockpile pizza. That's what I do with pecan pie. Pile it high. When Balaam was a child, no doubt, he piled pizza—and pie—as high as the sky! The goal? M-O-R-E.

Forrest Fenn was a wealthy art dealer who lived in New Mexico. And he loved adventure! Several years ago, Fenn filled a chest with gold, rare coins, and expensive jewelry—all worth at least a million dollars. He then hid the treasure in the Rocky Mountains. After ten years, it was found in 2020 by a former journalist and medical student named Jack Stuef.

Stuef was one of thousands who raced after Fenn's treasure. People journeyed through deserts, scaled mountains, forded rivers, and faced innumerable obstacles and dangers. Eighteen suffered broken bones. Six experienced acute dehydration. Three actually died in their quest for Fenn's valuables. What does Paul say about this? "Those who desire to be rich fall into temptation, into a snare, into many senseless and harmful desires that plunge people into ruin and destruction" (1 Timothy 6:9 ESV).

Balaam didn't buy it.

When Balaam listened to Balak, what did he hear? Abundance. Prosperity. Wealth. Money! Money! Money! Balaam defined life solely in financial terms. "Once I get that land; once I get that promotion; once I get that house; once I get that inheritance; once I retire, I'll finally be on easy street!" With his new gig with Balak, Balaam had struck gold!

Yes, money meets tangible needs. And yes, money meets intangible needs. But only Jesus hanging on the cross, outside the city of Jerusalem, meets our deepest needs—forgiveness, love, acceptance, purpose, and everlasting life.

Money is temporary. Jesus is eternal. Money comes and goes. Jesus stays through thick and thin. Money says, "Work to get more!" Jesus says, "I've done all the work for you." Money leaves us when we die. Jesus stays with us when we die and then welcomes us into His Father's house to live in resplendent beauty forevermore.

As we take a look at Balaam's four oracles, it's important to realize that—while Balaam utters stunning prophecies about Jesus—it's all done in the context of grimy, grubby, godless greed.

BALAAM'S FIRST ORACLE

What's the gist of Balaam's first oracle? Because the Israelites are different from every other nation, they can't be cursed. In other parts of the Bible, God reinforces this hold on Israel by lovingly calling His people *segulah*—that's a Hebrew word meaning "a prized and priceless possession." The term applies to God's people six times in the Old Testament (Exodus 19:5; Deuteronomy 7:6; 14:2; 26:18; Psalm 135:4; Malachi 3:17). Israel is God's one-of-a-kind treasure.

Let me explain it this way. I pull out a one hundred dollar bill, hold it up, and ask if you'd like it. Before you can answer, I crumple it in my hands, fold it, and bend it. I ask you again, "Would you still like this hundred dollar bill?" Before you can answer me, I step on it and rub my foot on it. Even with this, I ask, "Are you still interested in this hundred dollar bill?" You probably still want it because, even though the hundred dollar bill is messed up, it hasn't lost one cent of its value.

In God's eyes, Israel would never lose its value, though throughout the book of Numbers, the nation is dented, dinged, and damaged—all by self-inflicted wounds! They get pretty messed up! The Israelites make one harebrained decision after another, driving Moses crazy. By the time they get to the plains of Moab in Numbers 22, God's people must have thought, "Look how often we've blown it! We'll never amount to anything!"

But, through thick and thin, the Israelites never lost one cent of their value to God—and neither have you. Sound too hard to believe? Then take a look at what God says: "You are precious in My eyes, and honored, and I love you" (Isaiah 43:4 ESV).

Balaam has more to say. The Israelites can't be cursed because they're a nation God has blessed—that's why they're so numerous (Numbers 23:10a). In fact, Israel is so blessed that Balaam wishes he was part of it. Balaam even goes so far as to declare that he wants to "die the death of the righteous" (Numbers 23:10b). Yet, like all his professions throughout Numbers 22–24, Balaam's walk doesn't match his talk. If Balaam really wanted to die the death of the righteous, he could have joined the righteous. How? By turning a deaf ear to money's one word: M-O-R-E.

Israel's doors were open to everyone who wanted to abandon their false religion and trust in the one true God. Consider Rahab, Ruth, and Naaman the Syrian general. And don't forget the Ninevites as well as all their animals! For Balaam, however, boatloads of big bucks were more important than being blessed. Instead, he stayed among unrighteous Midianites and died by an Israelite sword (Numbers 31:8).

BALAAM'S SECOND ORACLE

Balak is furious with Balaam. How dare Balaam bless Moab's enemy! But Balak sticks with his high-powered hexer, inviting Balaam to try again. Balak thinks the number of Israelites overwhelmed Balaam the first time (cf. Numbers 23:10) so a new location—hiding some of God's people (Numbers 23:13)—will do the trick.

Within Balaam's second oracle, we come across these words: "God is not man, that He should lie, or a son of man, that He should *change His mind*" (Numbers 23:19 ESV). The ESV translates the Hebrew word *nacham* with "change His mind." In other verses, the ESV renders *nacham* with "relent." Either way, Balaam appears to say that God will never change His mind—period. No further comment. End of discussion.

God does, however, sometimes revise His plans (*nacham*). Some of these take place at key junctures in the Old Testament: the flood story (Genesis 6:6), at Mount Sinai (Exodus 32:12, 14), and when God institutes the monarchy (1 Samuel 15:11, 29, 35). Divine change, of course, is even incorporated into Israel's creedal statements. Both Joel 2:13 and Jonah 4:2 confess (with slight variations) that the Lord is gracious and merciful, slow to anger, and abounding in steadfast love; and He relents [*nacham*] over disaster. Most of the time, then, "relent" (*nacham*) appears in the context of God switching plans (e.g., Jeremiah 18:7–10).

However, the statement that God does *not* change or relent on previous decisions appears in eight verses (Numbers 23:19; 1 Samuel 15:29; Psalm 110:4; Jeremiah 4:28; 20:16; Ezekiel 24:14; Hosea 13:14; Zechariah 8:14). Of these, five describe God's refusal to change His decision concerning His judgment of Judah in 587 BC. One speaks of God's unwillingness to modify His commitment to Melchizedek's eternal priesthood (Psalm 110:4). The remaining two verses—Numbers 23:19 and 1 Samuel 15:29—appear to place God's unwillingness to change within a standard statement of principle. "God is not man, that He should lie, or a son of man, that He should change His mind" (Numbers 23:19 ESV).

So, which is it? Does God change His decisions or not? He does both. Huh? I often tell my students, "Context is king!"

Balaam's statement in Numbers 23:19 comes within the context of Balak hiring him to curse Israel. However, Balaam says God won't let that happen because of the divine promise to Abraham and his descendants (Genesis 12:2–3). Additionally, in 1 Samuel 15:29, God's unwillingness to change appears in the context of His final rejection of Saul. It's also connected to His refusal to adjust one specific decision: the choice of David as Israel's new king. Like God's covenant with Abraham, David's is also an unconditional covenant (cf. 2 Samuel 7:1–17; 23:5). What, then, are we to make of these two verses, Numbers 23:19 and 1 Samuel 15:29?

Though God can and does change from Law to Gospel (or vice versa), God will never revoke His promises to Abraham and David—the two covenants that form the backbone of the New Testament (e.g., Matthew 1:1; Luke 2:4; Galatians 3:29). God's unchanging intention is to bless all the families of the earth (His pledge to Abraham) through Jesus Christ (His pledge to David). Thus, when Balaam says, "God is not man, that He should lie, or a son of man, that He should change His mind" (Numbers 23:19 ESV), it means no one and nothing will ever remove God's promises to Abraham and his offspring, which, in the New Testament, includes us, the baptized. The deal is sealed! *On this, God will never change His mind!*

BALAAM AND THE LION

Balaam continues. He likens God's people to a lion (Numbers 23:24)—a motif that echoes Jacob's deathbed messianic prophecy: "Judah is a *lion's cub*; from the prey, my son, you have gone up. He stooped down; he crouched as a *lion* and as a *lioness*; who dares rouse him?" (Genesis 49:9 ESV).

Here are some fun facts about lions. A male lion can weigh nearly five hundred pounds and eat fifteen pounds of meat a day. The king of the jungle is seven times stronger than we are and takes down his prey with a single, powerful bite. Chomp! A lion's top speed is fifty miles per hour, while it's roaring can be heard from as far away as five miles. At 114 decibels, a lion's roar is almost as loud as thunder in the sky.

Have you ever seen a lion face to face? I hope it was at a zoo! In its "Big Cat Country," the St. Louis Zoo in Forest Park had one of the biggest lions I'd ever seen. His name was Oba. Now, if there was going to be a fight, I made it as clear as possible—I was on Oba's side! The only way to see a lion up close and personal, and live to see another day, is if he's behind bars. While my three children loved the zoo's "Penguin and Puffin Coast," I liked standing in front of this king of the jungle—as long as he remained in his cage!

That's what Balak thought as well. He hired Balaam to do just that. But lion Israel (*and all the more, Israel's Messiah*) will never be caged. John calls Jesus "the Lion of the tribe of Judah" (Revelation 5:5 ESV). Our Savior is far from being a tame, purring kitty cat. Jesus defeated Satan in the wilderness, cleansed the Jerusalem temple with a whip, and called down curses against His enemies. Jesus didn't step back from going toe to toe with anyone.

But Judah's roaring Lion became the slain Lamb. Christ's greatest power was made perfect in His weakness. Jesus allowed soldiers to march Him along as He shouldered His crossbar with blood dripping from His butchered back. Jesus let executioners strip Him naked, shove Him to the ground, and pin Him to wood with their tools of torture. Jesus absorbed the spit and insults without asking His Father to dispense twelve legions of angels.

Societies don't execute Captain Kangaroo, Mr. Rogers, or SpongeBob. They do, however, destroy people who shake their religious establishments to the very core. "There," the Jewish leaders said that Friday afternoon. "No need to call 911. There's no more Lion alert. He's crucified, dead, and buried!"

But, coming forth from the tomb, the Lion rumbles in His jungle! There's nothing dead about Jesus! By raising His Son bodily on the third day, God the Father accepted Christ's atoning sacrifice for our sin.

What Good News! We don't have to cry our sin away, eat our sin away, shop our sin away, or work our sin away. Jesus takes all our sin away. We're free from sin's condemnation as well as its hold on our lives. And there's more freedom to come. We believe in the resurrection of the dead and the life of the world to come.

In the meantime? In between? We have this promise from the Savior: "I am with you always, to the end of the age" (Matthew 28:20 ESV). Christ is on our side, fighting our battles, and leading us triumphantly to the new Jerusalem. The Lion of the tribe of Judah has conquered (cf. Revelation 5:5).

BALAAM'S THIRD ORACLE

Each of Balaam's four oracles goes deeper into God's destiny for His people. In his third vision, the prophet again describes himself as a man who sees clearly (Numbers 24:3–4; cf. Numbers 22:32). What does Balaam see? Israel is beautiful (Numbers 24:5), abundant (Numbers 24:6–7), and victorious in battle (Numbers 24:8–9). Balaam again echoes God's promises to Abraham—His plan to restore all things in Christ (Genesis 12:2–3; Ephesians 1:10; Colossians 1:20; Revelation 21:5). However, there's something new in Balaam's third oracle. God's Spirit descends upon him (Numbers 24:2).

We may think that the Holy Spirit is a latecomer in God's plan for the world who arrives on the day of Pentecost (Acts 2). However, the Spirit appears in the second verse in the Bible (Genesis 1:2), while Isaiah refers to the Holy Spirit two times in a lament (63:10, 11). Is the Spirit's work in the Old Testament confined to these few verses?

You tell me. The expression "the LORD's Spirit" appears twenty-seven times in the Old Testament, and the phrase "God's Spirit" comes sixteen times. The Holy Spirit empowers Joseph with the skill to interpret dreams (Genesis 41:38) and gives Israel rest in the Promised Land (Isaiah 63:14). The Spirit imparts the ability to excel in craftsmanship (Exodus 31:3; 35:31) and enables not only Balaam to prophesy but also Saul (1 Samuel 10:10), Azariah (2 Chronicles 15:1), Jahaziel (2 Chronicles 20:14), Zechariah (2 Chronicles 24:20), Micah (Micah 3:8), and Ezekiel (Ezekiel 11:5). In fact, Peter reminds us that all of God's prophets were empowered by the Holy Spirit (2 Peter 1:20–21). Most importantly, the Holy Spirit commissions the Davidic Messiah to carry out His ministry of saving the world (Isaiah 11:2–3; 42:1; 61:1; cf. Matthew 3:16).

At least thirty additional texts in Israel's Scriptures refer to the Holy Spirit. In these passages, we learn the following:

The Holy Spirit renews the earth (Psalm 104:30).

The Holy Spirit instructs Israel in the wilderness (Nehemiah 9:20).

The Holy Spirit offers direction (Isaiah 30:1).

The Holy Spirit kills (Isaiah 40:7) and makes alive (Ezekiel 37:1–14).

AGAG OR GOG?

In the middle of his third oracle, Balaam speaks of Israel's great king who will "be higher than *Agag*, and his kingdom shall be exalted" (Numbers 24:7 ESV). While many English versions—including the ESV—give us *Agag* in this verse, there is little reason to believe Balaam is prophesying about King Saul defeating Agag, king of the Amalekites (1 Samuel 15). In fact, Saul's failure to execute Agag doesn't result in an exalted kingdom for Saul; rather, God rejects him as king (1 Samuel 15:23). Noting this, many ancient translations of the Bible—like the Septuagint (the Greek Old Testament), as well as the Samaritan Pentateuch—have "Gog" instead of "Agag" in Numbers 24:7. Why is it important that we read "Gog" instead of "Agag"?

Ezekiel the prophet tells us. He writes about "Gog from the land of Magog, the chief prince of Meshech and Tubal" (38:2). Gog is Israel's great enemy whom God will destroy before He establishes His eternal kingdom at the end of time (Ezekiel 38–39; cf. Revelation 20:8).

When Gog goes down, the Messiah goes up. So do the Messiah's people—that's us!

Ezekiel further confirms that Numbers 24:7 refers to "Gog" and not "Agag." The prophet depicts God addressing this end-time enemy and asking, "Are you he of whom I spoke *in former days* by my servants the prophets of Israel, who in those days prophesied for years that I would bring you against them?" (38:17 ESV). Ezekiel mentions Gog as the subject of prophecy "in former days." However, Gog isn't mentioned anywhere else in the Old Testament before Ezekiel—except in Balaam's third oracle.

There you have it—the mystery of Agag and Gog is solved! With pinpoint accuracy, Balaam beholds Christ's final victory and ours as well.

BALAAM'S FOURTH ORACLE

Balak finally loses it. He can't believe what Balaam has just done—predicting that Israel's Messiah will defeat every enemy, even the great Gog! The Moabite king strikes his hands in frustration. He wants Balaam to leave, get out of Dodge immediately. But the famous seer isn't done seeing.

Balaam's last oracle begins like the previous one (cf. Numbers 24:3–4 with Numbers 24:15–16), yet his fourth oracle (Numbers 24:14–25) is different from earlier pronouncements—it's the most memorable and messianic. Additionally, the imagery in Balaam's first three oracles becomes more historically specific. He names nations and explains earlier metaphors. "I will let you know what this people will do to your people in the latter days" (Numbers 24:14 ESV). In the last days, God's kingdom will come on earth as it is in heaven.

PERFECT EYESIGHT

Have you ever seen that big *E* on the eye chart? I haven't. I wear contact lenses. Why? When your vision is as bad as mine, there are no good-looking glasses. You should see my eighth-grade class picture—the last time I wore glasses. On second thought, maybe you shouldn't see it. My black horn-rims might scare you to death!

What about Balaam's eyesight? He starts off his oracles needing prescription glasses. By the end? He's got perfect eyesight. Balaam moves from vagueness to crystal-clear clarity. In his first oracle, Israel looks like a dust cloud (Numbers 23:9–10). Then, he compares the nation to a lioness (Numbers 23:24). Next, Balaam likens Israel to beautiful tents—with trees, gardens, and abundant water (Numbers 24:5–7). Now, in his last and most stunning oracle, Balaam describes himself as "the man whose eye is open" (Numbers 24:15) and one "who sees the vision of the Almighty, falling down with his eyes uncovered" (Numbers 24:16 ESV). Then this climactic confession: "I see Him, but not now; I behold Him, but not near" (Numbers 24:17a ESV).

The Messiah will originate "from Jacob . . . from Israel." He is a rising star with a scepter—the symbol of royal authority (Numbers 24:17b). Balaam envisions this King defeating all the enemies of His people, symbolized by Israel's current enemy—the Moabites. The Messiah's scepter "shall *crush* the forehead of Moab" (Numbers 24:17c ESV). Balaam's use of the verb "crush" has overtones that go back to Genesis 3:15, where Moses tells us that an offspring of the woman will *crush* the head of the serpent. The prophet's point? "One from Jacob shall exercise dominion" (Numbers 24:19 ESV).

This is way too much for Balak. Why, Balaam just predicted Balak's demise and doom! The king quickly fires his hexer for breach of contract. There's no golden parachute or severance pay. Balak is simple and to the point. "You're fired!" The king had tried almost everything: messengers, altars, sacrifices, threats, and money—a whole lot of money. And what did it get him? Nothing.

The anticlimactic ending of Numbers 22–24 is spot on. "Then Balaam rose and went back to his place. And Balak also went his way" (Numbers 24:25 ESV). That's how evil leaves the presence of God— always like a popped balloon.

NATION WILL RISE UP AGAINST NATION

As Israel prepares to take its first steps on Canaan's soil, Balaam's last oracle looks beyond these current circumstances and to the Messiah's arrival. The seer's fourth and final oracle spans a large swath of history. Nation after nation will rise to dominate—only to fall in defeat. But when the King arrives, no one, other than Israel, will survive the Final Day. At the end of time, when history has played out its course, God's people will be the only ones standing.

Before that happens, the Israelites will occupy the Promised Land. Then, the Amalekites, who were "*first* among the nations," will be destroyed (Numbers 24:20 ESV). Because the Amalekites earlier fought the Israelites (Exodus 17:8–13), they're considered "first"—that is, the first to oppose God's people coming out of Egypt.

Next up? The Kenites, who eventually settle among the Israelites. In time, however, Ashur will take the Kenites into captivity (Numbers 24:21–22; cf. 2 Kings 17:6–23). Kenite secure locations will be no defense; Ashur will flush them out of their rocky lair.

God will then destroy Ashur—better known as Assyria—by a warlike power from across the sea (Numbers 24:24). Ships will come from Kittim—that is, Greece—to raid Syria and Lebanon. Yet the Greeks will also be destroyed (Numbers 24:23–24).

Is that enough biblical history for you? I hope not! There's one more nation that plays a part in God's restoration plan. Its name? Rome.

O LITTLE TOWN OF BETHLEHEM

If NBC, CNN, and Fox News had been around in 1809, their broadcasts would have originated from Austria. Austria? That's where all the action was. Napoleon Bonaparte was sweeping through Austria like a hot knife through butter. Bonaparte was making history!

But think about the baby boys born that same year—1809. Charles Darwin, Oliver Wendell Holmes Sr., Edgar Allan Poe. And, in a rugged log cabin in Hardin County, Kentucky—owned by an illiterate farmer—in the year 1809, one could hear the infant cries of a newborn son. His name? Abraham Lincoln.

What appeared to be super-significant with Napoleon ended up being no more important than a Sunday afternoon walk in the park. Today only a handful of historians can name Napoleon's 1809 Austrian victories. But most people have heard of Darwin, Holmes, Poe, and Honest Abe Lincoln.

Go back eighteen centuries before that—the heart of Balaam's last oracle. Who cared about the birth of a baby while the world was watching Rome in all its splendor? All eyes were on Caesar Augustus—the Roman emperor—who had just decided to raise everyone's taxes. Augustus was making history! While all eyes were focused on Rome's military might and political muscle, God arrived. *God arrived*—in silence, on straw, in a stable, under a star. The star that Balaam predicted.

Micah picks up where Balaam left off. "Bethlehem Ephrathah, you who are so *little* among the clans of Judah" (Micah 5:2a). No wonder the Christmas hymn by Phillips Brooks (1835–93) begins with the words "O *little* town of Bethlehem" (*LSB* 361:1). Even though Bethlehem was King David's hometown, at the time of Christ's birth, the backwater bungalow had a population of about two hundred people.

Micah goes on. "From you shall come forth for Me one who will be *ruler in Israel*, whose coming forth is from of old, from ancient days" (Micah 5:2b ESV). The "Ruler in Israel"—predicted by Balaam—will come from the house and lineage of David. What's more, the King will come "from of old, from ancient days." Hold on! This Ruler had a history before He arrived in history? The Ruler's existence stretches back into eternity? The Ruler was planned before the creation of the world? Yes, yes, and yes!

This Ruler—Jesus—is one with the eternal Father. A new person didn't come into existence when Jesus was conceived and born of the virgin Mary. Instead, the Second Person of the Trinity took on flesh. He became incarnate. God took upon Himself a body. God slept, burped, and cried. God became hungry, thirsty, and tired. God felt disappointment, sorrow, hurt, and loneliness. Christ's arrival is so much more than sugar plum fairies, old St. Nick, chestnuts roasting on an open fire, and Jack Frost knocking at your door. Christmas means God showed up—with a body.

Jesus understands when our bodies hurt and our hearts break. Jesus gets it when people ignore us, dismiss us, or reject us. Jesus can relate with our despair when we cry out, "It's too late to do anything about this train wreck called my life!"

The world was reeling from Alexander the Great, Herod the Great, and Augustus the Great—and the great God became one of us. *And people missed it!* The Bible has a word for that: *sin*. Sin makes us blind to the wonder, the majesty, the kindness, and the deep, deep love of Jesus.

Your sin—my sin, our sin—that's what led Jesus to stand before Pontius Pilate. Pilate has the Savior's body ripped, torn, shredded, dressed in purple, and crowned with thorns. God is crucified. God bleeds. God dies. God is buried. End of story? No way! Micah's not done. "And He shall stand and shepherd His flock in the strength of the Lord, in the majesty of the name of the Lord His God. And they shall dwell *secure*, for now He shall be great to the ends of the earth" (5:4 ESV).

Security. Isn't that finally what we want? Isn't that what we spend our lives trying to achieve? Isn't that why we invest money? Go to work? Watch what we eat, exercise, and triple lock our doors? We want to be secure—secure in life and secure in death.

Micah invites us to claim that gift, to open wide our eyes and see Jesus. Jesus—born in the little town of Bethlehem. Jesus—of the house and lineage of David. Jesus—God with a body, who comes forth from of old, from ancient days. Jesus—standing and shepherding His flock. In Christ, we're safe—safe and secure from all alarms.

BLESSING ISRAEL

Who is Israel today? Who receives Balaam's blessings? You do. So do I. That's what Paul preaches: "If you are Christ's, then you are Abraham's offspring, heirs according to promise" (Galatians 3:29 ESV). God's promise—articulated by Balaam—is to bless Abraham's offspring. That's the baptized, all who are in Christ Jesus.

This blessing is a solid rock, a firm foundation. People may come and go. Others may let us down and disappoint us—sometimes deeply. Fortunes may be made and lost, houses may burn, stock markets may crash, and cars may rust. Yet in Christ, we are blessed until the end of time—and after that, forevermore.

On the Last Day, our King will come, finally and fully, on the clouds of heaven, with thousands upon thousands of angels. Christ will be acclaimed King of kings and Lord of lords (Revelation 19:16). Inexpressible joy will fill our hearts as we stand before Him with robes washed white in His blood. Our song? "The kingdom of this world has become the kingdom of our Lord and of His Messiah, and He shall reign forever and ever!" (Revelation 11:15).

CHAPTER 16

MAYHEM ON THE PLAINS OF MOAB: NUMBERS 25

Flee from idolatry. (1 Corinthians 10:14 ESV)

That people went on a picnic wasn't surprising. After all, it was a Sunday afternoon in July. A picnic made complete sense. So, what was surprising? These people picnicked on a battlefield—with live ammunition flying hither and yon!

On July 21, 1861, a few folks who lived in Washington, DC, rode their horses and buggies to Manassas, Virginia. They wanted to watch Union soldiers bring an end to what they thought would be a short rebellion. The picnickers' intent was to sit on blankets, watch the battle from a distance, have a good time, then go home refreshed and ready for work on Monday morning. Were they in for a surprise!

It didn't take long before reality set in. With the sound of gunfire, the sight of blood, the screaming of wounded soldiers, and some dying, the onlookers from DC realized this was neither the place nor the time for an outdoor excursion.

This was the only time people had a picnic on a live battlefield. Right? Wrong. It happens to us when we think the Christian life is a picnic. Put up a few banners. Sing a few songs. Shake a few hands. Take an offering. Have a grand ol' time. Then go home refreshed and ready for Monday morning. But the Christian life isn't a picnic. The Christian life takes place in the middle of a bloody battlefield.

Who's the commander and chief of the enemy army? The devil and Satan—both words mean "accuser." He goes by other names as well. Jesus calls him "a liar and the father of lies" (John 8:44 ESV). John says that he's "Abaddon" and "Apollyon" (Revelation 9:11 ESV). Both of these words mean "Destroyer." And he's crafty. Paul warns us, "Satan disguises himself as an angel of light" (2 Corinthians 11:14 ESV).

It's easy for us to ignore all this. It's easy to stroll along, humming a happy tune, thinking the Christian life is pretty much what? A Sunday afternoon picnic. We're not alone. In Numbers 25, Moses and company also find out the hard way.

A RUDE AWAKENING

The surviving members of the exodus generation, along with their children, are camping on the plains of Moab when—unbeknownst to them—Balak and Balaam burst upon the scene. In spite of their insidious plans, God's care, protection, and love for His people is fervent throughout Numbers 22–24. What were the Israelites doing while God inspired Balaam to utter his slew of blessings? Nothing. They were completely uninvolved—just like Abraham when he slept through the covenant God established with him (Genesis 15:12). We do nothing. God does everything. That's called grace (cf. Ephesians 2:8–9).

Did Balaam's Spirit-inspired blessings mean that God had changed His mind about barring adults who left Egypt from entering Canaan? Had mercy triumphed over judgment? Was more grace on the horizon?

God's people were within a day's walk from Canaan—the place of their revered ancestors, Abraham, Sarah, Rachel, and Jacob. Can you imagine the excitement that welled up in their hearts? People must have breathed a deep sigh of relief and thought, "Finally! We're almost there! It's time for a picnic!"

Suddenly the picnic was over. Who crashed it? Moses tells us. "While Israel lived in Shittim, the people *began to whore* with the daughters of Moab" (Numbers 25:1 ESV). The story goes from the lofty heights of Balaam's blessings to the depths of Israel's sin at Shittim. If Israelite rebellions throughout Numbers 11–21 weren't bad enough, the events in Numbers 25 extinguish all hope for the remaining adults. This is the final nail in their coffin—literally.

What does it mean that the Israelites "began to whore"? Good question! It means Israelite men became unfaithful to their wives. It also means these same men were unfaithful to their God. They turned their backs on their wives and on their God. And, in both cases, the sin wasn't simply breaking some rules. The Israelites didn't discard the laws of a faceless government. The people didn't ignore commands from a nameless cosmic power. Instead, the Israelites turned their back on the God who had loved them, chosen them, rescued them, and given them great and precious promises. Thus, they betrayed two relationships—very personal and intimate relationships. "The people began to whore."

Not only that, but these same people also ate (Numbers 25:2). Why include this information? In the ancient Near East, when a sacrifice was made to a god, it was customary to eat part of the sacrifice. By eating with the Moabites, the Israelites joined themselves to Moabite deities—specifically a god named Baal Hadad.

BAAL HADAD

Baal Hadad was a member of the Canaanite religious system, one that was a threat to Israel—beginning with Numbers 25 and continuing through the rest of the Old Testament. Archaeological discoveries in 1929 of the Ras Shamra texts in northern Syria have greatly increased our understanding of this religion.

The Canaanite pantheon was led by the god El and his wife Athirat, who appears as Asherah in the Old Testament. Together, El and Athirat/Asherah are said to have had seventy children. Their most famous son was the storm god Baal Hadad. The couple's most influential daughter was a bloodthirsty woman named Anat.

The first part of the myth depicts conflict between Baal and Yamm, the god of the sea. Baal is victorious and is exalted as king. Baal Hadad not only defeats Yamm but also brings life-giving rain, which results in the growth of vegetation, at least until the summer drought.

The second part of the drama describes Baal's conflict with the god of the underworld, Mot. Mot swallows Baal and rain comes to a halt. Anat responds by unleashing her violent power, defeating Mot, and bringing Baal back to life. Rain returns and with it abundant fertility.

By engaging in sex at a high place—a hill or mountain—Canaanites believed they could manipulate Baal Hadad and Asherah into having sexual relations. This would produce rain that would water the crops, thus producing a handsome paycheck.

Can you see the sickness? Canaanites deified sex and money. Sex and money—when enjoyed within the boundaries of the Ten Commandments—are great gifts. Deify them, though, and they destroy people. Every. Single. Time.

WHAT A RIDE!

In June of 2007, Ben Carpenter got the ride of his life. His electric wheelchair got lodged in the grille of a semitrailer, and Ben was pushed down a highway for several miles at about fifty miles per hour. Ben's dad, Don Carpenter, who witnessed the ordeal, couldn't believe it when police called to tell him his twenty-one-year-old son was okay.

How did this wild ride begin in the first place?

Carpenter started crossing an intersection in Paw Paw, Michigan, about 140 miles west of Detroit. The light changed while Ben was still in front of a truck. The truck driver didn't see Ben, so his truck bumped into the side of Ben's wheelchair. Its handles then became enmeshed in the truck's grille. The ride had begun! Ben told others it was pretty scary. I can only imagine!

In Numbers 25, Israelite men become enmeshed with idolatrous Midianite and Moabite women. The ride, however, didn't end like Ben Carpenter's. The men brought down God's curses on themselves. It got ugly—really ugly. Idolatry takes us for a ride every single time.

FLEE FROM IDOLATRY

The pagan prophet Balaam blessed Israel. His donkey showed great spiritual insight . . . for a donkey! But Israel? How did God's people respond to divine gifts—especially the Messiah's coming? With idolatry. The last of the adults to leave Egypt are found wanting, *again*.

Balaam, unsuccessful in his attempts to curse the Israelites, advised Balak that he could overcome God's people through coaxing them to worship Baal Hadad. If the front door is locked, you can always try the back door. Note these words: "Behold, these [Midianite women in league with the Moabites], on Balaam's advice, caused the people of Israel to act treacherously against the Lord in the incident of Peor" (Numbers 31:16 ESV). Moab and Midian joined forces against Israel again, just like they did when Balak summoned his nomadic neighbors to defeat God's people (Numbers 22:4, 7). The coalition failed the first time. The second time? A stunning success.

The ancient Near East, Israel's cultural context, had never heard of worshiping the one true God. That's right. Monotheism was unknown. Moabites, Canaanites, and other people groups had a full menu of gods and goddesses to pay homage to. Today? Sacrifice to Baal. Tomorrow? Burn some incense to Asherah. On the weekend? Show your devotion to El.

When it comes to bowing down before other gods, Paul doesn't mince words. Writing to the church in Corinth, he bluntly mandates, "Flee from idolatry" (1 Corinthians 10:14 ESV). Leave compromising spiritual entanglements and don't look back. Paul looks at idolatry as an out-of-control fire, a nuclear leak, or a ticking time bomb. The apostle doesn't say, "Don't get too close!" No. It's more like, "Run for your life!"

At the root of idolatry is blurring the distinction between the Creator and His creation. We never break the other Commandments without first breaking the First Commandment—declaring created things to be godlike absolutes.

The word *idolatry* often evokes pictures of primitive people worshiping statues. We think of Paul in Athens, noticing that it was a city filled with gods and goddesses (Acts 17:16). But idolatry wasn't just a problem in biblical times. It's a human problem for all times.

Buddhism says get your karma right, and you'll be reborn into a different body after you die. Deism says God made the world then went missing in action. Hinduism says that if you become virtuous, you'll get another whack at life in another life. Moralism says try harder.

Idolatry dominates our culture. Anywhere sacrifices are offered to achieve ultimate happiness, there's an idolatrous shrine. Counterfeit deities are more than just false lovers and pseudo-saviors. They're slave masters that are never satisfied. Idols never speak the Gospel. Law is their only theological category. "Is that the best you can do?" "Come on! Try harder!" "If you bring your best game, you'll become more popular, more beautiful, more affluent, more athletic." "Get up earlier. Swim more laps. Run more miles. Get with the program!" Idolatrous shrines can be found in libraries and gyms—and they're out of control on the internet.

Often an idol isn't evil in and of itself. It might be some God-given gift that we use as a substitute for the real God. My idol may be a job, a person, a hobby. False gods are something or someone of value, but we ascribe to them ultimate value. Idolatry takes *good* things—vocation, money, love, ministry, health—and turns them into *ultimate* things. It takes *valuable* things and deems them *supreme* things. Often the object of our worship becomes another person. Affection turns into adoration.

At that point we've become a slave to our god. "You said, 'It is no use! I love foreign gods, and I must run after them'" (Jeremiah 2:25). It's tempting to think that money, sex, and power will liberate us. But counterfeit gods always torment us, and, if left unchecked, they will most certainly destroy us.

The problem with idolatry is that often we're blind to it. Our nation, government, military, or economy can become our idol, and we don't realize it. But the most popular counterfeit god today is Eros. Our society elevates romantic love to the status of eternal savior. This idol, too, is bound to disappoint. Then the hurt goes on for longer than long.

The only solution to entanglement in false gods is to turn to the true God—the God revealed at Sinai and at Calvary. This is the only God who, when He's in our lives, will fulfill us. And this is the only God who, when we fail Him, completely forgives us. No one else is worthy of our ultimate attention, affection, allegiance, and adoration. Jesus. Jesus. *Only Jesus.*

THE GOLDEN CALF PART TWO

There's only one other story in the Pentateuch where God is working for His people while they're working against Him. It's the story about the golden calf. While God and Moses are going over the tabernacle's blueprint at the top of Mount Sinai (Exodus 25–31), the Israelites descend into idolatry and sexual promiscuity. It happened again in Shittim (Numbers 25)—call it "Golden Calf Part Two."

The adults that leave Egypt, therefore, fail at the beginning of their journey to Canaan (the golden calf) and at the end (worshiping Baal Hadad). Ironically, recorded right after the account of building the calf and worshiping it, God's instructions in Exodus 34:15–16 warn His people not to make a covenant with another nation, lest they prostitute themselves to their gods. On the plains of Moab in Shittim, Israel jettisons these commands. Everything falls apart.

How much progress did these adults make? None. They ended up where they began. The only glimmer of hope is that, while Aaron instigated the making of the golden calf in Exodus 32, his grandson Phinehas ends Israel's flagrant rebellion (Numbers 25:7–13).

PHINEHAS TO THE RESCUE

Moses was a prophet without equal (Numbers 12:6–8). Now Phinehas becomes the priest par excellence. Phinehas appears earlier in a genealogy (Exodus 6:25) where we learn he's Eleazer's son and Aaron's grandson.

The tipping point at Shittim happened when an Israelite man escorted a Midianite woman in front of Moses and the Israelites. While the faithful are mourning God's judgment, a guy and a gal become involved sexually—right before their eyes! What a brazen act of rebellion. The couple has no regard for what God has said, nor for the distraught Israelites.

The word *behold* in Numbers 25:6 focuses attention upon Phinehas and his zeal. Although the ESV (and other translations) tells us about "a Midianite woman," more literally, the Hebrew indicates she is "*the* Midianite woman." This woman isn't anyone. She's *that* one. She's the ringleader. And she's now in the middle of the Hebrew camp! Her name is Cozbi, and she's Midianite royalty. Her father, Zur, is one of Midian's five kings (Numbers 31:8). This Cozbi is having public sex with an Israelite named Zimri, from the tribe of Simeon (Numbers 25:14–15). Who will step up and do something? Anything? Phinehas answers the call!

Phinehas's "jealousy" for the Lord (Numbers 25:11 ESV) doesn't imply envy; instead, it denotes his zeal and passion for God's honor. Not willing to tolerate idolatry, Phinehas proceeds to execute Cozbi and her Israelite paramour Zimri on the spot. What does God say about Phinehas? "It was counted to him as righteousness from generation to generation forever" (Psalm 106:31 ESV).

Just as Aaron went among the congregation with incense to atone for sin, thus stopping the plague (Numbers 16:46–48), so now Phinehas's quick action cuts short another plague. God looked on his deed and relented from further judgment—though by this point Moses writes, "Those who died in the plague were twenty-four thousand" (Numbers 25:9). The last of the old generation has passed away.

While most of the rebellions in Number 11–25 include the entire nation, sometimes several tribes are singled out. These include the tribes of Levi and Reuben (Numbers 16) along with the tribe of Simeon (Numbers 25). Jacob promised as much. When blessing his sons before his death, Jacob denounced his first three sons because of their violence and defiance (Genesis 49:1–7). Jacob's curses come to fruition in the book of Numbers.

We already know—through the narrative in Numbers 16—what happened to Korah and his crowd (Levites) along with Dathan, Abiram, and On (Reubenites). What was God's judgment against the tribe of Simeon—in large part because of Zimri's blatant sin? In the first census, there were 59,300 Simeonite fighting men (Numbers 1:23). In the second census? Only 22,200 (Numbers 26:14). The Simeonites never recovered from this decimating loss of people—narrated in Numbers 25. Once in Canaan, Judah absorbed Simeon, and we never again hear about this tribe.

PUT SIN TO DEATH

Put sin to death. That's God's message in Numbers 25. Sin isn't something to tolerate. Sin isn't something to wink at, agree on, or compromise with. God wants sin put to death. God *has* put sin to death. God used Phinehas. Now God uses Holy Baptism.

We died when we were baptized. That's how Paul puts it. "Do you not know that all of us who have been baptized into Christ Jesus were baptized into His death? We were buried therefore with Him by baptism into death" (Romans 6:3–4a ESV). Through water and the Word, God unites us with Christ's death. But that's not all. That's only part of Baptism. Here's the second half of what God does: "In order that, just as Christ was raised from the dead by the glory of the Father, we too might walk in newness of life" (Romans 6:4b ESV). Yes, we die in Holy Baptism. Yes, we rise again, all the more!

Baptized and born anew, everything changes! *I'm now empowered to renounce idolatry.* What does that look like? My job isn't my life. My investments aren't my life. My relationships aren't my life. My health isn't my life. My hobbies and interests and teams and sports and education and goals aren't my life. There's nothing wrong with any of these, but none of them can forgive me, restore me, or ultimately delight me and fill me. And none of them can raise me from the dead to present me washed, cleansed, and righteous before the Father. Only Jesus can do that. That's why Christ is my life (Colossians 3:4).

Paul maintains that Christ is the very image of God, the Lord of creation, the Head of the church, the Reconciler of the universe, the One who has all the treasures of wisdom and knowledge, the fullness of God, the Victor over all cosmic powers (Colossians 1:15–20; 2:3–9). *This* Christ is *my* life!

Once I'm baptized, how do I keep fleeing from idolatry? More dying. "Put to death therefore what is earthly in you: sexual immorality, impurity, passion, evil desire, and covetousness, which is idolatry" (Colossians 3:5 ESV). A false god pops up, and we go to war against it. We refuse to cave in or capitulate. We attack them daily through repentance, faith, and God's Word. "If by the Spirit you put to death the deeds of the body, you will live" (Romans 8:13 ESV).

Here's the baptized life. God kills. God resurrects. God empowers us to keep idols from ruling our life. Martin Luther has this to say:

> [Baptism] works forgiveness of sins, rescues from death and the devil, and gives eternal salvation to all who believe this, as the words and promises of God declare. (Small Catechism, Baptism, Second Part)
>
> There is no work done here by us, but a treasure, which God gives us and faith grasps. (Large Catechism, Part 4, paragraph 37)
>
> But here in Baptism there is freely brought to everyone's door such a treasure and medicine that it utterly destroys death and preserves all people alive. (Large Catechism, Part 4, paragraph 43)

WE HAVE A BETTER PRIEST

The words *jealous* and *jealousy* are apt descriptions for what happened when Phinehas stood in the gap and stopped God from condemning more Israelites. "Phinehas the son of Eleazar, son of Aaron the priest, has turned back My wrath from the people of Israel, in that he was *jealous* with My *jealousy* among them, so that I did not consume the people of

Israel in My *jealousy*" (Numbers 25:11 ESV). God then gives Phinehas "a covenant of peace" (Numbers 25:12 ESV). His actions weren't those of a vigilante out of control. Instead, they brought much-needed peace to God's people (Numbers 25:11–12).

While Phinehas is a zealous and faithful priest, he would eventually die—just like his grandfather Aaron and his father, Eleazar. We have a much better priest! The writer of Hebrews says that Jesus continues as "priest forever" (e.g., Hebrews 5:6; 6:20; 7:3, 17, 21). God's covenant of peace with Phinehas reaches its climax in Jesus.

Here's what that means. As our priest, Jesus forgives sin. We sometimes find ourselves talking like this: "I shoulda made a better decision. I coulda been more loving. I woulda helped out—but I came up with a bunch of really lame excuses." In the Old Testament, priests forgive sin, but their sacrifices had to be repeated—every day, every week, every month, every year.

In Hebrews, the author expounds upon some of David's most weighty words to teach that Christ's sacrifice for sin doesn't need to be repeated: "The Lord says to my Lord: "*Sit* at My right hand, until I make Your enemies Your footstool" (Psalm 110:1 ESV, cited in Hebrews 1:13). Following His ascension to heaven, Jesus now sits at the Father's right hand. "Sit" is the key. It's done. Salvation is won—once and for all time. Jesus sits at the Father's right hand with sin—our greatest enemy—under His feet. It's all forgiven. It's all forgiven, forever.

As our priest, Jesus also feels our pain. We might think that, because Jesus has passed through the heavens and now sits at the right hand of God the Father Almighty, He doesn't feel our pain. That's wrong. Jesus feels all our pain. "For we do not have a high priest who is unable to *sympathize* with our weaknesses, but we have one who has been tempted in every way, just as we are, yet was without sin" (Hebrews 4:15). The word *sympathize* literally means "to suffer with." Do you feel rejected? Jesus felt that. Do you feel lonely? Jesus felt that. Do you feel discouraged? Jesus felt that. Do you feel abandoned? Jesus felt that too.

When we feel hopeless, our Priest hears our prayer. "Let us then approach *the throne of grace* with confidence [*parresia*]" (Hebrews 4:16). The throne of grace is synonymous with the Most Holy Place—the very presence of almighty God. Only the high priest entered the Most Holy Place—once a year on the Day of Atonement (Leviticus 16). Number symbolism is an important feature in this chapter. Blood is sprinkled seven times (vv. 14, 19). Both the Holy Place (vv. 2, 3, 16, 17, 20, 23, 27) and mercy seat (vv. 2 [twice], 13, 14 [twice], 15 [twice]) are mentioned seven times. Throughout the Bible, the number 7 denotes completeness.

When we approach the throne of grace, we do so because of blood—Christ's blood. That's why we approach with *parresia*—translated "confidence" in the ESV. In ancient Greece, *paressia* described the right of a citizen to speak his mind in the town assembly. Only full citizens had this right—slaves didn't. As used in the book of Hebrews, *parresia* stands for our freedom of speech when we approach God with our prayers. We're full citizens in the Kingdom. We can tell Him anything.

Sin can't defeat us. Our high priest forgives it. Pain can't defeat us. Our high priest feels it. Hopelessness can't defeat us. Our high priest hears our prayer. And our weakness can't defeat us. Our high priest gives us grace "so that we may receive mercy and find *well-timed grace* to help us" (Hebrews 4:16). "Well-timed grace." It's grace at the perfect time.

There are times when I try to help people by doing something when I shouldn't do anything. There are other times when I try to help people by saying something when I shouldn't say anything. Not Jesus. He gives perfect grace at the perfect time. With a Scripture verse, with a Christian friend, with a song or a hymn, with a miracle—a blessing out of nowhere!

Well-timed grace helps us when we're weak. What are your weaknesses? Is it your health? Your old age? Maybe it's raising teenagers. Whatever it is, that weakness can't defeat you. Our High Priest gives well-timed grace. He sends the right word, the right text, the right person at just at the right time.

Phinehas is great. Jesus is grand!

PAUL AND MARRIAGE

Numbers 25 shows the negative side of sex and marriage. Everything went to hell in a handbasket. Paul, in Ephesians 5, shows the positive side—the upside—of the union between one man and one woman.

The apostle's teaching? Make more deposits than withdrawals. That's a fundamental truth in banking. No one likes to bounce checks. When it comes to marriage, we're empowered by Christ's love to make more deposits than withdrawals. In marriage, a deposit is anything positive. A gentle touch, a listening ear, a kind word. A withdrawal is anything said or done that's negative. An unkept promise, an outright lie, a harsh word. Some marriages are in tough shape because spouses are making more withdrawals than deposits. Do that long enough, and your marriage will become bankrupt.

Marriage was a mess in Moses' day. Marriage was a mess in Paul's day. Marriage is a mess in our day. Is there any hope? Yes. Make more deposits than withdrawals. Paul shows us how.

Let me address wives first. Before marriage, you thought your husband was as good looking as Brad Pitt, as smart as Albert Einstein, as athletic as Tom Brady, as noble as Ralph Nader, and as funny as Woody Allen. But now that you've been married a while, you know he's as good looking as Woody Allen, as funny as Ralph Nader, as athletic as Albert Einstein, and nothing at all like Brad Pitt or Tom Brady. How can you make more deposits than withdrawals? "Now as the church submits to Christ, so also wives should submit to their husbands in everything" (Ephesians 5:24).

I would guess that for some women, when you read this passage, alarms go off, warning lights begin to flash, and you feel a knot of dread in your gut. You might think, "Submit? To my husband? Why, I'm more fit to lead our family than he is. If I submit to him, we'll be broke before the end of the month and all he'll do about it is change the channel on the television!"

I must admit that, in a society where more women graduate from college than men, with higher grade point averages, women are more likely than men to go to graduate school, advance in the workplace, and buy a home, and women are increasingly out-earning men, "submit" sounds strange.

We need some context. The Bible also teaches that citizens are to submit to their government, that Christ submitted to the Father, that Christians are to submit to one another, that employees are to submit to their employers, and that Christians are to submit to God. Submission, then, is another word for what? Humility.

Wives be humble before your husband, not because he's wise and unselfish and a wonderful leader, but because God commands it. Just as we'll see in a moment, God commands husbands to love their wives as Christ loves the church.

Wives, when you let your husband lead, you make a huge deposit in your marriage because at the core of most men is the need to be what? Respected. Why is the passive, self-absorbed, emotionally distant, uninvolved male stereotypical of men today? It's because men are afraid they won't be respected. "Why initiate when I may be attacked? Why stick my neck out and lose my head? Why make the first move just to set myself up to fail?" Men are afraid of being criticized, argued with, second-guessed, and rejected. That's why some men think that if they passively go with the flow, their wives will be happy.

No, they won't. Wives want husbands to lead. Wives, you can make significant deposits in your marriage by affirming your husband, encouraging him, being humble with him, and, yes, submitting to him. That's a win-win. He's affirmed, and you get the leader you want.

Men, now it's your turn to learn from Paul. "Husbands, love your wives, just as Christ loved the church and gave Himself up for her" (Ephesians 5:25). Men were never exhorted to love their wives in either first-century Greco-Roman literature or in first-century Jewish texts. If Paul had said, "Husbands, rule your wives, control your wives, and manipulate your wives," no one would have given it a second thought. But Paul says that a Christian husband's primary duty is to love his wife just as Christ loved the church. And notice that this command isn't followed by "if"—if she loves you or if she's easy to get along with. Regardless of his wife's behavior, appearance, health, or personality, the Christian husband is commanded not only to love his wife but to love her like Christ loves the church.

How does Christ love the church? Christ took the initiative. He didn't wait until we loved Him. He didn't wait until we were lovable. "But God demonstrates His own love for us in this: While we were still sinners, Christ died for us" (Romans 5:8). Real love doesn't wait until it's safe. Real love doesn't wait until it knows there will be a response. Real love initiates. And men, that's what women want. Husbands, when you sacrificially love your wife, you make a huge deposit in your marriage because at the core of most women is the need to be what? Sacrificially loved.

Often it's small sacrifices: filling her car with gas, eating at her favorite restaurant rather than Dairy Queen (unless you're blessed with a wife whose favorite restaurant is Dairy Queen!), taking time to check in and find out about her day when you're tired and just want to crash, being the one to get up with the crying baby in the middle of the night, talking about the things she's interested in instead of the St. Louis Cardinals (unless you're blessed with a wife whose favorite team is the St. Louis Cardinals!).

Sometimes, though, the sacrifices are huge. I once read about Robertson McQuilkin, who was president of Columbia International University from 1968 until 1990. When his wife of forty years was diagnosed with Alzheimer's disease, McQuilkin resigned his position to care for her full time until her death in 2003. He said that when they were married, he promised to care for her until death, and he kept that promise, even when she no longer knew who he was.

In 1996, one of the space shuttles was grounded by—of all things—woodpeckers. Woodpeckers found the insulating foam on the shuttle's external fuel tank irresistible material for pecking. What's my point?

Most marriages aren't grounded by the big things (abandonment, physical abuse, infidelity) but by the little things—the daily withdrawals that peck away at the balance. Wives, husbands, to keep your marriage from going bankrupt, you need to maximize daily deposits and minimize senseless withdrawals. How do you do that? Wives, submit, be humble. Husbands, love, lead, be sacrificial. You'll be surprised at how quickly your balance grows. In fact, it's something you can bank on!

CHAPTER 17

THE NEW GENERATION: NUMBERS 26–32

> That they should not be like their fathers, a stubborn and rebellious generation. (Psalm 78:8 ESV)

In May of 2007, the Alabama legislature issued a formal apology for the state's role in its history of slavery and subsequent lawlessness perpetrated upon its black citizens. This was a dramatic decision for a state from whose capitol the telegram initiating the Civil War was sent—the state whose capital city was the site of the beginning of the civil rights movement in 1955, when Rosa Parks refused to give up her seat to a white man on a Montgomery city bus. One state senator commented in 2007 that people can't move forward without first taking account of their past. Being willing to look at a failed past isn't easy, but it's the only way to begin anew—and succeed.

Numbers 1 lists the first census in the book. The ensuing chapters, though chapter 10, prepare Israel to travel to Canaan with God in their midst—vis-à-vis the tabernacle. Israel's camp consisted of concentric rings of holiness that were designed to protect people from getting too close to God—lest His anger burst forth and they die. How did all this work once the cloud lifted and the people began their journey? *Everything went to the dogs.*

Then, in Numbers 21, a ray of light dawns! For the first time in their journey, God's people confess their sin (Numbers 21:7); defeat foes on the east side of the Jordan River: Sihon, king of the Amorites, and Og, king of Bashan (Numbers 21:21–35); and are blessed by God through Balaam (Numbers 22–24). Are these events a foretaste of better things to come?

Yes, but first the last of the old generation launches their last rebellion (Numbers 25)—a tragic end for all the adults who came out of

Egypt. Apart from Joshua and Caleb (and Moses, who will die soon), this is the last we hear of them. Numbers 26 begins a new era for Israel through its second generation.

Will these Israelites fare any better than their ancestors? Is the past a prologue to the future? Do the sons and daughters learn from their parents' mistakes or slide back into the same sins? And what about God? Will He stay with Israel if things go south again?

FINALLY, SUCCESS!

Israel's second generation is willing to look at its parents' failed past. This couldn't have been easy, but it was the only way to begin anew—and prevail. Realizing the age-old adage "What got you here won't get you there," the children (now adults) make several course corrections. And they succeed in grand fashion!

When compared to Numbers 11–25, the rest of the book paints a vastly different portrait. The contrast couldn't be greater. The most stunning example is that, while chapters 11–25 narrate the exodus generation's death, Numbers 26–36 doesn't record *any* deaths of their children. Even when they engage in combat with the Midianites, no Israelite soldiers are killed (Numbers 31:49).

Moses highlights additional accomplishments in the book's last eleven chapters. Military engagements succeed (Numbers 28; 31), potential problems are solved (Numbers 32), and legislation looks to the nation's future life in the Promised Land (Numbers 34). Moreover, according to Numbers 28–29, once in Canaan every year, Israelite priests will sacrifice 113 bulls, 32 rams, and 1,086 lambs. Yearly, they will also offer more than a ton of flour and a thousand bottles of oil and wine. God planned for His people to be agriculturally prosperous! And remember Balaam's oracles? God will remain completely faithful to Israel—no matter what. God's commitment and devotion to His people—and His greater plan of using them to bless the nations—is unchanging.

Yet while the second generation succeeds spiritually, it doesn't make progress geographically. Israel doesn't get any closer to the Promised Land in Numbers 26–36 (that happens in Joshua 3).

THE SECOND CENSUS

The book of Numbers provides several connecting words and phrases that help us follow the storyline. For instance, Numbers 11:1–3 provides an overview of Numbers 11–25, while Numbers 15:1 announces that, in spite of Israel's spy calamity, God will still bring His people into the Promised Land. Here's another verse that helps us follow things: "After the *plague*, the Lord said to Moses and to Eleazar . . ." (Numbers 26:1 ESV).

This "plague" refers to God's judgment in Numbers 25, when the last of the rebellious generation died. Moses, though barred from Canaan because of his hubris (Numbers 20:10–11), stays on to pass the leadership baton to Eleazar, one of Aaron's sons, as well as to Joshua. And don't forget Caleb. He's still standing strong! These new leaders engender hope in the next generation. It's possible to live faithfully and inherit God's promises.

COMPARING NUMBERS 1 AND 26

CENSUS OF THE NEW GENERATION	
Reuben	46,500—43,730
Simeon	59,300—22,200
Gad	45,650—40,500
Judah	74,600—76,500
Issachar	54,400—64,300
Zebulun	57,400—60,500
Ephraim	40,500—32,500

CENSUS OF THE NEW GENERATION (CONTINUED)	
Benjamin	35,400—45,600
Manasseh	32,200—52,700
Dan	62,700—64,400
Naphtali	53,400—45,400
Asher	41,500—53,400
TOTAL	603,550—601,730
TOTAL CHANGE	**DOWN 3 PERCENT**

The first census in Numbers sets the stage for chapters 1–25, which focus on the adults who came out of Egypt. They began well (Numbers 1:1–10:11) and ended miserably (Numbers 10:12–25:18).

The book's second census (Numbers 26) introduces the next generation. This counting unfolds a lot like the first—with several exceptions. First, the sequence Ephraim-Manasseh (Numbers 1:32–35) changes to Manasseh-Ephraim (Numbers 26:28–37). Second, in Numbers 1, Moses uses the phrase "who are able to go to war" fourteen times. The second census in Numbers 26 employs the expression just once (Numbers 26:2). Numbers 26 also doesn't mention the chieftains who are so prominent in the first census (Numbers 1:16). Why the difference? The second counting isn't focused on warfare; instead, its goal is to prepare Israel to divide the land in Canaan and live in it. "No need to worry about fighting for the land; just get ready to live in it!" The city of Jericho functions as a frame around the second census (Numbers 26:3, 63), thus increasing Israel's expectations. "Canaan, here we come! First stop? Jericho!"

Also, unlike Numbers 1—which doesn't have any anecdotal comments—Numbers 26 weaves in five asides (Numbers 26:5, 9–11, 19, 33,

46). These short comments instruct the new generation on what they need to learn from their rebellious parents. Three of the five warnings are dire. Moses mentions ringleaders in a rebellion—Dathan, Abiram, and Korah (Numbers 26:9–11; cf. Numbers 16:1–35). Er and Onan, Judah's evil sons, also appear (Numbers 26:19; cf. Genesis 38:6–10). Add Nadab and Abihu to the list (Numbers 26:61; cf. Leviticus 10:1–2). What do these people have in common? "The wages of sin is death" (Romans 6:23 ESV).

But that's not the end of the story. The second counting includes words of hope: "But the sons of Korah did not die" (Numbers 26:11 ESV). Are they traumatized by the death of their father? No doubt. Are they at a loss as to what the future holds for them? Most certainly. Do they lose faith, give in to despair, and throw in the towel? Not at all. Korah's sons composed Psalms 42; 44–49; 84–85; and 87–88. There's a word for this: *Redemption*.

The second census also includes a counting of the Levites (Numbers 26:58–61). It's also surprising that Moses mentions women (Numbers 26:33, 46, 59)—in large part to prepare us for the key role of Zelophehad's five daughters in Numbers 27 and 36.

In addition to reminders about unfaithfulness in Numbers 26, more appear throughout Numbers 27–33:

Moses' imminent death (Numbers 27:13; 31:2)

Apostasy at Peor (Numbers 31:14–16)

Temptations that may come to Reuben, Gad, and half the tribe of Manasseh (Numbers 32:6–15)

Consequences for failing to drive out Canaan's inhabitants (Numbers 33:50–56)

PATRILINEAL

Here's probably a new word for your vocabulary: *patrilineal*. It means something related to your father. In Israel's case, land inheritance was patrilineal—it passed down through a father to his son(s). What would happen, though, if a father didn't have any sons? The question is hinted at in Numbers 26:33–34, where Manasseh's genealogy goes back seven generations, ending with Zelophehad, who had five daughters and no sons.

The story of Zelophehad's daughters (Mahlah, Noah, Hoglah, Milcah, and Tirzah) is more than a one-off in the last part of Numbers—it weaves a thread throughout the rest of the book:

> The daughters' names are listed three times (Numbers 26:33; 27:1; 36:11).
>
> God makes His decision about the daughters in front of Israel's elders (Numbers 27:7).
>
> The law regarding Zelophehad's daughters impacts all similar future claims (Numbers 27:11).
>
> The daughters are described as exemplars of faithfulness (Numbers 36:10–11).

Moses frames Numbers 27–36 with stories about Zelophehad's daughters and their inheritance (chapters 27 and 36). In between are matters related to Israel's sacrificial calendar (Numbers 28–29), making vows and oaths (Numbers 30), taking vengeance against the Midianites (Numbers 31), the distribution of land to the tribes on the east side of the Jordan River (Numbers 32), Israel's wilderness travel itinerary (Numbers 33), and matters pertaining to Israel's life in the Promised Land (Numbers 34–35). That's quite a potpourri of subjects. Let's focus on a few of them.

A DIVINE INHERITANCE

God gave Korah's sons a new beginning. What about Zelophehad's daughters? Their dilemma appears in the second census. "Now Zelophehad the son of Hepher had no sons, but daughters" (Numbers 26:33 ESV). The daughters' economic future is at risk, so they bring the dilemma to Moses (Numbers 27). Their argument goes something like this: "True, our father was part of the failed first generation of those who came out of Egypt, and he died in the wilderness. But he wasn't a complete apostate like Korah, Dathan, Abiram. Neither did he fall under divine judgment at Peor. So, why should our father's inheritance be lost just because he didn't have any sons?"

Think back to the first generation. How did they approach obstacles and complications? The list is long. They complained, became impatient, wanted to go back to Egypt, worshiped other gods, were envious of one another, and in general were a very cantankerous group to work with! What do Zelophehad's daughters do? Are they carbon copies of the rebellious generation? Do the women start spreading unfounded rumors about Moses' unwillingness to work with them? Does the community rise up and demand the brotherless daughters stand down and go home? Not even close.

Zelophehad's daughters exhibit humility and faithfulness. They're prompted not by selfish desires but by the desire to do what's good for families, tribes, and the nation. Moses brings the case to God, who rules in favor of the women. They're promised land in Canaan. And that's that. No drama. No revolt. No cries to stone Moses or go back to Egypt. Why this emphasis on Zelophehad's daughters? They model how to solve problems. They conserve past traditions and follow Moses' teachings. *This is the new generation.*

RECEIVING AN INHERITANCE

I'm not a huge Green Bay Packers fan—after all, I live in Minnesota, home of the Vikings. I do, however, fondly remember some Packers players from my childhood: Bart Starr, Jerry Kramer, Ray Nitschke, Boyd Dowler. More recently, Brett Favre and Aaron Rodgers have worn the green and gold. Love them or hate them, there's no other professional sports team like the Packers.

The population of Green Bay, Wisconsin, is a little over 107,000. Lambeau Field—the home of the Packers—seats 81,441. With so few people in town, and that many seats in the stadium, we might conclude there are always plenty of seats available for games. That would be a completely wrong conclusion!

The waiting list for Green Bay Packers season tickets has more than 110,000 names on it. If you put your name on the list today, you will have to wait an estimated 955 years for season tickets. Good luck! It's common for Green Bay residents to put a baby's name on the list as soon as he or she is born. The one exception to the waiting list is the transfer of tickets from an owner, upon death, to a relative. For Packers fans, that's the greatest inheritance of all!

What if you were an Israelite? In the book of Numbers? What would be your greatest inheritance? The Promised Land. That's what Zelophehad's daughters say.

God promised the land to Abraham and his descendants (Genesis 12:2–3). The adults who left Egypt forfeited the land (Numbers 13–14). But, by the end of Numbers, their children are poised to enter Canaan. That's Numbers in a nutshell. Its focus? *Inheritance.*

Because of Christ's resurrection, we have a more glorious inheritance. Peter tells us that it's "an inheritance that can never perish, spoil or fade, kept in heaven for you" (1 Peter 1:4). Imagine that! Our inheritance is untouched by death, unstained by evil, and unimpaired by time. And God vigilantly guards it in heaven for us. Peter goes on to sprinkle seven end-times promises of heaven throughout his letter. What's it mean? Our future isn't defined by our past. Isn't that the best news you've ever heard? Past sins and shortcomings are not the last word on our lives. Our future is defined by God's guarantee of a heavenly inheritance.

The 2006 novel *Black Swan Green* by David Mitchell is about thirteen-year-old Jason Tyler, who lives in England in the early 1980s. Jason's family falls apart, England goes to war (against Argentina over the Falkland Islands), and finally—at the end of the book—his family moves from their home. Jason's big sister, Julia, tries to comfort him, saying that in the end it will be all right. Jason, not convinced, tells Julia that it sure doesn't feel all right now. Julia's response? "That's because we're not at the end."

Peter is with Jason Tyler. Sometimes life doesn't feel very good!

> For a little while, if necessary, you have been *grieved* by various trials. (1 Peter 1:6 ESV)
>
> For to this you have been called, because Christ also *suffered* for you, leaving you an example, so that you might follow in His steps. (1 Peter 2:21 ESV)
>
> But even if you should *suffer* for righteousness' sake, you will be blessed. Have no fear of them, nor be troubled. (1 Peter 3:14 ESV)
>
> Let those who *suffer* according to God's will entrust their souls to a faithful Creator while doing good. (1 Peter 4:19 ESV)

Julia's response to Jason is Peter's response to us: "Set your hope fully on the grace that will be brought to you at the revelation of Jesus Christ" (1 Peter 1:13 ESV). *We're not at the end, but the end is worth waiting for.* That's when we will fully possess our eternal inheritance (Revelation 21–22). My! What a day that will be!

A 2016 survey asked Americans, "What words give you the most hope?"[5] Here are the answers. Number one: "I love you." Number two: "I forgive you." Number three: "Supper's ready." These three expressions

---

5 Dennis Turner, "What Words Do We Most Want to Hear?" *The Times-Mail*, June 17, 2016, https://www.tmnews.com/story/lifestyle/faith/2016/06/17/what-words-do-we-most-want-to-hear/47892435/ (accessed January 3, 2025).

summarize the hope of our inheritance. On the Last Day, God will say, with a gleam in His eye, "I love you! I forgive you! Supper's ready!" In the marriage feast of the Lamb, we will sing an endless and deathless hallelujah. Zelophehad's daughters were looking forward to their inheritance. *So are we.*

GETTING ORGANIZED TO WORSHIP

What's next in Numbers? Two chapters with laws and regulations about worship. Numbers 28:2 provides a fitting summary—offerings (God calls them "My" offerings) are a "pleasing aroma" (ESV), which must be offered at the proper time. The phrase "pleasing aroma" occurs eleven times in Numbers 28–29 (Numbers 28:2, 6, 8, 13, 24, 27; 29:2, 6, 8, 13, 36). Why all the details? Moses is instructing the new generation.

The offerings are summarized as follows: daily (Numbers 28:1–8), weekly (Numbers 28:9–10), and monthly (Numbers 28:11–15). Annual offerings focus on festivals or special occasions: the Passover (Numbers 28:16–25), the Feast of Weeks (Numbers 28:26–31), the feast of trumpets (Numbers 29:1–6), the Day of Atonement (Numbers 29:7–11), and—the most complex celebration of all—the Feast of Booths (Numbers 29:12–40). Numbers 30 then repeats several features from the vow requirements listed in Numbers 6.

Now on to the mighty, menacing Midianites!

VICTORY OVER THE MIDIANITES

In Numbers 31, Israel gains a sensational victory over the Midianites. The triumph is the exact opposite of what the adults did when they were confronted with Midianites in Numbers 25—a total collapse on Israel's part. Moses' response to this defeat? He commands their children to enact vengeance (Numbers 31:2), which is also the Lord's vengeance (Numbers 31:3). The Israelites are God's covenant people. The two can't be separated. Offend one, and you offend the other.

Each tribe in Israel commits one thousand warriors for the battle—for a total of twelve thousand (Numbers 31:5). This is a relatively small army, given that thirty-two thousand Midianite nonfighters were captured (Numbers 31:35). It's fitting that Phinehas—the valiant priest who saved the day at Peor (Numbers 25)—leads the charge against the Midianites (Numbers 31:6). The Israelites kill every male; then the five kings of Midian; and last, but not least, Balaam.

Yet Moses becomes angry. Israel's soldiers "let all the women live" (Numbers 31:15 ESV). Moses sends troops out for part 2 of the battle. His orders? Kill Midianite boys as well as sexually active Midianite women (Numbers 31:17–18). Moses allows young women to live. They're consigned to a life of slavery.

Time out. Let's be honest. It's hard to read about Israel's killing and enslaving. We need some historical context. First, killing young men was a common military practice in the ancient Near East. They're the ones who would become soldiers and take vengeance on those who had killed earlier generations. The Israelites, however, didn't kill every Midian male. Note how the Midianites terrorize the Israelites in Judges 6:1–6.

Second, the fight is more than geopolitical. It's also spiritual. Remember? Moses describes the sin at Peor is "whoring" (Numbers 25:1 ESV). Israelite men broke faith—both with their wives and their God. Moses' command to execute divine vengeance against women who have "known man by lying with him" (31:17 ESV) fits within this context. Judgment is carried out against guilty Midianite women.

Third, although it's possible to read Moses' mandate to keep young women as a form of sexual slavery, there's nothing in the text that says that. Here's another option. Moses' qualification for mercy ("have not known man") doesn't make them sexual slaves; instead, he's separating these women from those who were guilty of the sins in Numbers 25.

As divine judgment, the whole episode is coherent, though still hard for us living in the twenty-first century. The long and short of it all? There's no escaping from God's righteous judgment.

Additionally, historians point out that—when compared to surrounding nations—Israel's approach was more merciful. Also worth mentioning is that later Old Testament texts don't exhort the Israelites to wipe out their enemies. Instead, these sections of the Bible promote peace and harmony (e.g., Isaiah 2:2–4)—the paradigm that the New Testament follows.

UNITED WE STAND

Minnesotans Abigail and Brittany Hensel are conjoined twins. They're one of the rarest set of dicephalus twins in the world. It's very unlikely to be born conjoined (1 in 40,000), and it's even rarer to survive after birth (1 percent of the 1 in 40,000). The fact that Abby and Brittany are alive and well is miraculous!

The twins have two hearts, two spines joined at the pelvis, four lungs, two esophagi, three kidneys, one ribcage, one liver, a partially shared nervous system, and a shared circulatory system. From their waist down, all organs are shared, including the reproductive system, intestines, and the bladder. Abby, the right twin, can't feel anything on the left side of body, while Brittany, the left twin, can't feel anything on the right side of the body. Neither survives without the other. Separation isn't an option. Cooperation is an obligation. That's the lesson in Numbers 32.

Following Israel's earlier victories over Sihon and Og (Numbers 21:21–35), the entire Transjordan is ready for the taking. Numbers 32:1–5 describes the request made by two tribes—Reuben and Gad, later joined by part of Manasseh (Numbers 32:33)—to settle to the east of the Jordan River. To get Moses on board, tribal leaders make the case that

> God has decisively conquered the land (Numbers 32:4),
>
> they will help in the fight for Canaan (Numbers 32:17–18, 20, 29–30), and
>
> their inheritance has changed to the east side of the Jordan (Numbers 32:19, 20–22, 27, 29–30).

Moses' initial reaction is one of anger, but after some discussion, he reaches a settlement with the tribes. Their request is reasonable, and the fact that Moses accommodates it gives evidence of divine approval.

Here's how it unfolds.

Unlike their parents, who had great difficulty solving problems and often resisted authority, these tribal leaders of Reuben and Gad listen to Moses. They follow his guidance and offer a compromise. Their wives, children, and livestock will stay in the Transjordan while their warriors fight with the rest of Israel to secure Canaan. Moses accepts the win-win proposal, and the crisis is resolved (Numbers 32:16–27). Both Joshua 4:12 and 22:1–4 indicate that the two and a half tribes followed through and carried out their obligations to Israel.

In fact, throughout Numbers, Moses emphasizes tribal unity. From beginning to end he calls the tribes "the *sons* of Israel"—an expression often abbreviated in English Bibles as "Israelites." This is unfortunate because the shortened form loses the idea that the nation consists of blood relatives—a fact on display in a handful of ways.

While Israel's tribes differ in size, they each bring the same gifts (Numbers 7:10–88) and send out one man to form a team in order to survey the Promised Land (Numbers 13:2). Following the same pattern, every tribe musters one thousand soldiers to fight Midian (Numbers 31:4). The overall thrust in Numbers 32, therefore, is that Moses keeps the twelve tribes together.

WE'RE ALL IN THIS TOGETHER

Before takeoff, Virgin America would play on their planes an animated short called "We're All in This Together." Some of the lyrics included "Flying through the air, clear skies and bad weather, like birds of a feather, we're all in this together. Hey kid kicking that seat! Hey guy with the five burritos to eat! Hey soft-drink sipper! Hey over-zealous nail clipper! Reality stars, men from Mars, guy sprawling like a hog, gal sleeping like a log. And don't make fun of the guy in leather! We're all in this together!"

Like Numbers 32, Ephesians 4:1–6 has much to say about unity. In the first three chapters of Ephesians, Paul talks about our wealth in Christ (Ephesians 1:3). In the last three chapters, Paul describes our walk in Christ. Beginning in Ephesians 4, the apostle's focus changes from belief to behavior, from doctrine to duty, from the root of salvation to the fruits of salvation. "As a prisoner for the Lord, then, I urge you to *walk* worthy of the calling you have received" (Ephesians 4:1).

The first item Paul takes up in our walk is church unity. When Christ brings us into relationship with Himself, He brings us into relationship with one another. In fact, the expression "love one another" appears twenty-three times in the New Testament. The church isn't a social network. It's not an activist group. It's not a collection of close friends. If we look at the church as merely a human organization, we'll probably watch from a distance.

Paul says the church is a Body (Ephesians 4:4). We're cemented together by the blood of Jesus. There's no stronger bond. The ties that bind us to one another as Christians are stronger than ties to work, country, and friends. I realize that most of us don't think this way. It's much more comfortable to look at the church like any other organization we belong to; that way we can come and go when we feel like it. That's a lot more comfortable, isn't it? But flying through the air, clear skies and bad weather, like birds of a feather, we're all in this together.

Paul discusses church unity from two different angles. The first is promoted through our behavior. The apostle writes, "Be completely humble and gentle; be patient, bearing with one another in love" (Ephesians 4:2).

Almost every bone in our body longs to live by the opposite of humility. And what would that be? Pride. Pride shows up when I think I really don't need the church or its singing or its preaching, or its fellowshipping. I'm doing just fine on my own, thank you very much. That's why I show up when I want, on my terms, when I feel like it. The opposite is humility—to admit that I need the church with its life-saving Gospel and Sacraments.

Next on Paul's list is to "be gentle." In Greek, the term literally means "strength under control." When the New Testament was written, "gentle" referred to a wind that would push a boat along at just the right speed. It was also used when describing a horse that had been broken so people could ride it. When winds and horses are out of control, they're destructive. But under control, they're beautiful. God says, "This is what brings people together. Not brute strength. Not, 'My way or the highway or get out of the way.'" God calls us to be gentle; that's strength under control.

Add patience to humility and gentleness. The Greek word is *macrothumia*. *Macro* means long, and *thumia* is where we get words like *thermometer* and *thermostat*. Get it? Patience means it takes a *macro* time to become *thumia*. When we're patient, we have a long fuse.

Paul continues teaching about church unity. His next expression is "bearing with one another in love" (ESV). Sometimes people rub us the wrong way. They make decisions that we don't like. They say stuff that makes us cringe. When that happens, bearing with one another in love means that I won't pout like a child, take my marbles, and go home.

Joe was dying, and he wanted to make everything right with Bill, who had been one of his best friends at church. But they hadn't spoken to each other in years. Wanting to resolve the conflict, Joe asked Bill to visit him in the hospital. When Bill arrived, Joe told him that he was afraid to die with bad feelings between them. He wanted to make things right. Joe reached out for Bill's hand and said, "I forgive you, Bill. Will you forgive me?" Bill said he would, but just as Bill started to leave, Joe shouted, "Hey, Bill. If I get better, this doesn't count!" That's neither humble, gentle, patient, nor bearing with one another in love!

Church unity is promoted by our behavior. It's also promoted by our beliefs. Paul continues, "Be eager to keep the unity of the Spirit through the bond of peace" (Ephesians 4:3). How do we preserve unity? Through our shared doctrines. What are those? "We are built on the foundation of the apostles and prophets, with Christ Jesus Himself as the chief cornerstone" (Ephesians 2:20). Paul's countrymen rejected Christ on Good

Friday. But on Easter, God made Him the chief cornerstone. When Christ becomes the cornerstone of our salvation, other beliefs follow. There are seven of them:

> One Body. Unity doesn't mean uniformity. The body has eyes and ears and hands and feet. We each have different gifts but live together as one Body.
>
> One Spirit. The Holy Spirit works through the means of grace—the Gospel, Baptism, and the Lord's Supper.
>
> One hope. The free gift of eternal life.
>
> One Lord. There's one Lord. It's not me. It's not you. It's Jesus.
>
> One faith. There aren't multiple faiths, multiple truths, multiple paths to eternal life.
>
> One Baptism. Baptism is what God does to save us, so we only need it once.
>
> One God and Father. The use of *Father* implies we're in the same family.

Throughout the New Testament, plural pronouns describe the church. The *we*'s outnumber the *I*'s, and the *our*'s outnumber the *my*'s. That's what Paul preaches. Separation isn't an option. Cooperation is an obligation. We've been baptized into God's family. We're all in this together!

CHAPTER 18

LET'S GET ON OUR WAY: NUMBERS 33–36

> I press on toward the goal for the prize of the upward call of God in Christ Jesus. (Philippians 3:14 ESV)

Matt Steven played on the basketball team at Pennsylvania's Upper Darby High School. Matt's also blind. Because his older brother, Joe Steven, was the coach, Matt got to play as the team's designated free-throw shooter during a tournament. Joe and Matt practiced consistently, with Joe hitting the rim with a wooden cane for his brother, who is blind.

Fast-forward to the second game of the tournament. Upper Darby was down by one point with seconds left in the game. Matt was on the free-throw line. The crowd was sitting on pins and needles. So far in the game, Matt was 0 for 6 on free-throw shots. He didn't want to take any more. Matt told Joe to put in someone else.

Have you been in a situation like that? God has a purpose for you, but you're 0 for 6 and you feel utterly hopeless. Every bone in your body says, "I'm done! Put someone else in!"

Because his brother believed in him, Matt stayed at the free-throw line. He shot his first free throw. Swish! The game was tied! Fans screamed. If Matt made the next shot, his team would win. Joe again hit the iron rim of the basket with a cane. Swish number two!

The Bible encourages us to believe in God. That's important. But what's even more important is to know that God believes in us. He stands—not with a cane but with His Word, guiding us to walk in His ways. That's true throughout the book of Numbers. God's determined to get His people to the Promised Land—even if it's the children of the adults who left Egypt.

A RECAP OF NUMBERS 25–32

Let's recap where we've been since the Balaam and Balak episode in Numbers 22–24. God's final judgment against the first generation happens on the plains of Moab. Moabite and Midianite women coax Israelite men into sexual immorality and idolatry (Numbers 25). The catastrophe, however, is followed by a new beginning that commences with a counting of Israel's second generation (Numbers 26).

This cohort took note of their parents' sin and rebellion and chose instead faithfulness to the Lord. They solve the problems of Zelophehad's daughters and confirm that Joshua will serve as Moses' replacement (Numbers 27). Following these successes, God issues directives for their worship life in Canaan (Numbers 28–29) as well as instructions regarding vows (Numbers 30). Moses then documents their war with the Midianites (Numbers 31) and assigns land to the tribes of Reuben, Gad, and half of Manasseh (Numbers 32).

It's now time to reflect on how far Israel has come—from slavery in Egypt to Canaan's southern border. That's Numbers 33. Moses hits pause to reminisce. The highlight? God repeatedly believes in Israel. He never loses faith in His people.

THE LONG AND WINDING ROAD

Numbers 33 details Israel's long and winding road. It recalls God's guidance to Israel in Egypt (Numbers 33:1–4), through the Sinai wilderness, and to the plains of Moab (Numbers 33:5–49). Moses also prepares the new generation for the last leg of their trip—settling in Canaan (Numbers 33:50–56). Along the way, he mentions forty-two places. Why forty-two?

Perhaps we should understand forty-two not only literally but also figuratively—six sevens. Six times seven equals forty-two. And six sevens suggests that Israel's journey is incomplete. Seven sevens is the goal. A biblical story can't end with six sevens. That's not a complete story. There must be a final seven.

Note, for instance, that Israel's Jubilee year begins after forty-nine years, or seven sevens (Leviticus 25:8). Daniel, for his part, announces that the Messiah will come in seventy weeks—or seventy sevens (Daniel 9:24). Also consider what Matthew 1:17 teaches us: "There were fourteen generations from Abraham to David, fourteen from David to the exile to Babylon, and fourteen from the exile to the Christ." Matthew summarizes biblical history in three sets of fourteens—or six sevens. It's a story that lacks an ending. That's Matthew's point. Jesus brings the biblical story to completion. Jesus ushers in the final stage in God's plan of salvation (Matthew 1:18–25).

Thus, Moses' itinerary fits within this larger biblical pattern. Israel had "worked" six days and was now poised to enter her land of rest on the "seventh" day. The real work, the hard work, had been done—forty-two camping sites! Rest now awaits them in the Promised Land—Israel's seventh seven is on the horizon. Canaan's within reach!

Some campsites in Numbers 33 are unknown today. The general gist, though, is clear. Numbers 33:6–15 chronicles Israel's travels in Exodus 13:17–19:1—from Succoth to Sinai. Numbers 33:19–29 cites places that don't appear anywhere else in the Bible. These verses also recall locales where Israel failed badly—places like Marah (Numbers 33:8) and Rephidim (Numbers 33:14). Overall, the chapter offers three different kinds of campsites: (1) where God was faithful, (2) where Israel was faithless, and (3) where nothing of great import occurred.

All of that said, I need to be honest with you. Moses' list of locations isn't very interesting. It may be fascinating to a handful of biblical scholars who use it to create a more accurate account of Israel's forty years in the wilderness. But for us? It's just a list of obscure places.

Not so, of course, for the Israelites themselves! Every one of the names would have evoked memories. The itinerary was an Ebenezer of sorts. You remember. Ebenezer was a stone memorial that Samuel set up at Mizpah to commemorate God's faithfulness and His power to deliver His people from their enemies (1 Samuel 7:5–14).

At the end of Numbers 33, Moses writes these encouraging words: "*When* you pass over the Jordan into the land of Canaan" (Numbers 33:51 ESV). Moses concludes the book by addressing life in the Promised Land.

Land boundaries (Numbers 34:1–15)

List of leaders who will allot the land (Numbers 34:16–29)

Levitical cities (Numbers 35:1–8)

Cities of refuge (Numbers 35:9–34)

Zelophehad's daughters (Numbers 36:1–12)

Conclusion (Numbers 36:13)

CHARTING OUR JOURNEY

Like the Israelites, our journey can be slow and meandering—like the muddy Mississippi River. At other times, we're clinging to the steering wheel as we hurl around a sharp curve—feeling like we're driving in the Indy 500. Maybe you're raising young children, seeing them off to college, or now trying to pay for it all. Wherever you are on life's journey, chances are you're still in between.

Baptized into Christ, we're between being new creations in Christ Jesus and longing for Him to return and renew all things. Peace is ours right now, but much more awaits us. We know that Good Friday gives way to Easter, but it's as though we're stuck in Holy Saturday, waiting for the fullness of resurrection promises to unfold. In-betweenness is the quintessential Christian condition.

Much like Moses and company, we travel from the bondage of our own Egypt through the waters of Holy Baptism and finally to our heavenly promised land. How will we get there? There's only one road. God only gives us one way—through the wilderness. I wish I could choose my own road to get to the new Jerusalem. It would be flat—with a gentle hill now and then. Lush trees and foliage would line each side of the boulevard. A gentle breeze would blow on my face. Comfortable hotels and a wide variety of restaurants would be readily available.

Nope. That's not how it works. God's plan is to sanctify us, not amuse us. His goal is our holiness, not our happiness. We have our own forty-two stations—just like Israel—the ups and downs of our journey through the wilderness of this world, even as we long for our seventh seven, our heavenly Canaan. "Blessed are the dead who die in the Lord from now on. 'Blessed indeed,' says the Spirit, 'that they may *rest* from their labors'" (Revelation 14:13 ESV). Rest, at last!

But not yet.

In the meantime, it's wise to remember where God has taken us. Every now and then, just like Moses in Numbers 33, it's good to call a time out to recall where we've been and what God has shown us, as well as where we're headed. Then our grind transforms into a story of pilgrimage, a great adventure where we begin to see the presence of our loving God. Why not do what Moses did? Write up a list of locales—the euphoric as well as the darkest places in your life.

How important is it that we periodically pause to get our bearings? I'll put it this way: Often our biggest problem is that we keep having the same problem. When I chart my life, I begin seeing patterns; I begin understanding the painful events that keep repeating themselves. Then I can be more strategic. And repentant. And mindful. And prayerful. As we all know, the definition of insanity is doing the same thing and expecting different results. Making a map keeps me sane!

There's a story about a woman who was complaining about her six failed marriages, as well as her six lousy ex-husbands. Another woman insightfully responded, "Honey, you've not been married to six different men. You've been married to the same man with six different last names." Do you catch her drift? I'm going to keep having the same problem unless I pause to understand what's good, what's bad, and what God invites me to change.

But change is difficult—especially if we've experienced trauma. Then we become frozen in time, stuck in one place, going in circles, replaying the nightmare. Traumatic events threaten to rob us of our ability to sketch our journey and tell others about it. We have snapshots and memories—even smells and tastes—but we can't put them together. It's a bunch of mumbo jumbo.

Insidiously, perpetrators of trauma encourage—and in some cases insist on—secrecy and silence. When this fails, they launch attacks against our credibility. "How could you believe that?" "What an exaggeration!" "You're making that up!" Powerful forces render us voiceless, unable to talk about our pain. There's a term for this—*shell-shocked*. Then comes what? Denial. Living in the land of make believe creates even more angst and anguish. Choosing fiction over reality never works—but that doesn't keep us from trying to beat the odds. Denial finds a million ways to cope with painful memories.

What does Moses say to that? Refuse to whitewash what happened. Face the music. Be honest. His list in Numbers 33 includes both failures and foibles, as well as God's faithfulness. Moses insists that we take the past seriously. Dig it up. Remember it well. First things first. Repentance then faith. Weeping then joy. Death then resurrection. So go ahead. Name your pain. Lament your loss. Truth will begin to surface. Trauma will begin to loosen its iron grip.

This is also the way of Jesus. He welcomes honesty. "Blessed are those who mourn, for they will be comforted" (Matthew 5:4). God pours out immeasurable comfort and consolation on those who walk and talk through their sorrows.

There's something very godly about acknowledging deep distress. God the Father looks at the sin of the world in Noah's day, and His heart is grieved (Genesis 6:6). Jesus approaches Jerusalem and weeps over the city (Luke 19:41). Paul writes that sin grieves the Holy Spirit (Ephesians 4:30). So, go ahead. Look back on your past, but also look up to the triune God, who knows about deep pain and is with you every step of the long and winding road.

NUMBERS 35

The motif of allotting land from Numbers 34 continues into Numbers 35, where Moses mandates that Israel gives the Levites cities and pastureland. This follows a template. The census in Numbers 26 is followed by counting the tribe of Levi. And, after the tribal allotments of land (Numbers 32 and 34), God now provides space for the Levites (Numbers 35). Do you see the pattern? Israel first. Levites second.

The Levites are different from the rest of the Israelites. They're a tribe, but the Levites aren't considered part of the twelve tribes. While God gives land to Israel's other tribes (Numbers 34), the Levites receive forty-eight cities and their pasturelands (Numbers 35:1–6), which were spread throughout Canaan (Joshua 21:1–48). Six of these cities were called cities of refuge (Numbers 35:9–34).

Numbers 35 thus has two parts: (1) towns and pastures for the Levites (Numbers 35:1–8) and (2) sanctuary cities for those who accidentally kill someone—what we call involuntary manslaughter (Numbers 35:9–34). I'm going to expand on the second section, the cities of refuge.

CITIES OF REFUGE

Safe places exist for a variety of people—troubled youth, battered women, homeless men. You can find asylums in fast-food restaurants, convenience stores, fire stations, libraries, and bus stations. They connect people who are in danger to safety and supportive services.

We all know how this works. When we were kids, to get away from our big sister, we ran to a closet or a fort in our backyard. Men, to get away from let's just say a spirited discussion with your wife, you seek refuge in your garage or a workshop in your basement. Others, to get away from something called a polar vortex, hightail it out of the Midwest every winter for a refuge called Phoenix, Arizona.

The Israelites had their own version of a safe place. They called them cities of refuge—places for "the manslayer who kills any person without intent" (Numbers 35:11 ESV). There were six safe havens: three "beyond the Jordan, and three cities in the land of Canaan" (Numbers 35:14 ESV). Kadesh, Shechem, Hebron, Bezer, Ramoth, and Golan (Joshua 20:7–8). Spread out over the Promised Land, the cities were an ever-present help in trouble.

HOW IT WORKED

If someone in your family was killed, your relatives would call a meeting, and somebody would be appointed as a "blood avenger" (Numbers 35:19–27). This blood avenger was to chase down the killer and—to put it bluntly—release the killer's neck from the burden of having to carry a head. Admittedly, this was crude, but it kept law and order. Of course, a major problem with such a system was an accidental death.

Let's use Deuteronomy 19:5 as an example. A man goes into a forest with his neighbor to chop down a tree. He swings his axe, and the axe's head flies off, hits his neighbor, and kills him. Now what happens? The dead man's family calls a meeting. They appoint a family blood avenger. And they don't choose rotund Uncle Earl. No, they pick fleet-footed Cousin Kurt. And Kurt's orders are clear: "Chase down the guy with the loose axe-head and kill him!"

I bet you're thinking, "That's not fair. He didn't mean to kill his neighbor. The guy just had a loose axe-head!" Fair enough, but the unintentional killer had to hightail it to a city of refuge before the avenger of blood could catch up with him and kill him. Once in the safe place, if the killer was deemed guilty, he was executed. If he was innocent, he remained in the city "until the death of the high priest" (Numbers 35:25 ESV). The high priest's death paid the price—after which, the accidental killer was free. The high priest's blood was an atoning sacrifice.

ON THE RUN

A big, brute, bruising bully is as American as baseball, hot dogs, apple pie, and Chevrolet. You know the kind. He's twelve years old and he's already shaving. Some 90 percent of the male voices in your junior high school sounded like altos and sopranos, but this guy's voice bellowed out like a bazooka. One of the bullies in my boyhood backyard was Duane Houts.

One day, in seventh-grade gym class, I made a move in flag football that upset Duane—I dodged him, then ran by him. It ended up with me scoring a touchdown. My friends cheered. I was the hero for the day. Duane? Let's just say Duane didn't join my fan club. In fact, after gym class, he confronted me and uttered two of the most dreaded words in my junior high, "Choose ya!" For the uninitiated, that meant he wanted to fight me after school. The word got out. These fights happened behind a shoe repair shop with at least fifty students forming a circle, with the fighters in the middle. A one-round knockout fight was inevitable, with my two front teeth hanging on for dear life!

What did I do? The flag football hero raced home after school as fast as I could—clocking a four-minute mile! Once home, with sweat pouring down my face, I caught my breath, took a deep breath, and realized I had made it, safe and sound!

In the battle hymn of the Reformation, "A Mighty Fortress Is Our God," Martin Luther describes the one chasing us. Do you recall these words?

The old evil foe now means deadly woe.

Though devils all the world should fill, all eager to devour us.

This world's prince may still scowl fierce as he will.

Deep guile and great might are his dread arms in fight; on earth is not his equal.

(*LSB* 656:1, 3)

The avenger of blood comes to kill and steal and destroy. The devil's first move in Genesis 3 was to speak. Sticks and stones may break my bones, but Satan's words break my heart, my home, and my church. We see him in our rearview mirror. We feel his hot breath behind us. We know what it's like to run for our lives.

As tempter, he chases after us, screaming, "Whatever it is you want to do, just do it. Have some rage? Act it out. Have some sexual fantasies? Go ahead, full throttle. Have some juicy gossip? Let it fly." He continues, "There are no limits, no consequences, and no commandments. Ready, set, go!" When we give in, the devil plants his foot upon our neck and says, "Now that you said this, thought this, did this, drank this, smoked this, saw this, God is finished with you!"

Numbers 35 describes safe places for those who kill accidentally and unintentionally. That leaves us out. Countless times we've sinned with malice aforethought. Then we become sitting ducks for the roaring lion—the devil himself (1 Peter 5:8). No one knows what to do, except the Lord, the God of Israel and the Father of our Lord Jesus Christ. It's in His heart to provide a refuge—an ever-present help in times of trouble.

Old Testament cities of refuge are fulfilled in Jesus, who is similar to, yet greater than, Joshua and Jonah, Melchizedek and Moses, the tabernacle and the temple. Jesus Christ is God's final expression for a safe place, an asylum, a sanctuary, a haven, and a mighty fortress. "God is our refuge and strength, a very present help in trouble" (Psalm 46:1 ESV).

Jesus says, "Now is the judgment of this world; now will the ruler of this world be cast out. And I, when I am lifted up from the earth, will draw all people to Myself" (John 12:31–32 ESV). Here is your Savior. Lifted up on the cross, casting out the prince of this world—the ancient serpent who is the devil and Satan. "He can harm us none. He's judged; the deed is done; one little word can fell him" (*LSB* 656:3).

HOLY COMMUNION

Martin Luther was once debating about Christ's real presence in Holy Communion when he wrote these Latin words upon a table: *Hoc est corpus meum,* "This is My body." Jesus' true body and blood in the Holy Supper are our ever-present help in trouble. By the power of God's Word, the forgiveness and mercy purchased for us on the cross are now present in, with, and under bread and wine.

To the casual observer, the Holy Supper must sound strange. Following *Lutheran Service Book*, pages 161–63, we sing "Holy, holy, holy Lord God of power and might"; hear our pastor speak the Words of Our Lord; and approach Christ's altar, singing, "Lamb of God, You take away the sin of the world." It may look like a list of Israel's cities of refuge: Kadesh, Shechem, Hebron, Bezer, Ramoth, and Golan. But to the baptized; to the catechized; to those of us who know what it's like be tempted, deceived, accused, chased, and harassed; to those of us who know the run; this refuge, this gift of the Sacrament, means . . . why, it means absolutely everything!

PLUS ULTRA

Throughout the book of Numbers, Israelites frequently lose sight of God's pledge to give them the Promised Land. All they saw was wilderness. All they heard was blowing sand. And the food? Don't ask again about the food! All they ate was manna, manna, and more manna.

The first section of Numbers (1:1–10:10) is upbeat, positive, and optimistic. God's people are careful to do "just as the LORD commanded" (Numbers 1:54; 2:34; 4:49; 8:3, 22; 9:5). This part of the book describes God's presence in the tabernacle as well as Israel's military preparations for their upcoming battles. What about the next section? "They murmured in their tents" (Psalm 106:25 ESV).

We can relate. Sometimes our journey can seem random and meaningless—with little or no progress. We get up. Eat. Shower. Commute. Work. Go home. Eat. Sleep. Repeat. It feels like we're going nowhere. And we never have enough time, money, energy, or hope. "Face it," a sinister voice whispers to us during a restless night. "That wilderness you see? That's all you'll ever get." Life in the wilderness can look *non plus ultra*. That's Latin for "nothing more beyond."

Non plus ultra. That was King Ferdinand of Aragon's slogan. He lived in Spain from 1452 to 1516. "You can only go so far west into the Atlantic Ocean. Then that's it. Don't you understand? The earth is flat. You'll come to the end, and then you'll fall off the planet. There's nothing more beyond."

That's how the Israelites looked at things. We can't blame them. Throughout Numbers, they endure lengthy censuses, laws, and legislations, with endless detailed lists. Their travels meander to and fro. Sometimes they camp in the same location for days on end. No wonder God's people callously criticize, perpetually complain, and are often blind to God's ongoing mercies. Longing to go back to Egypt, they're unwilling to endure hardship. They reject Moses' leadership, have little faith in divine promises, and even get caught up in worshiping other gods.

God's response? *Plus ultra*—there *is* more beyond!

Christopher Columbus believed that. Remember the jingle? "In fourteen hundred ninety-two, Columbus sailed the ocean blue!" In doing so, he poked a hole in King Ferdinand's flat earth argument. *Plus ultra!* More beyond! This is the promise that enlivens Israel's second generation in the book of Numbers. Though not perfect, these Israelites emerge as a formidable nation ready to enter the Promised Land.

But Moses doesn't complete their story. Why not? Israel's next chapter is left open ended—just like your life and mine. We're also in the middle, in between. We're still in the wilderness with its highs and lows, hints of hope, and crushing setbacks. There are many reasons to lose heart, give up, go through the motions, and go back to Egypt. God's response? *Plus ultra!* There's more beyond our present pain and deep disappointments. Jesus puts it this way: "I go and prepare a place for you, I will come again and will take you to Myself, that where I am you may be also" (John 14:3 ESV).

What a day that will be! William Williams (1717–91) captures the joy with these hymn lyrics: "When I tread the verge of Jordan, bid my anxious fears subside; death of death and hell's destruction, land me safe on Canaan's side. Songs of praises, songs of praises I will ever give to Thee; I will ever give to Thee" (*LSB* 918:3).

Our land is waiting. Let's get on our way!

STUDY GUIDE

CHAPTER 1. NAVIGATING NUMBERS: AN OVERVIEW OF THE BOOK

1. How does Philippians 1:6 summarize this chapter?
2. What tempts you during your in-between times in life?
3. What stands out for you in the section on 1 Corinthians 10 and Hebrews 4?
4. How are you planning to leave a Christian legacy?

CHAPTER 2. I HAVE CALLED YOU BY NAME: NUMBERS 1

1. How does John 10:3 summarize this chapter?
2. What does Numbers 1:1 teach you?
3. How does Romans 6–8 connect to Numbers?
4. What insights did you glean from the section on spiritual warfare?

CHAPTER 3. GOD WITH US: NUMBERS 2–3

1. How does Jeremiah 14:9 summarize this chapter?
2. What stands out for you in the discussion on Ezekiel?
3. What interests you the most about the Levites? What confuses you the most?
4. How does the doctrine of substitution work in the Bible?

CHAPTER 4. BOUNDARIES: NUMBERS 4–5

1. How does Romans 5:2 summarize this chapter?
2. Why is God's gift of access so valuable?
3. How important are boundaries in the book of Numbers? How important are boundaries in your life?
4. What does 1 Peter teach you about God's mission?

CHAPTER 5. THE LORD BLESS YOU: NUMBERS 6–7

1. How does Ephesians 1:3 summarize this chapter?
2. What does the Bible teach about God's blessings?
3. What parts of the Aaronic benediction most inspire you?
4. Define *shalom*. How does God deliver it to you?

CHAPTER 6. ARISE, O LORD: NUMBERS 8–10

1. How does Psalm 132:8 summarize this chapter?
2. How important is "Vitamin F"? Why?
3. What are some new insights related to Christ's final coming?
4. Why is the ark of the covenant so important?

CHAPTER 7. COMPLAINING 101: NUMBERS 11

1. How does Psalm 78:18 summarize this chapter?
2. Why is it so easy to begin? Why is it so hard to finish?
3. How does Numbers 11:1–3 preview the central section of the book?
4. What is the role of the Holy Spirit in Numbers? In the rest of the Bible?

CHAPTER 8. GREEN WITH ENVY: NUMBERS 12

1. How does 1 Peter 2:1 summarize this chapter?
2. How does envy show up in your life? What can you do about it?
3. What happened to Miriam? How does God's grace to her comport with His grace to you?
4. How does James's teaching about the tongue address your use of words?

CHAPTER 9. TWELVE MEN WENT TO SPY ON CANAAN: NUMBERS 13

1. How does 1 John 4:18 summarize this chapter?
2. Why is Numbers 13–14 the heart of the book?
3. Define fear. Define faith. What's the difference between the two?
4. How can you follow in Caleb's footsteps?

CHAPTER 10. SHIPWRECKED: NUMBERS 14

1. How does Psalm 78:42–43 summarize this chapter?
2. What are your takeaways from the discussions about the Gospel?
3. Discuss "unbelieving Christianity."
4. Define *hesed* and talk about how you see the gift in your life.

CHAPTER 11. KORAH'S COUP: NUMBERS 15–17

1. How does Philippians 2:3 summarize this chapter?
2. What happens when all we want is to go up?
3. Where do you see division in your life? Unity?
4. What do you think about God's wrath as it's taught in the New Testament?

CHAPTER 12. LOOSE LIPS SINK SHIPS: NUMBERS 20

1. How does Psalm 106:33 summarize this chapter?
2. Describe the worst day in Moses' life. What does it teach you?
3. How does the section "Christ, Our Rock" give you hope?
4. What can you implement in your life from the section on mourning Aaron's death?

CHAPTER 13. IN THE WAITING ROOM: NUMBERS 21

1. How does John 3:14 summarize this chapter?
2. Respond: God's delays aren't God's denials.
3. Discuss how God turns curses into blessings in Numbers and in the rest of the Bible.
4. What part of the section on God's love surprises you the most?

CHAPTER 14. BALAAM AND BALAK: NUMBERS 22

1. How does Revelation 2:14 summarize this chapter?
2. Describe Balaam, Balak, and God's Messenger. What are their similarities? Differences?
3. How important is God's covenant with Abraham? Why?

CHAPTER 15. A STAR IS BORN: NUMBERS 23–24

1. How does Revelation 22:16 summarize this chapter?
2. What role did money play in Balaam's life? What role does it play in your life?
3. Define *nacham*. What does it teach you about God's will and ways?
4. What promise about Christ in Balaam's oracles fills you with the greatest joy?

CHAPTER 16. MAYHEM ON THE PLAINS OF MOAB: NUMBERS 25

1. How does 1 Corinthians 10:14 summarize this chapter?
2. Who is Baal Hadad? Why should we care?
3. Define idolatry. How does it show up in your life? What can you do about it?
4. Do you agree with Paul's teaching about marriage? Why or why not?

CHAPTER 17. THE NEW GENERATION: NUMBERS 26–32

1. How does Psalm 78:8 summarize this chapter?
2. Compare and contrast the two generations in Numbers.
3. How does the promise of inheritance appear in Numbers? In your life?
4. What does Paul say about Christian unity?

CHAPTER 18. LET'S GET ON OUR WAY: NUMBERS 33–36

1. How does Philippians 3:14 summarize this chapter?
2. Why is Numbers 33 so applicable to our lives?
3. How do the cities of refuge point to Christ?
4. Use five words to summarize the book of Numbers.